Chongqing's Red Culture Campaign

Between 2009 and 2012, the city of Chongqing came into the national, and even international, spotlight, as it became the geographical centre of the 'Singing Red, Smashing Black' campaign, and later the political storm that swept China. Chongqing's Red Culture Campaign drew an incredible amount of interest at the time, but speculation and prejudice has since blurred the public understanding of the sensational story that ties the campaign with the rise and fall of a political star, Bo Xilai.

This book, therefore, seeks to study the nature of Chongqing's Red Culture Campaign, and the interaction between the political programme and the practices of its participants. Based on fieldwork conducted in Chongqing, it seeks to question whether the Red Culture Campaign was actually a return to Maoist revolutionary mass campaigning whilst examining the relationship between the CCP's political power and the lives of the ordinary people as reflected in the case of the campaign. Ultimately, it highlights that the campaign was not in fact a real Maoist mass movement. Although it followed the pre-existing model of past mass campaigns in China, containing a series of frequent and highly performative operations, Xiao Mei argues that it essentially demonstrated critical features of 'simulation'.

By contributing to our understanding of the discrepancies between a designed political programme, and what it actually becomes when implemented on the ground, this book will be of use to students and scholars of Chinese Studies, Politics and Sociology.

MEI Xiao recently obtained her PhD in Sociology from the University of Cambridge.

Routledge Research on the Politics and Sociology of China
Series Editor: Reza Hasmath, University of Oxford, UK

The modern Chinese state has traditionally affected every major aspect of the domestic society. With the growing liberalization of the economy, coupled with an increasing complexity of social issues, there is a belief that the state is retreating from an array of social problems from health to the environment. Yet, as we survey China's social and political landscape today we see not only the central state playing an active role in managing social problems, but state actors at the local level emerging in partnerships with relatively new actors such as social organizations and private enterprises.

The Routledge Research on the Politics and Sociology of China series is interested in examining the sociology and politics of this 'new' China. The series will engage with contemporary research that explores the intricacies of institutional interactions, and analysis of micro-level actors such as migrant workers, ethnic minorities, and women, who are shaping China's future. The book series seeks to promote a discourse and analysis that views state and society as contested spaces for power, authority, and legitimacy. As a guiding principle, the series is notably interested in books that use China as a laboratory for confirming, modifying or rejecting existing mainstream theories in sociology and politics.

For a full list of titles: www.routledge.com/Routledge-Research-on-the-Politics-and-Sociology-of-China/book-series/RRPSC

Social Entrepreneurship and Citizenship in China
The rise of NGOs in the PRC
Carolyn L. Hsu

Chongqing's Red Culture Campaign
Simulation and its social implications
MEI Xiao

Chongqing's Red Culture Campaign

Simulation and its social implications

MEI Xiao

LONDON AND NEW YORK

First published 2018
by Routledge
2 Park Square, Milton Park, Abingdon, Oxon OX14 4RN

and by Routledge
711 Third Avenue, New York, NY 10017

Routledge is an imprint of the Taylor & Francis Group, an informa business

© 2018 MEI Xiao

The right of MEI Xiao to be identified as author of this work has been asserted in accordance with sections 77 and 78 of the Copyright, Designs and Patents Act 1988.

All rights reserved. No part of this book may be reprinted or reproduced or utilised in any form or by any electronic, mechanical, or other means, now known or hereafter invented, including photocopying and recording, or in any information storage or retrieval system, without permission in writing from the publishers.

Trademark notice: Product or corporate names may be trademarks or registered trademarks, and are used only for identification and explanation without intent to infringe.

British Library Cataloguing-in-Publication Data
A catalogue record for this book is available from the British Library

Library of Congress Cataloging-in-Publication Data
A catalog record for this book has been requested

ISBN: 978-1-138-22231-1 (hbk)
ISBN: 978-1-315-40806-4 (ebk)

Typeset in Times New Roman
by Apex CoVantage, LLC

Printed and bound in Great Britain by
TJ International Ltd, Padstow, Cornwall

This book is dedicated to my parents MEI Guohong and LIU Li.

Contents

**1 Chongqing under the spotlight: the 'Chongqing Model'
and its controversies**   1

Chongqing under the spotlight 1
The 'Chongqing Model' 2
The controversies over Bo's 'Chongqing Model' 4
Aims of the book 6
Data collection 9
Structure of the book 9

2 Putting the Red culture campaign into perspective   15

Social movement studies in the Chinese context 16
The 'state-society' framework in China studies 18
Domination and legitimacy 20
Power of resistance – collective action and the
   'weapons of the weak' 22
Theoretical concepts 25
Summary 29

3 Chongqing's Red culture campaign as simulation   37

Simulation 37
Implications of Chongqing's Red culture campaign
   as simulation 47
The problematic of characterising Chongqing's
   Red culture campaign as simulation 49

**4 Who were the participants in Chongqing's Red
culture campaign?**   53

The participants in the campaign 53
Different generations of participants 55
Institutional conditions 57
Summary 62

viii   *Contents*

**5   Experiencing the campaign: patterns of practices by
the local people in Chongqing**   66

First level of participation 66
Second level of participation 69
Third level of participation – exclusively for retirees 72
*Levels of participation, organization, and quality
    of performance 75*
Working as participating – employees type II 77
Summary 80

**6   How the official programme interacted with the practices
of the local participants: exchange**   82

The official programme as strategy 82
*What the Red culture campaign needed from its
    participants 84*
*What the participants offered to and received
    from the Red culture campaign 84*
The participants' practices as tactics 92
Summary 93

**7   How the official programme interacted with the
practices of the local participants: framing**   96

Framing processes by the official programme 96
*Framing processes by the participants – primary
    frameworks 98*
*How frames are appropriated and contested – the
    keying processes 105*
Summary 108

8   Conclusion   111

Chongqing's Red culture campaign as simulation 111
*Patterns of the participants' practice and how it
    interacted with the official programme 113*
Social and political implications 115

Epilogue: understanding the case of Chongqing   117
Appendices   121
Index   148

1 Chongqing under the spotlight

The 'Chongqing Model' and its controversies

Chongqing under the spotlight

In early 2009, Hong Kong-based magazine *Asian Weekly* published an article introducing and praising the 'Chongqing Model'[1] as a breakthrough in China's pursuit of economic revival.[2] A subsequent article, describing Chongqing as 'Chicago on Yangtze' and revealing its startlingly fast development to the outside world, appeared in the prestigious magazine *Foreign Policy*,[3] Over the next three years, Chongqing waltzed into the national, even international spotlight, not only because of the ambitious 'Chongqing Model' but also because it became the geographical centre of the political storm that swept China in 2012.

Chongqing had been a relatively low-profile megacity in southwestern China, despite its once substantial political status in China's modern history. Chongqing, cradle of the ancient *Bayu* (巴渝) culture, has a proud history of more than 3,000 years. Nesting at the congruence of the Yangtze River and Jialing River, Chongqing has always been an important river port that connects China's west to the rest of the nation and the outside world. With a total population of almost 30 million and covering an area of 82,400 km², Chongqing is currently divided into 38 administrative districts. More than 70 per cent of its landscape is mountainous. The political significance of Chongqing reached an unprecedented height when the then-ruling Nationalist Party (*Kuomingtang*) made Chongqing the wartime capital in 1937 during China's anti-Japanese war. As a consequence, Chongqing quickly rose to become the political, economic, and cultural centre of *Kuomingtang*-ruled China. After Chongqing was 'liberated' by the People's Liberation Army (PLA) of the Chinese Communist Party (CCP) in November 1949, Chongqing had been a centrally-controlled municipality within the Southwest Bureau. In 1954, it was downgraded to a provincially-governed city under the jurisdiction of Sichuan Province. In the 1960s, however, Chongqing became a key site of the 'Third Front' (*sanxian* 三线) development project.[4] During the large-scale industrial relocation, heavy industry developed swiftly in Chongqing. As part of the unforeseeable consequences of this development, Chongqing's 'armed struggle' (*wu dou* 武斗) during the Cultural Revolution (CR), especially in the most violent periods of 1966 and 1967, was one of the most violent, destructive, and lethal due to the relatively easy access to heavy weapons. In the era of

2 *Chongqing under the spotlight*

reform and opening up since 1978, Chongqing became one of the pilot cities for the national comprehensive reform of the economic system in 1983. In 1997, Chongqing was once again separated from Sichuan Province and became one of the four municipalities with a provincial status in China.[5] In the past two decades, under the directives of the central government, such as the '314' plan,[6] Chongqing is making ardent efforts to turn itself into an economic and business centre in China's western area and prides itself for being a pioneer in the 'Open up to the West' (*xibu da kaifa* 西部大开发) movement. Chongqing now hosts the largest industrial compound near the upper Yangtze River and is one of the most important trade and transport ports in South-western China.[7] As the largest municipality with a provincial status, Chongqing occupies a critical position in China's modernisation project. Yet Chongqing still trails coastal cities, such as Beijing and Shanghai, in economic prosperity and international presence.

Chongqing's sudden rise to fame might seem unexpected. Yet there is an important political context for its ascendance. That is, the CCP's 18th National Congress was taking place in November 2012, during which the standing committee of the Political Bureau (Politburo Standing Committee [PBSC]) welcomed a new generation of leaders. Chongqing's then-Party secretary Bo Xilai, before his fall from grace in 2012, was widely speculated to be a strong contender for a seat on the PBSC, the most powerful position in the country. The PBSC is the ruling body of the CCP and effectively China's top decision-making mechanism. Although the National Party Congress is the Party's highest power organ in theory, in reality the CCP's Politburo and its Standing Committee make the final decisions concerning policy making, implementation, as well as discipline inspection.[8] Changes in the CCP's leadership have always been extremely important in Chinese politics because political power in China is highly concentrated at the top.[9] During the pre-Jiang Zemin era, leadership changes were accompanied by dramatic institutional transformations in China's socio-economic policies, foreign relations, and state-society dynamics.[10] The change of leadership often resulted in significant changes in policies. Since the CCP's 16th National Congress, however, the leadership transition procedures have become more institutionalised and far calmer. Nevertheless, the leadership selection remains largely behind closed doors.[11] Although the CCP's most recent leadership transition officially took place during the 18th National Congress in November 2012, the real contending process occurred in the informal elite arena, where 'retiring incumbents and prospective successors maneuvered, typically with elaborate subtlety and political opacity', long before the actual congressional meetings.[12]

The 'Chongqing Model'

Bo Xilai, Party secretary of Chongqing Municipality (2007–2012), is the son of the Chinese Communist Party revolutionary leader Bo Yibo. A celebrated member of the 'princeling' fraction of China's ruling elites, Bo Xilai built his own political career as the mayor of Dalian in the 1990s, governor of Liaoning Province (2001–2004), minster of commerce (2004–2007), and Party secretary of Chongqing from

2007 until his prosecution.[13] His relocation to Chongqing after the 17th National Congress was widely considered a demotion, and Bo was forced out of the most inner circle of the Party leader hopefuls. It was believed that the 'Chongqing Model' and the conspicuous display of Chongqing's 'success' was Bo's attempt to get back into the game on the eve of the 18th National Congress.

The so-called 'Chongqing Model' consisted of a series of economic, social, and cultural policies. Chongqing's economic policies combined efforts to attract outside investment, increase government investment, and boost domestic consumption. A new export-processing model, 'one end outside, one end inside' (*yi tou zai wai, yi tou zai nei* 一头在外，一头在内),[14] successfully attracted a large number of parts companies to settle in Chongqing's new-fledged special industrial zones. HP, Ford, Foxconn, and many of the world's biggest corporations came to invest in Chongqing. Moreover, the government invested greater than 30 billion *yuan* (≈£3 billion) in the infrastructure every year, building extensive transportation networks of highways, bridges, and subways. As elsewhere in China, 'land financing' (*tudi caizheng* 土地财政) constituted a key force in driving urban development.[15] As a result, Chongqing maintained a startling GDP growth rate of around 15 per cent during the few years for which Bo was Party secretary.[16] The social policies implemented in Chongqing included the construction of 40 million m² of affordable public housing, special assistance for children and the elderly who had been left behind in the rural areas, and an attempt to reduce the discrepancies between the urban and rural areas and improve people's standard of living. The slogan 'Five Chongqings' vowed to build a metropolis that was green, safe, healthy, pleasant, and convenient to live.[17] The cultural policies aimed to enrich the city's cultural life and improve people's mental outlook, including promoting the Red culture campaign. At the same time, Chongqing was committed to enforcing better discipline and a 'mass-line' approach to work among the Party cadres in the city.[18] All levels of cadres in Chongqing were requested to participate in three activities: '*da xia fang*' (大下访, visiting the masses and asking about their difficulties), '*san jin san tong*' (三进三同, getting involved at the grass-roots level by visiting villages and eating, living, and working with peasants in their households), and '*jie qiong qin*' (结穷亲, building long-term assisting relationships with households suffering hardship).

The most controversial endeavour among the various policies carried out as part of the 'Chongqing Model' was a pair known as 'Singing Red, Smashing Black' (*chang hong da hei* 唱红打黑). The 'Smashing Black' campaign, led by the chief of police, Wang Lijun, was a relentless crackdown on alleged organized crimes.[19] The campaign started in June 2009 and was said to have cracked more than 2,000 criminal cases, leading to arrests of more than 1,500 suspects and confiscation of billions of Chinese *yuan* over the duration of four months. The campaign evoked both approval from local residents, applauding the significant improvement in public security in the city, as well as heavy criticisms from China's legal community, who accused it of violating legal procedures and tampering with human rights. During the campaign, the vice director of the Police Bureau and director of the Justice Bureau, Wen Qiang, was sentenced to death along with a dozen alleged

4 *Chongqing under the spotlight*

mafia bosses.[20] Many wealthy businessmen were targeted and sentenced following hasty trials, and the trial of Li Zhuang, a lawyer who had defended one of the businessmen, spurred huge controversy.[21]

Equally eye-catching was the Red culture campaign (June 2008–March 2012), which featured four elements: 'Singing Red, Reading Classics, Telling Stories, and Spreading Mottos' (*chang du jiang chuan* 唱读讲传). 'Singing Red' appeared to be the most prominent and controversial aspect of the programme. Popular activities included singing competitions organized by all levels of the Chongqing government, regular Red-themed singing and dancing performances in public squares, TV programmes featuring Red songs produced by the Chongqing satellite TV channel, and so on. The 'Reading Classics' section of the programme focused on the publication of small pocket books edited by Chongqing's Propaganda Department. The intention was to encourage the officials and masses to read classic works that 'represent the fruits of civilization and wisdom of humanity'.[22] The first collection of 'Reading Classics' was published in December 2008. In the subsequent years, 28 series of small booklets were published, with a total issuance of more than 17 million units. The third element – 'Telling Stories' – was launched in March 2009. Pamphlets of 'Telling Stories' (*jianggushi* 《讲故事》), containing up to 8,000 stories, were printed and disseminated among the public. The fourth part – 'Spreading Mottos' – involved sending Red-themed text messages. The most famous was probably the one that Bo sent to millions of mobile phone users in Chongqing on 28 April 2009. He quoted several of Mao Zedong's famous dictums, including 'Humans need to have some spirit' (*ren shi yao youdian jingshen de* 人是要有点精神的). In 2008 and 2009, Chongqing organized two consecutive 'Red text-message composition contests' to encourage 'the study, composition and transmission of Red mottos'.[23]

The controversies over Bo's 'Chongqing Model'

Comments on the 'Chongqing Model' by both public intellectuals in China and observers of China abroad, were split at the time. In the context of the Chinese intellectual field, 'Left' and 'Right' have specific meanings and carry connotations different from the ones they have in Western political discourse. On the spectrum from 'Left' to 'Right', one can identify four basic categories of political factions in post-CR China: the ultra-Left (Maoist); the new-Left; the reformist; and the far-Right (Liberals). The ultra-Left (Maoist) insists on the rule of the CCP, a planned socialist economy and supports, or is at least sympathetic to the CR and Mao's doctrine of continuous revolution under the dictatorship of the proletariat. The Left does not necessarily like the CR but supports the ruling of the CCP, the socialist nature of the country, and economic policies adopted prior to the CR. The new-Left often adheres to populist or nationalistic causes and engages actively in critiques of neo-liberalism and globalisation. The new-Left is nostalgic for the orthodox form of socialism and criticises the economic reforms that occurred during the post-Mao era. There may be some overlap between the ultra-Left and the new-Left. Moving towards the Right, there is the reformist, who still evokes socialism as the legitimate political ideology for CCP rule but abandons the previous economic policies and supports the liberalisation of the Chinese economy by allowing elements of capitalism into it. The far-Right (liberals) wants to adopt a free market economy and tends to demand a liberal democracy modeled on the West.[24] There are many other ways to categorise the different political camps that exist in China's intellectual and political fields. Let it suffice here to point out that much of the political analysis of the 'Chongqing Model' was intrinsically linked to the political standing of the commentators. In general, the 'Leftists' tended to be supportive, or at least sympathetic, to Bo's policies in Chongqing, whereas the 'Rightists' were far more critical.

The 'Leftists' attempted to provide analytical and theoretical support for Chongqing's policies. They saw Chongqing's practices as constituting a specific genre of governance and potential direction for China's future reforms on a national scale.[25] Tsinghua University professor, Li Xiguang,[26] in an article written in 2010, praised many of Chongqing's policies, such as its effort to increase farmers' income, the public housing project, the provision of free lunches and milk for children who had been left behind in rural areas, and so on. According to Li, these policies not only improved people's welfare but also strengthened the soft power of China's Party-state governance. The significance of the 'Chongqing Model/Practice' was elevated to such a level that it was believed to have successfully rejected market fundamentalism and proved the superiority of socialism.[27] The UCLA-based historian, Professor Philip C. C. Huang, also discussed the possibility of the 'Chongqing Model' spearheading China's next stage of reform. He saw Chongqing's economic model as a new combination of the specific components of market capitalism and a planned socialist economy that made good use of the 'third hand' – the government- and the state-owned enterprises (SOEs).[28] Cui Zhiyuan, a Tsinghua University professor, was also an enthusiastic supporter of the 'Chongqing experiment', which he regarded as an attempt to achieve balanced development between the urban and rural areas and between public and private business.[29] When the then-premier, Wen Jiabao, launched a thinly-veiled attack on Bo Xilai during the press conference at the culmination of the National People's Congress and the Political Consultative Conference in March 2012, Tsinghua University professor Wang Hui expressed concerns that the dismissal of Bo signalled a suppression of different interpretations of the Chongqing practices and would discourage social experimentation with China's reform.[30] Criticism of the 'Chongqing Model', on the other hand, was more likely to come from the more 'liberal' public intellectuals and appeared in the form of newspaper articles or online blogs rather than academic articles. For example, Professor Sun Liping described the 'Chongqing Model' as 'the wrong answer to the right question'.[31] Zhongshan University-based researcher Rong Jian offered a series of commentaries that critically reflected upon the 'Chongqing Model'.[32] The criticism centred on a wide variety of issues, including the radicalisation of the 'Singing Red, Smashing Black' campaigns, the squandering of public money purely for the purpose of image construction (such as the large-scale planting of gingko trees), the swelling government deficits, and the strict control over the

6 *Chongqing under the spotlight*

media and public opinions (in some cases, resulting in citizens being sentenced to hard labour). These analyses and commentaries offered interesting insights for comprehending the case of Chongqing.[33] Nonetheless, they were of varied levels of scholarly quality, and most fell short of rigour demanded of academic research.

Aims of the book

This book is not a political analysis of the fate of the politician or the political climate in which the 'Chongqing Model' was carried out. It is, however, a timely effort to document the details of one specific part of the 'Chongqing Model', that is, Chongqing's Red culture campaign. The Red culture campaign, given its spectacular scale and methods of mass mobilisation, has drawn serious criticisms linking it to the infamous mass campaigns in the history of China's politics. Throughout the first three decades of CCP's ruling of the country, mass campaigns underpinned by ideological doctrines used to dominate the political life of the Chinese people. It is widely considered a major source of political legitimacy in 'communist' regimes. Even in the post-Mao era, ideological campaigns continue to be employed as a key tool of governance in contemporary Chinese society, although the aim has changed from mobilising people to participate in political actions to producing 'passive consent' during the reform era.[34] In any case, it is widely believed that the power of ideology, in particular Marxism and Maoism, to regulate social life in current Chinese society has declined dramatically. Yet the image of millions of people singing Red in unison during Chongqing's Red culture campaign brings back the memories of China's past political campaigns. In this context, Bo's Red culture campaign aroused a considerable amount of curiosity as well as concerns and criticisms. Therefore, the first task of the book is to analyse the nature of the campaign, that is, whether it is a genuine mass campaign that alerted a return to stricter ideological controls as in the past.

Moreover, this book focuses on the actual experiences of the participants during the implementation of the ideological programme. The campaign not only drew the most of media attention at the time but also was the specific section of the 'Chongqing Model' that permeated into the majority of ordinary people's daily lives. Yet serious research on Chongqing's Red culture campaign that was driven by serious scholarly interest has so far been scanty. Commentators rushed to offer diagnostics on the political implications of the campaign before mapping out the contours and collecting the specifics of the campaign. Few seemed to care enough to ask whether the people who actually participated in the campaign experienced it in the same way as the political commentators imagined for them. In fact, the experiences of the ordinary people during the implementation of the campaign constituted a layer of the 'fact' of the campaign that was consistently left out of political analysis. Missing this facet of the campaign would hinder our understanding of the *effect* of a political programme.

This book asks the question of whether Chongqing's Red culture campaign is a genuine Maoist mass campaign and what it implies about the relationship between the political programme and the everyday lives of the ordinary participants of the

Chongqing under the spotlight 7

campaign. For sure, the particular case of Chongqing's Red culture campaign cannot represent all contemporary political or cultural campaigns in China. I do not attempt to generalise the findings of this case to other cultural and political campaigns in China, either past or present. However, it exhibits some shared features with other mass campaigns that have occurred during the history of the CCP and at the same time demonstrates sufficient uniqueness to merit special, detailed scholarly treatment. Thus, the findings about Chongqing's Red culture campaign can be compared to those other campaigns, past or future. The specific questions asked in this book are as follows:

Was Chongqing's Red culture campaign a return to Maoist revolutionary mass campaigns?

Mass campaigns consist of a series of continuous operations that involve the participation of the general public to achieve certain social or political goals. The CCP has a long history of adopting mass campaign as a major method of mobilisation. The technique of mass mobilisation developed in the CCP's rural bases in North China before 1949 was later adapted to various campaigns.[35] From the 1950s to the 1970s, the list of mass campaigns ran long: the land reform campaign, the campaign to suppress counter-revolutionaries, the Three-Antis, the Five-Antis, the Thought Reform campaign, the Great Leap Forward (1958–1961), the Red Guard Movement (1966–1967), the Criticise Lin, Criticise Confucius Movement (1973–1974), and so on. Mao believed in the importance of political struggles in solving perceived political, social, as well as economic problems. He popularised the concept of 'continuous revolution' in China and proposed to institute the mass campaigns as a regular part of people's daily lives.[36] In the post-Mao era, a number of ideological campaigns, such as the 'antibourgeois liberalisation' campaign (1981, 1986–1987), the 'anti-spiritual pollution' campaign (1983–1984), and the 'anti-imperialist peaceful evolution' campaign (1989) continued to have a significant impact on the political arena. Entering the 21st century, although communist doctrines are increasingly de-emphasised in the political teachings of the CCP, it nevertheless continues to search for new theoretical advancement. The 'Three Represents',[37] 'socialist harmonious society', and 'Chinese Dream' are examples of how the official ideology continues to engineer long-term visions of social transformation and wield huge influence on Chinese politics.[38] At the forefront of ideology construction, enormous efforts are devoted to building a causal link between the Party-state and the prosperity and well-being of the Chinese society.

However, despite that ideological campaigns, as shown, continue to exist as an important political tool and educational method for the CCP, it no longer occupies such a critical position in the CCP's political culture as it did in the pre-reform era. Even when ideological campaigns are carried out, it is no longer used to create a brand-new society but to defend the CCP's status as the sole ruling party.[39] The mechanisms employed for idea transmission and thought control in recent decades have aimed at achieving better management than indoctrination. China's thought management in the 21st century has shown features of flexibility, market

8 *Chongqing under the spotlight*

friendliness, and reliance on new communication technologies. These changes have contributed to the CCP's so far relatively successful management of a society haunted by increasing social fragmentation and unrest.[40]

At the surface, it seems to be the case that Chongqing's leader Bo Xilai is mobilising a Maoist-style mass campaign to inject revolutionary beliefs back into society for the sake a building a 'better' society. If this were what truly happened in Chongqing, Chongqing's Red culture campaign would be contradicting the general trend in the recent development of China's political culture, during which the ideology of Maoism and the mechanism of mass mobilisation have suffered a severe decline in significance. Was Chongqing's Red culture campaign a return to Maoist revolutionary mass campaigns? Was it meant to re-educate the population with revolutionary ideals? Did it indicate an attempt to revive Maoism in today's political life in China? This book argues that Chongqing's Red culture campaign was not a return to Maoist revolutionary mass campaigns. By appearing to be re-educating the population with revolutionary ideals, it attempted a simulation of a Maoist mass campaign to enhance the legitimacy of Chongqing's leadership in his pursuit of political power.

What kind of relationship between the CCP's political power and the everyday lives of ordinary people was reflected in the case of Chongqing's Red culture campaign?

The interaction between a political programme and the actions of the participants can take different forms. These specific forms of interaction are underpinned by different forms of power relations. Typical ones include oppression, resistance, and collaboration. Often it is a combination of these different sets of power relations that underlie the particular case of a political campaign. What kind of relationship between the CCP's political power and the everyday lives of ordinary people was reflected in the case of Chongqing's Red culture campaign? This book tries to show that the interplay between the state and the participants of the Red culture campaign cannot be characterised simply as oppression or resistance. Collaboration cannot accurately summarise this relationship either as this would suggest that a far higher level of equality exists between the two as well as a higher level of voluntariness on the part of the participants. In the space where this specific form of interaction takes place, there is a high level of conformity observed on the part of the participants. At the same time, it is also a space where compliance entails reappropriation and creativity.

The interaction between the Red culture programme in Chongqing and its practitioners entails a unique combination of both forms of association and disassociation. In this book, I use the concept of 'simulation' to characterise the nature of the Red culture campaign. I also use the pair of concepts – 'strategy' and 'tactics' – to refer to the top-down political programme of the Red culture campaign and the practices of the participants in everyday life. I describe their interactive relationship as simultaneously associative and disassociative under the effects of simulation, resources exchange, and framing processes.

Data collection

This book is based on fieldwork taken place in Chongqing during two main periods between September 2011 and June 2013.[41] The first phase lasted for seven months, between September 2011 and March 2012. A total of 74 participants in the Red culture campaign were interviewed for this research project. Twenty-three of them were retirees, 25 university students, and 26 employees. In Chapter 4, I will offer a detailed account of the generational differences in terms of socio-economic status, life stage, and values among the three social groups. See *Appendix II* for the biographical details of the interviewees. Three main techniques were used during the data collection process: interviews, observation, and documentary analysis.

Structure of the book

There are eight chapters in this book. In Chapter 1, I have introduced the case study of the Red culture campaign by offering a brief account of the 'Chongqing Model', of which the Red culture campaign was a crucial component. I raised the questions to be answered in this book and proposed the composition of an answer to it. Chapter 2 presents a theoretical framework adopted in this book to help the readers comprehend the case of Chongqing's Red culture campaign at the conceptual level. Two major themes dominate literatures on China's social and political movements: 1) the dominating power of the Party-state and 2) the masses and the possibility of resistance. Responding to the theoretical inadequacies identified in the existing literature, I propose a theoretical framework for the current research project, designed to capture the unique interactive relationship between the political programme of the Red culture campaign and its participants. In Chapters 3 through 6, I present the main findings of this book and offer answers to the questions raised earlier in this chapter. In Chapter 3, I argue that Chongqing's Red culture campaign exhibited critical features of simulation, which conditions the disassociative element of the interaction between the political programme of the Red culture campaign and its participants. By the end of Chapter 3, I also point out the problematics of applying the concept of simulation and explain where simulation falls short of fully accounting for the whole of the Red culture campaign. Chapter 4 provides a description of the participants of the campaign and in particular those interviewed for this book. Their experiences of the campaign are discussed in the context of the different generations to which the participants belonged and the institutional conditions under which the campaign were organized. Chapter 5 further supplements the description of the participants' practices by formulating the general patterns of participation according to the level of the organization, the quality of the performance, and the amount of publicity given to the performance. In Chapters 6 and 7, I tackle the problematics of applying the concept of simulation in Chapter 3 by further introducing two forms of interaction between the political programme of the Red culture campaign and its participants: exchange and framing. By exchanging and framing, the two parties appropriated each other's existence as the political programme was being implemented and

10 *Chongqing under the spotlight*

practiced in everyday life. In Chapter 8, I summarise the findings and implications of this research project, and discuss how these can contribute to a deeper understanding of the Chinese society and China's politics.

Notes

1 Then-Party secretary Bo Xilai denied the existence of the 'Chongqing Model' at a press conference during the 2009 National People's Congress meeting. See '*Zhongwai meiti quanguo lianghui jujiao Chongqing*' (National and Foreign Press Focus Attention on Chongqing During the 'Two Meetings'), *Chongqing Daily*, 11 March 2009.

2 Mingshuo Ji, '*Chongqing moshi chuang zhongguo jingji fangong xinlujing*' (The Chongqing Model Is the New Road to China's Economic Fight-back), *Asian Weekly*, no. 6, February 2009.

3 Christina Larson, 'Chicago on Yangtze', *Foreign Policy*, September/October 2010, <www.foreignpolicy.com/articles/2010/08/16/chicago_on_the_yangtze?page=0,3> [accessed 09 January 2014].

4 The 'Third Front' development project refers to the preparation for the perceived possibility of warfare when China faced a hostile international environment in the 1960s. In particular, it faced dramatic worsening of relations with the Soviet Union and threats from the United States.

5 The other three are Beijing, Tianjin, and Shanghai.

6 In 2007, the then-general secretary of the CCP and president, Hu Jintao, mapped out the future development plan for Chongqing. The '314' plan urged Chongqing to become a major driver of growth in western China, the economic centre close to the upper Yangtze River, a centrally-governed municipality with balanced urban-rural development. Chongqing should be a role model in building 'a comprehensive well-off society in all-round way' (*quanmian xiaokang shehui* 全面小康社会). Chongqing was given four tasks: to use industrial development to nurture agriculture, to draw on the support of the city in developing rural areas to construct the 'socialist new countryside'; to reform the model of economic growth and reform the old industrial bases; to improve people's livelihoods and build a socialist harmonious society; and to strengthen urban construction and improve the quality of urban governance.

7 Jianhong Li, 'Chongqing: Opportunities and Risks', *China Quarterly*, 178 (2004), 448–66.

8 Gang Lin, 'Ideology and Political Institutions for a New Era', in *China After Jiang*, ed. by Gang Lin and Xiaobo Hu (Stanford, CA: Stanford University Press, 2003), p. 55.

9 The Party structure of the CCP primarily follows a Leninist model and adopts the principle of democratic centralism. More than 3 million 'primary Party organizations', established in neighbourhoods, workplaces, schools, and so on form the basis of the Party structure. At the top of the Party hierarchy, the principle of 'collective leadership' has been reinstalled in the aftermath of the Cultural Revolution in an attempt to root out personality cult. See Tony Saich, *Governance and Politics in China* (London: Palgrave Macmillan, 2011), p. 108.

10 Gang Lin and Xiaobo Hu, 'Introduction', in *China After Jiang*, ed. by Gang Lin and Xiaobo Hu (Stanford, CA: Stanford University Press, 2003), p. 2.

11 Lowell Dittmer, 'Chinese Leadership Succession to the Fourth Generation', in *China After Jiang*, ed. by Gang Lin and Xiaobo Hu (Stanford, CA: Stanford University Press, 2003), p. 11.

12 Dittmer, 'Chinese Leadership Succession to the Fourth Generation' p. 13.

13 The flamboyant years of Chongqing's Red culture campaign ended with the downfall of its leader Bo Xilai. At the time, Bo's fell from grace was said to be the biggest political scandal in China for at least two decades. The drama unfolded in February 2012, when Chongqing's former chief of police, Wang Lijun, fled to the US Consulate in the neighbouring city of Chengdu. He was said to be in fear of his life after conflicting with

Bo Xilai over the murder of the Englishman Neil Heywood by Bo's wife, Bo Gu Kailai. Bo Xilai was sacked as Party secretary of Chongqing in March 2012. His membership of the prestigious Central Committee and Politburo was terminated in April, amidst allegations of 'severe discipline violations'. Four months later, Bo Gu Kailai was convicted of murdering Neil Heywood and received a suspended death sentence. In September 2012, Wang Lijun was sentenced to 15 years in prison for bending the law, the abuse of power, and accepting bribes. Later that month, Bo was expelled from the Party, accused of the abuse of power, corruption, and violations of Party's discipline. In October, he was stripped of his position at the National People's Congress, China's top legislature. Bo was subjected to a high-profile, five-day trial in Jinan, Shandong Province, between 22 August 2013 and 26 August 2013, before receiving a sentence of life imprisonment on 22 September 2013. Bo Xilai's appeal was rejected by the court on 25 October 2013. He is now serving his sentence.

14 This refers to the arrangement whereby the components of products will be manufactured and assembled on site in Chongqing before export, in contrast to the previous model whereby components had to be imported to China to be assembled for export. The previous model is called 'two ends out' (*liang tou zai wai* 两头在外).

15 Philip C. C. Huang, 'Chongqing: Equitable Development Driven by a "Third Hand"?' *Modern China*, 37 (2011), 569–622.

16 Chongqing's GDP grew by 14.5 per cent in 2008, 14.9 per cent in 2009, 17.1 per cent in 2010, and 16.4 per cent in 2011. Accessed 23 November 2013 at www.cqtj.gov.cn/html/sjxx/rdsj/11/12/5691.html.

17 'Five Chongqings' refer to '*yiju Chongqing, changtong Chongqing, senlin Chongqing, ping'an Chongqing, jiankang Chongqing* （宜居重庆，畅通重庆，森林重庆，平安重庆，健康重庆）

18 Ji, '*Chongqing moshi*'.

19 For an analysis of the political implications of the 'Smashing Black' campaign, see Joseph Fewsmith, 'Bo Xilai Takes on Organized Crimes', *China Leadership Monitor*, 32 (2010), 1–8.

20 Wei Su, Yang Fan & Liu Shiwen, *Chongqing Moshi* (*The Chongqing Model*) (Beijing: Zhongguo jingji chubanshe, 2011).

21 For detailed discussion on Chongqing's 'Smashing Black' campaign, see Zhiwei Tong, '*Chongqing dahei xing shehui guanli fangshi yanjiu baogao*' (Report on Chongqing's Social Management in the Style of the 'Anti-Crime' Campaign), *Zhongguo xianfa xue yanjiu hui*, 22 October 2011, <www.21ccom.net/articles/zgyj/ggzhc/article_2012021353482.html?1329286156> [accessed 09 January 2014]. See also a series of reports on the campaign and its controversies published in *Southern Weekend*, for example, '*Bei quan ding de "hei laoda" daodi you duo hei?*' (How Black Are the Accused 'Black Mafia'?), 18 March 2010, www.infzm.com/content/42718[accessed 09 January 2014]; '*Li Zhuang an: fating wai de jiaoliang*' (The Case of Li Zhuang: Struggles Outside of the Court), 7 January 2010, www.infzm.com/content/39771[accessed 09 January 2014].

22 '*He Shizhong: "Chang hong" shi jiankang youyi de qunzhongxing wenhua huodong*' (He Shizhong: Singing Red Is a Beneficial Cultural Activity for the Masses), *Chongqing Daily*, 11 July 2011.

23 'Decision on Promoting Vigorous Development and Prosperity of Culture' (*Zhonggong Chongqing shiwei guanyu tuidong wenhua dafazhan dafanrong de jueding*), June 2009.

24 Jisheng Yang, *Zhongguo Gaige Niandai de Zhengzhi Douzheng* (Political Struggles in the Era of China's Reform) (Hong Kong: Excellent Culture Press, 2004).

25 For example, Weiwei Zhang, '*Chongqing guilai hua Chongqing*' (Talking about Chongqing after a trip to Chongqing), *Hongqi Wengao*, 2 (2012), 36–37; Shaoguang Wang, '*Tansuo zhongguoshi shehuizhuyi 3.0: Chongqing jingyan*' (To explore Chinese socialism 3.0: Chongqing experiences), *Makesi Zhuyi Yanjiu*, 2 (2011), 5–14.

26 Li Xiguang is the president of Tsinghua's International Centre of Communications Studies.

12   *Chongqing under the spotlight*

27 Xiguang Li, '*Chongqing meng yu zhongguo moshi*' (The Dream of Chongqing and the China Model), *Phoenix Finance* website, 5 September 2010 http://finance.ifeng.com/news/20100905/2588460.shtml [accessed 09 January 2014].

28 Huang, 'Chongqing'.

29 Zhiyuan Cui, 'Partial Intimations of the Coming Whole: The Chongqing Experiment in Light of the Theories of Henry George, James Meade, and Antonio Gramsci', *Modern China*, 37 (2011), 646–60; Zhiyuan Cui, '*"Chongqing jingyan" jingxingshi: guozi zengzhi yu cangfu yu min bingjin*' ('Chongqing Experiences': concurrent increase of wealth between national property and the masses), *China Review of Political Economy*, 1 (2010), 73–80. Zhiyuan Cui, '*Chongqing "shi da minsheng gongcheng" de zhengzhi jingji xue*' (The Political Economy of Chongqing's 'Ten Projects for Public Welfare'), *Institute for Advanced Historical and Social Research*, 19 June 2011, <www.lishiyushehui.cn/modules/topic/detail.php?topic_id=362> [accessed 09 January 2014].

30 Hui Wang, 'The Rumor Machine', *London Review of Books*, 34 (2012), 13–14.

31 Liping Sun, '*Youguan Chongqing de liangdian kanfa*' (Two Thoughts on the Chongqing Model), *Aisixiang* website, 16 March 2012, www.aisixiang.com/data/51299.html [accessed 09 January 2014].

32 Jian Rong, 'Looking Back on Chongqing 1–5', *Sina Blog*, http://blog.sina.com.cn/s/blog_49f32b3f0101a9az.html[accessed 09 January 2014].

33 For other articles, see Fan Zhongxin's speech '*fazhi zhuiqiu yu Chongqing moshi de jiaoxun*' (Pursuit of the Rule of Law and Lessons to Be Learned from the Chongqing Model) at Central South University, 23 May 2012, http://blog.sina.com.cn/s/blog_89aa0dcd010131d8.html[accessed 09 January 2014]; Weifang He, '*Weile fangzhi, wei le women xinzhong de nayifen lixiang*'(Rule of Law – For the Ideal in Our Heart), <www.chinaelections.org/NewsInfo.asp?NewsID=225346> [accessed 09 January 2014].

34 Anne-Maire Brady, 'Introduction', in *China's Thought Management*, ed. by Anne-Maire Brady (London: Routledge, 2012), p. 4.

35 Frederick C. Teiwes, 'The Establishment and Consolidation of the New Regime, 1949–1957', in *The Politics of China: The Eras of Mao and Deng*, 3rd edition, ed. by Roderick MacFarquhar (Cambridge: Cambridge University Press, 1997), p. 86.

36 Tyrene White, *China's Longest Campaign: Birth Planning in the People's Republic, 1949–2005* (London: Cornell University Press, 2006), p. 2.

37 Three Represents: the CCP should 'always represent the developmental requirement of China's advanced productive forces, represent the developing orientation of China's advanced culture, and represent the fundamental interests of the overwhelming majority of the Chinese people'. See Lin, 'Ideology and Political Institutions for a New Era'.

38 Lin, 'Ideology and Political Institutions for a New Era' p. 64; Patricia M. Thornton, 'Retrofitting the Steel Frame: From Mobilizing the Masses to Surveying the Public', in *Mao's Invisible Hand: The Political Foundations of Adaptive Governance in China*, ed. by Sebastian Helimann and Elizabeth J. Perry (London: Harvard University Asia Center, 2011), pp. 237–68.

39 Anne-Maire Brady, 'Conclusion: The Velvet Fist in the Velvet Glove: Political and Social Control in Contemporary China', in *China's Thought Management*, ed. by Anne-Maire Brady (London: Routledge, 2012), pp. 185–6.

40 Brady, 'Introduction'.

41 Due to geographic constraints and financial limitations, this research was carried out exclusively in the central urban area of Chongqing, which covers 650 square kilometers and has a population of 8 million.

Bibliography

'*Bei quan ding de "hei laoda" daodi you duo hei?*' (How Black Are the Accused 'Black Mafia'?), *Southern Weekend*, 18 March 2010, <www.infzm.com/content/42718> [accessed 09 January 2014]

Brady, Anne-Maire, 'Conclusion: The Velvet Fist in the Velvet Glove: Political and Social Control in Contemporary China', in *China's Thought Management*, ed., Anne-Maire Brady (London: Routledge, 2012), 183–205

―――― 'Introduction', in Anne-Maire Brady, ed., *China's Thought Management* (London: Routledge, 2012), 1–8

Cui, Zhiyuan, ' *"Chongqing jingyan" jingxingshi: guozi zengzhi yu cangfu yu min bingjin*' ("Chongqing Experiences": Concurrent Increase of Wealth Between National Property and the Masses), *China Review of Political Economy*, 1 (2010), 73–80

―――― '*Chongqing "shi da minsheng gongcheng" de zhengzhi jingji xue*' (The Political Economy of Chongqing's "Ten Projects for Public Welfare"), *Institute for Advanced Historical and Social Research*, 19 June 2011, <www.lishiyushehui.cn/modules/topic/detail.php?topic_id=362> [accessed 09 January 2014]

―――― 'Partial Intimations of the Coming Whole: The Chongqing Experiment in Light of the Theories of Henry George, James Meade, and Antonio Gramsci', *Modern China*, 37 (2011), 646–60

Dittmer, Lowell, 'Chinese Leadership Succession to the Fourth Generation', in Gang Lin and Xiaobo Hu, eds, *China After Jiang* (Stanford, CA: Stanford University Press, 2003), pp. 11–38

Fewsmith, Joseph, 'Bo Xilai Takes on Organized Crimes', *China Leadership Monitor*, 32 (2010), 1–8

'*He Shizhong: 'chang hong' shi jiankang youyi de qunzhongxing wenhua huodong*' (He Shizhong: Singing Red Is a Beneficial Cultural Activity for the Masses), *Chongqing Daily*, 11 July 2011

He, Weifang, '*Weile fazhi, wei le women xinzhong de nayifen lixiang*' (Rule of Law – For the Ideal in Our Heart), <www.chinaelections.org/NewsInfo.asp?NewsID=225346> [accessed 09 January 2014]

Huang, Philip C. C., 'Chongqing: Equitable Development Driven by a "Third Hand"?' *Modern China*, 37 (2011), 569–622

Ji, Mingshuo, '*Chongqing moshi chuang zhongguo jingji fangong xinlujing*' (The Chongqing Model Is the New Road to China's Economic Fight-Back), *Asian Weekly*, no. 6, February 2009

Larson, Christina, 'Chicago on Yangtze', *Foreign Policy*, September/October 2010, <www.foreignpolicy.com/articles/2010/08/16/chicago_on_the_yangtze?page=0,3> [accessed 09 January 2014].

Li, Jianhong, 'Chongqing: Opportunities and Risks', *China Quarterly*, 178 (2004), 448–66

Li, Xiguang, '*Chongqing meng yu zhongguo moshi*' (The Dream of Chongqing and the China Model), *Phoenix Finance* website, 5 September 2010, <http://finance.ifeng.com/news/20100905/2588460.shtml> [accessed 09 January 2014]

'*Li Zhuang an: fating wai de jiaoliang*' (The Case of Li Zhuang: Struggles Outside of the Court), *Southern Weekend*, 07 January 2010, <www.infzm.com/content/39771> [accessed 09 January 2014]

Lin, Gang, 'Ideology and Political Institutions for a New Era', in Gang Lin and Xiaobo Hu, eds, *China After Jiang* (Stanford, CA: Stanford University Press, 2003), pp. 39–65

Lin, Gang, and Xiaobo Hu, 'Introduction', in Gang Lin and Xiaobo Hu, eds, *China After Jiang* (Stanford, CA: Stanford University Press, 2003), pp. 1–10

Rong, Jian, '*Huiwang Chongqing 1–5*' (Looking Back on Chongqing 1–5), *Sina Blog*, <http://blog.sina.com.cn/s/blog_49f32b3f0101a9az.html> [accessed 09 January 2014]

Saich, Tony, *Governance and Politics in China* (London: Palgrave Macmillan, 2011)

Su, Wei, Yang Fan, and Liu Shiwen, *Chongqing Moshi (The Chongqing Model)* (Beijing: Zhongguo jingji chubanshe, 2011)

14 *Chongqing under the spotlight*

Sun, Liping, '*Youguan Chongqing de liangdian kanfa*' (Two Thoughts on the Chongqing Model), *Aisixiang* website, 16 March 2012, <www.aisixiang.com/data/51299.html> [accessed 09 January 2014]

Teiwes, Frederick C., 'The Establishment and Consolidation of the New Regime, 1949–1957', in Roderick MacFarquhar, ed., *The Politics of China: The Eras of Mao and Deng*, 3rd edition (Cambridge: Cambridge University Press, 1997), pp. 6–86

Thornton, Patricia M., 'Retrofitting the Steel Frame: From Mobilizing the Masses to Surveying the Public', in Sebastian Helimann and Elizabeth J. Perry, eds, *Mao's Invisible Hand: The Political Foundations of Adaptive Governance in China* (London: Harvard University Asia Center, 2011), pp. 237–68

Tong, Zhiwei, '*Chongqing dahei xing shehui guanli fangshi yanjiu baogao*' (Report on Chongqing's Social Management in the Style of the 'Anti-crime' Campaign), *Zhongguo xianfa xue yanjiu hui*, 22 October 2011, <www.21ccom.net/articles/zgyj/ggzhc/article_2012021353482.html?1329286156> [accessed 09 January 2014]

Wang, Hui, 'The Rumor Machine', *London Review of Books*, 34 (2012), 13–14

Wang, Shaoguang, '*Tansuo zhongguoshi shehuizhuyi 3.0: Chongqing jingyan*' (To Explore Chinese Socialism 3.0: Chongqing Experiences), *Makesi Zhuyi Yanjiu*, 2 (2011), 5–14

White, Tyrene, *China's Longest Campaign: Birth Planning in the People's Republic, 1949–2005* (London: Cornell University Press, 2006)

Yang, Jisheng, *Zhongguo Gaige Niandai de Zhengzhi Douzheng (Political Struggles in the Era of Reforms in China)* (Hong Kong: Excellent Culture Press, 2004)

Zhang, Weiwei, '*Chongqing guilai hua Chongqing*' (Talking About Chongqing After a Trip to Chongqing), *Hongqi Wengao*, 2 (2012), 36–37

'*Zhongwai meiti quanguo lianghui jujiao Chongqing*' (National and Foreign Press Focus Attention on Chongqing During the "Two Meetings"), *Chongqing Daily*, 11 March 2009

2 Putting the Red culture campaign into perspective

Chongqing's Red culture campaign is not a typical social movement, as defined in Western social movement literature. Social movements are collective challenges to elites or authorities in the name of certain 'justified' common purposes. They require constant recruitment and mobilisation of supporters to carry out contentious collective actions towards antagonistic forces within the movement. Gamson and Meyer define social movements as 'sustained and self-conscious challenge to authorities or cultural codes by a field of actors'.[1] In China, the Communist Party (CCP) has always been the sole power that was capable of mass mobilising. Campaigns are one of the key mechanisms of political sanctions that help to eliminate hostility towards the Party.[2] It is extremely rare for autonomous interest groups to form, not to mention countering the power of the state. Collective action faces extreme difficulty in achieving satisfactory results as most will be nipped in the bud. What Andrew Walder argues in the 1980s still largely holds true even in today's China – that the Chinese state has an 'extraordinary ability to prevent organized political activities even from reaching the state of collective action'.[3]

In fact, Chongqing's Red culture campaign is more of a form of mass activity (*yundong* 运动) which exhibits both similarities and disparities with social movements. It is similar with social movements in that Chongqing's Red culture campaign contains organized and purposeful mass-mobilised activities. It is different from social movements for that as a Chinese '*yundong*', the Red culture campaign was sponsored by Chongqing's local government, not as contentious challenges towards authority but as actions to reinforce it. Thus, the theoretical framework of social movement studies is not entirely applicable to the study of Chongqing's Red culture campaign. Yet I share a number of inspirations from the previous studies of China's movements. For one thing, individual participants of a movement or mass activity are rational human beings who are well aware of the benefits and costs of getting involved in such events. They are capable of making rational judgment. For another, the ways in which individuals and the state interact condition the effectiveness of the movement or mass activity. Lastly, despite all the rational judgment and calculating effort, there are always emotions and the need to construct identities involved in the process of mass mobilisation. Thus, studies on social movement provide a rich source of theoretical framework for the study of social mobilisation in the case of Chongqing's Red culture campaign. In

16 Red culture campaign in perspective

the following section, I mainly draw on studies of a most important movement in the recent history of the Republic of China, that is, the Cultural Revolution (CR), to illustrate how the interaction between the state and the individual participants have been tackled in past research.

Social movement studies in the Chinese context

Typical examples of social movements examined in Western academic literature include the American civil rights movement, feminist movements, gay rights movements, environmental protests, and so on. All social movements require constant production, negotiation, and transmission of meanings to mobilise individuals, sustain social networks, and incur pressure on opponents.[4] Studies of social movements have gone through different stages, evolving from focusing on mass grievances to deciphering the complex organizational structure and resources mobilisation of the movements. In the 1990s, researchers became interested in the function of culture and identity in mobilising participants of social movements. During the theoretical evolution of social movement studies, 'individuals' are treated differently in different stages of studies. The 'maddened crowd' becomes rational human beings as the researchers identify the significance of organization and the fact that individuals make rational decisions when choosing whether to get involved in certain movements. Gradually, however, researchers realise that the 'personal judgment' is not based on pure self-interest or rational calculation. Social identities and emotions play crucial roles shaping and framing these judgments.[5]

The study of social movements in China generally follows the same developmental trajectory of Western social movement studies, encompassing themes of social grievances, organizational structure, identity and emotions, and so on. It has been observed across different localities that pre-existing social grievances are important motivation behind such violence, and the nature of such grievances are often conditioned by specific, ordinary, local factors.[6] Lynn White explores the organizational causes of violence during the CR. The happening of a political movement is normally the function of interweaving individual actions, group consciousness, and institutional structures. According to White, turbulence of such scale and intensity could not be possible unless the power of the masses is sufficiently unleashed. Individual participants are believed to attach different meanings to the CR, which are conditioned by personal political ideals, local environment, or the availability of resources. The organizational structure of such violence, on the other hand, is conditioned by certain administrative policies, such as the labeling policies, which create distinctive status groups such as the 'rightists', 'the 'capitalists', and so on, and the patronage policies, which require people to choose sides and remain royal to a particular 'boss'.[7] Perry and Li, in their careful examination of the experience of local people in Shanghai during CR, argue that the power of the proletarian masses is no less important than that which comes from the top-down political structure. Mass activism has traditionally been explained by socio-economic status, political networks based on patronage, or

Red culture campaign in perspective 17

psychological factors. Perry and Li are convinced that mass activism, despite its seeming disorder and chaotic appearance, is in fact the result of organizational effort. Popular activism is never unorganized but consistent with the specific patterns of organization formed under contextual constraints and personal concerns.[8] Guobin Yang in his research examines the students' experiences in the movement as an emotional process. He argues that emotions are capable of affecting and shaping micro-level mobilisation, and individuals sometimes gain emotional, satisfying experiences from participating in the movement.[9] Studying also from the perspective of culture, Pfaff and Yang investigate the role of political commemorations as a form of symbolic resources in mobilising collective action. They confirm that symbols are crucial for establishing shared identity, which in turn empower social and political movement. They argue that rituals enforced top-down can simultaneously reinforce domination and provide room for dissenting voice and action.[10]

There has also been a constant interest in documenting and analysing the personal experiences of individual participants as well as the interaction between such experiences and larger structural factors, such as economic conditions, traditional culture, incomplete political reform, and so on. Since the late 1970s and early 1980s, scholars of China studies have begun to realise the inadequacy of studying China's social movements merely from the perspective of the leader's intention or political struggle among the elites. Research that studies the CR from the perspective of those below, that is, the experience of the masses, starts to emerge. Researchers are interested in how local people are split into different fractions and why struggles contain different levels of violence. As a critical response to the previously adopted 'totalitarian model' that focuses on the role of the Party and its almighty leader in CR literature, this approach turns to the dynamics of the everyday practices of local people in the political movement. For example, abundant research has been dedicated to searching for the sociopolitical conditions for the grass-roots conflicts in China during the 1966–1968 Red Guard movement. As a typical example of studies focusing on the *individuals*, Wang Shaoguang in his treatment of the CR in Wuhan, argues that the rationality of the local residents during the revolution is in fact the determinant factor for them to choose to, or not to, get involved in a mass movement. Wang also draws the conclusion that the behaviour of the masses, which is based on calculations of costs and benefits, to a large extent limits the effect of Mao's power as a charismatic leader.[11] Sharing a similar focus on the individuals' experiences, Yin Hongbiao, who devotes an entire career to investigate the grass-roots experience of the CR, also focuses on the young people's development of ideas. He examines the emergence of new ideas that contradict with the official narrative and slogans.[12]

One commonly shared focus that underlies all research is the interaction between individuals and the institutional structure of the state. For instance, in Vivienne Shue's exploratory essay on the politics of China's rural society during the CR, she uses the concept of 'cellularity' to explain the interstices between the state and rural society. She argues that the limited effect of state penetration during the CR in the countryside is the function of fragmented, parcellised, and cellular

18 *Red culture campaign in perspective*

structure of the local economy and society. Moreover, by tracing the process of political life in the rural area, Shue also demonstrates the mutually conditioning effects between the state and society, in particularly, how 'the peasant society left its imprint on contemporary state organization and routines.[13]

In the next section, I specifically discuss the 'state-society' framework in China studies. Drawing upon existing major themes of research on China's state-society, several important questions should be raised when pondering the case of Chongqing's Red culture campaign: 1) Is mass mobilisation witnessed in Chongqing's Red culture campaign a form of 'domination'? If so, is it carried out in forms of oppression or legitimation? 2) Do participants of Chongqing's Red culture campaign practice 'resistance'? If so, is it carried out in forms of overt or tacit resistance?

The 'state-society' framework in China studies

Decades of scholarly work that aspires to understand the relationship between China's Party-state and its people are informed by the 'state-society' paradigm. Focusing on topics such as state building, the civil society, and social governance, the framework gained prominence in China studies in the late 1980s. It marked a clear break from the totalitarian model and CR studies, constituting the 'third generation' of scholarship working on China.[14] At the same time, the framework has been criticised for its overly generic and dichotomised orientation towards the notions of 'state' and 'society'. As a result, much effort has been devoted to reconfiguring, or even transcending, this dominant framework in the field of China studies. Some have attempted to disaggregate the concept of the 'state' because it is believed to be far more fractured than is normally assumed. The state is not a coherent, goal-oriented, single entity. Research, such as Shi and Cai's study on collective resistance in Shanghai, has shown that state power is profoundly fragmented at the local level. It is this fragmentation that has led to opportunities for the people on the ground to engage in successful resistance.[15] Emphasising the important role of the local state in the '(re-)negotiation of the state-society relationships', other research has examined specifically how the Chinese state has been 'shaped by local forces'.[16] Migdal, for instance, introduces a new 'state-in-society' approach and tries to redefine the notion of the state. According to Migdal, the interaction between the state and the multiple groupings in society is heavily laden with conflicts, and each side is capable of utilising various forms of strategy or tactics to promote a specific version of values and norms. He sees the state as 'a contradictory entity that acts against itself'. The state contains an image of itself which is often unified and singular as well as its actual practices, which are fragmented and sometimes conflicting.[17] This approach rebels against the classic notion of an autonomous state, which was once popularised by classic political theorists such as Rueschemeyer and Skocpol.[18] Stern and O'Brien, inspired by Migdal's work, propose another 'state reflected in society' approach to discern the characteristics of the Chinese state. They rely on popular experiences with the state power to examine how the Chinese government and the people negotiate

Red culture campaign in perspective   19

and interpret the boundaries of permissible actions. The researchers found that the messages given out by the 'state' about the limits of activism are often mixed and inconsistent. Different levels of authorities speak with different voices.[19]

Likewise, the concept of 'society' has been argued to be extremely vague. It encompasses a wide variety of social actors, including social organizations of different kinds, the masses, and individuals. Moreover, in the case of China, society is often deeply intertwined with the state structure and entrenched within the Party's political system. Research on Chinese nongovernmental organizations (NGOs), for example, illustrates that the theoretical framework that artificially separates the state and society is inappropriate, or at least insufficient, to account for the state-NGO relationship. As Teets argues, 'a model of state-society collaboration may be more useful in helping the burgeoning civil groups to deliver a better service for public welfare'.[20] In fact, the relationship of the NGOs with governments of all levels remains a key factor in the effectiveness of such organizations and social groups. Cheng et al., for example, find that many, if not all civic associations in China must cultivate a good relationship with the local officials and the administrative networks. Informal politics remain necessary and effective techniques for ensuring the survival and success of civic organizations.[21] Similarly, Hsu has argued that social organizations in China are much less interested in gaining 'independence' from the state than looking for possibilities of mutual reliance and benefits.[22] In the case of China, there is no clear demarcation between state and society and little public space in which people are free to join associations, debate public issues, or influence political decisions.[23] When analysing the interaction between NGOs and the local state, Hsu and Hasmath argue that the local government preserves its own relevance in the sector of NGOs by employing corporatist measures to manage the NGOs. The state's corporatist approach is underpinned by the logic of tacit sanctioning, under the effect of which the state manages NGOs by actively granting certain privilege to NGOs of its own selection in exchange for compliance. The authors suggest that although the local state still exerts significant impact on the life course of the NGOs, the state and the NGOs can be complementary in providing social services to their constituencies.[24] In addition to the continual effort to revise the 'state and society' model by taking into account the interactive and collaborative aspects of their relationships, a more radical move tries to dismantle this framework altogether. Researchers have proposed a more grounded approach to examine the dynamics between the concrete and specific players within China's social and political life. For example, Gui et al., by examining the development of neighbourhoods in Shanghai, argue that the grass-roots level of the political system in today's China is neither 'state' nor 'society' but a network of social actors with distinctive interests of their own.[25]

In this book, the relationship between the political power that initiated and implemented the Red culture campaign and the practices of the ordinary participants is much more restricted in scope than the broad notion of 'state-society' relations. The political power that pushed through the programme was not operated at the level of the central leadership of the Party-state but embodied in the position of an official of the local municipality. This creates a complex situation because, on

20 *Red culture campaign in perspective*

the one hand, the political power that supports the Red culture campaign did not exist in isolation but was rooted in the power matrix of the authoritarian Party. On the other hand, it should not be conflated with the central leadership of the Party as there was individual ambition at stake, and one should also take into account the uniqueness of the structure of the local government. It is also worth mentioning that the Red culture campaign was terminated as the central leadership of the CCP decided to remove Bo from office.[26] That meant there might be some conflicts regarding how ideological issues should be handled among different levels of the state. Most of the research on China's politics in the reform era observes a tendency for the Party-state to relax its ideological control. There has certainly been a decline in the use of mass mobilisation as a major method for acquiring political legitimacy. The emergence of Chongqing's Red culture campaign, however, seemed a counterexample of this tendency. There has rarely been an ideological campaign initiated by a local official that could wield so much influence over the ideological discourse of the Party. Usually, when researchers study ideological campaigns, they examine the goals and actions of the Party as a singular and holistic executor of political power. In this case, there was clearly a distinction to be made between the ambition of Bo Xilai and the central leadership of the CCP.

Similarly, 'society' is obviously too broad a notion to account for the participants involved in the Red culture campaign. There are some complications here as well. Most of the participants did not take part in the campaign out of a purely *individual* volition. They participated as members of local residential communities, students of a university, or employees of a company. In most cases, they sang in groups and *performed* collective actions. Moreover, there were shared patterns of participation among the three different social groups studied for this project. At the same time, there was a distinctively *individualistic* element in the practices of these participants. The ways in which people rationalise and judge their own participation in the campaign in terms of their personal needs and interests were largely individually-oriented. Each participant should be treated as an individual who was aware of the choices he/she made regarding whether one should get involved in the political campaign.

Although I do not directly engage with the broad concepts of 'state' or 'society' in this book, it is worth acknowledging that this book does inherit inspirations from the decades of scholarly deliberation on the 'state-society' relationship, especially the more recent effort to decipher the collaborative and interactive aspects of this relationship. Moreover, the underpinning concern with the issues of power inequality and struggles shared by this book and previous studies on the 'state-society' relationship is the same. In particular, the issues of domination and resistance underpin the theoretical interpretation of the case of Chongqing's Red culture campaign.

Domination and legitimacy

Studies on the interaction between the Party-state and its people are often underpinned by concepts of domination and resistance. Scott defines domination as

Red culture campaign in perspective 21

'where power is structured into the stable and enduring social relations that make up large-scale social structures'. It works through institutions 'to produce regular and persistent patterns of action'. Domination is an inherently unequal form of social interaction. It entails power relations that are formed under actions of force, manipulation, or legitimation.[27] The research on the CCP's sources of power in the reform era is increasingly focused on legitimation instead of oppression or overt manipulation.

Legitimation is one form of domination that builds upon the subalterns' emotional commitment to a specific set of values that will persuade them to follow a specific pattern of conduct.[28] Political legitimacy is 'the capacity of the system to engender and maintain the belief that the existing political institutions are the most appropriate ones for the society'.[29] It is considered a key criterion for measuring the success of the ruling party and future prospects of the stability of the political regime.[30] In the case of China, analysts are particularly interested in the source of power that has enabled the Party-state to remain in control for more than 60 years. Many political analysts see authoritarian rule as 'inflexible and unlikely to endure'. Based on this understanding, they predict that 'intraparty splits, economic development, changing class structure, and/or pacts' will lead to the collapse of authoritarian regimes.[31] Yet, the CCP seems to enjoy a high level of political legitimacy despite the dramatic changes in the political and social conditions in the past decades. A large volume of scholarly work is dedicated to analysing the nature of the CCP's legitimacy and, in particular, how it has changed and endured.

According to Guo, for example, the political legitimacy of the CCP during Mao's era relied on the narrative of the 'historical mission' of communism, the charismatic leadership of Mao, the principle of 'democratic centralism', the method of 'proletarian dictatorship', and the goal of 'serving the people'.[32] In Mao's era, his mass-line approach corresponded well with the traditional beliefs in the pursuit of equality and the importance of popular consent.[33] Moreover, the CCP relied on the mobilisation mode to legitimise its authority. Mao Zedong's concept of 'continuous revolution' is such an example.[34] In the post-Mao era, however, political analysts found that the use of mobilisation had drastically decreased. Instead, China adopted completely different socio-economic priorities, whereas class struggles and the mass movement gave way to rational-bureaucratic administration and no longer acted as the main source of political legitimacy.[35] Charismatic legitimacy has also declined significantly since the passing away of Mao Zedong and Deng Xiaoping.[36] Technocrats replaced the 'strongmen' as the leaders of the party and the nation. Many China observers were puzzled by the CCP's ability to maintain a high level of legitimacy despite the tremendous challenges it faces in the political environment of a market economy.[37] One of the main arguments is that the CCP now largely relies on 'performance legitimacy' to remain in power.[38] The CCP combines 'economic nationalism, political conservatism, and the rehabilitation of the individual pursuit of personal happiness' as the new strategy for maintaining its status and relevance as the ruling party.[39] Most notably, economic prosperity took over as the predominantly utilitarian rationalisation for the people to

22   *Red culture campaign in perspective*

accept the authority of the Party. Scholarly attention therefore starts to focus on the relationship between China's political system and its economic reforms. For example, Gordon White argues that economic reform was a means for the CCP to reclaim 'hegemonic authority' and generate a new form of legitimacy that is predicated on the Party's ability to improve people's welfare.[40] Xinmin Pei points out that institutional flexibility at the local level enhanced economic performance and strengthened support for the government.[41] Jean Oi examines the institutional foundations of China's economic growth, in particular how rural industrialisation has brought about dramatic growth without triggering substantial political changes.[42] Victor Nee et al. investigate the delicate relationship between the state and China's firms as China adopts what they call a 'politicized capitalism' in its market transition.[43]

In addition to economic reform, an increasing amount of research has begun to examine how the CCP responds and adapts to the challenges by introducing new modes of governance and social management. In fact, good governance starts to emerge as another major source of legitimacy pursued by China's Part-state.[44] In part, this is the reaction of the Party-state towards an increasingly estranged and confrontational relationship with the angry 'society'.[45] Governance at the local level, such as the rural village or *shequ* in the cities, has become a popular subject for research. Jamie Horsley, for example, examines the legal context and administrative procedures for public participation taking place at the local level. She points out that some of these mechanisms (e.g., the administrative and legislative hearings) have helped to soothe the tension between the local government and residents on sensitive issues such as land acquisition and housing demolition.[46] Xu Feng, for instance, explores the Party's effort to build 'harmonious' communities in the cities that provide essential social services for the residents. Self-governance at the community level not only provides essential social services for the residents but also functions as a mechanism for strengthening the Party's network organization. She argues that the CCP's resilience to challenges and crises relies on a pragmatic adoption of new methods of governance despite their incompatibility with the Party's official ideology.[47]

Power of resistance – collective action and the 'weapons of the weak'

The domination practiced by the Party-state over its people has nevertheless been countered by resistance in a wide variety of degrees and forms. Power relations always contain the possibility of conflict. Domination, therefore, rarely sustains without evoking forms of resistance or counteraction. According to Scott, fully developed counteraction refers to 'co-ordinated or collective action' against the dominator, but resistance does not always take place in the form of overt struggles. 'Resentment, hostility, or withdrawals' are also elementary forms of counteraction.[48] Studies on the power of resistance against the domination of political power in China fall correspondingly into roughly two genres. The first type concerns more formal forms of resistance, that is, collective action.

Most notably, studies have been carried out to examine social unrest and mass incidents in China, which increased tenfold from 1993 to 2005.[49] It was estimated that about 180,000 incidents of social unrest took place in 2010, some of which started to spread to the major cities rather than being restricted to the rural areas.[50] With regard to rural protests, O'Brien and Li write about 'rightful resistance' by the peasants. According to the authors, the peasants in rural China used the state policies and laws directly to challenge the local cadres. These challenges were conducted in public and conspicuously visible.[51] Other research has studied the phenomenon of urban labour unrest following the extensive restructuring of the state-owned enterprises (SOEs) in the 1990s, which resulted in widespread unemployment among urban workers. Many working-class people still hold onto residues of the revolutionary culture, evoking ideas of 'anticapitalism, antiexploitation, equality, and state welfare' as weapons to struggle with the 'evils' of the market economy and ensuing social problems.[52] Lee argues that labour unrest during this period makes up a 'force of political challenge and social change' that is mainly constrained at a local level.[53] On the other hand, they do manage gradually to change the dynamics between the local officials and residents.[54]

The mass incidents occurring in today's China typically concern land disputes, mass layoffs, pollution, or ethnic conflict. Yu Jianrong sees these conflicts as social actions of the subaltern. The subaltern is seen as not only the object of political management but also the actor of what Yu calls 'contentious politics'. The root of contentious politics is the conflicts of interest resulting from the widespread social inequality between the disadvantaged masses and the elite groups who possess a disproportional amount of political and economic resources.[55] Frustrated people increasingly adopt more disruptive measures to express their economic and social grievances. As Yu points out, the workers and peasants are capable of employing both traditional political rhetoric and the current state laws as their weapons for challenging the local authority. Cai, in his study on collective resistance in China, identifies several strategies used by protesters to achieve success in protests, including seeking support from an upper-level authority, asking for help from external sources such as the media and foreign foundations, and carrying out disruptive action.[56] At times, disadvantaged social groups in China have to employ 'troublemaking' tactics to gain leverage in their bargaining games with the local governments, to whom maintaining social stability is the most important political priority.[57]

As discussed earlier in the chapter, collective actions that aim to challenge the state are rather rare in today's China. What is most likely to take place is tactical resistance. A key task faced by the studies on China's masses is to assess to what extent their actions constitute a transformative political force in China. Alan Liu, in his book on mass politics in China, argues that the public opinion of the non-elite groups is capable of 'shaping major political outcomes' through the people's everyday interaction with the state, despite the constraints of the Party-state structure.[58] Lee, on the other hand, points out that although the conduct by protesters is capable of opening up space for the voices of the masses on issues they deem

24 *Red culture campaign in perspective*

critical, labour unrest in China has nevertheless been 'more effective as a force for social change than as a force for political change'.[59] In fact, because these protests are deemed as posing a threat to the normative order of society and face retaliation by the state,[60] workers often adopt a realistic and pragmatic approach, having convinced themselves that the odds of defying the deeply-entrenched system is extremely slim, whereas the consequences could be severe. Therefore, protestors often identify themselves as 'loyal member(s) of the regime' who operate within the boundaries circumscribed by the political system. As Chen acutely observes, ordinary citizens who engage in contentious actions against the government often display 'resistance while somehow remaining submissive'. Characterised as 'protest opportunism', the mass incidents have not caused any fundamental challenge to the existing political structure.

The other genre of resistance is identified as containing everyday actions that are quiet, dispersed, and often invisible. Research on this type of resistance is typically influenced by James Scott's influential works on the weapons of the weak and the hidden transcriptions of the subalterns.[61] Yuhua Guo, for example, works on the 'telling of suffering' by peasants in China. For her, focusing on the individuals in the lower social stratum builds links between the individual experiences and the transformation of the social structures of the larger society. It is believed that the stories of the 'silent majority' can act as a counter-narrative to the official history and contain forms of resistance in themselves.[62] Wanning Sun, in her ethnographic study on Chinese migrant workers' consumption practices, identifies ' "subversive" behaviours *within* rather than *in opposition to* the capitalist commercial logic and space'.[63] Such research tends to focus on marginalised groups in society and normally identifies human agency as heavily constrained by the structural conditions.

In sum, studies on the relationship between China's Party-state and the practices of its people have come to appreciate the complexity of this relationship. Domination can occur in the form of not only force and manipulation but also legitimation. Legitimacy can be acquired through many channels as well, including political mobilisation, economic development, social governance, and ideological control. On the other hand, resistance can also take on different appearances. It contains both dramatic and disruptive actions as well as struggles of a quieter and subtler nature. In the next section, I will follow the lead of the existing research to emphasise that the interaction between the Party-state and its people can happen in various forms and with varying intensity and therefore produce different effects on society.

Chongqing's Red culture campaign, which seemed very much like a mass campaign, demonstrated features of neither forceful domination nor outright resistance. In the next section, I use the concept of 'simulation' to characterise the nature of the Red culture campaign. I use the pair of concepts – 'strategy' and 'tactics' to characterise the top-down political programme of the Red culture campaign and the practices of the participants in everyday life. I describe their interactive relationship as simultaneously associative and disassociative under the effects of simulation, resources exchange, and framing processes.

Theoretical concepts

Simulation

I draw on Baudrillard's concept of simulation to characterise Chongqing's Red culture campaign to decipher the interactive relationship between the political power underpinning the campaign and the practice of the ordinary participants. Baudrillard's theory of simulation is useful in this case for it facilitates a better understanding of the nature of both the Red culture campaign and political power that supported and sustained the programme. Baudrillard devises a theory of simulation as a radical critique of the capital, which he believes has 'cancelled the *principle* of reality' and had a particularly hallowing effect on modern life.[64] Baudrillard's theory of simulation concerns a specific kind of power and its organization in modern society. It is a form of organizing power that dominates in a very specific way. According to Baudrillard, simulation is a process during which models of reality are produced. Simulation artificially generates systems of signs that are used to substitute the representations of reality, firstly, to simulate means pretending to possess something that does not exist. It indicates an absence of *the real*. Secondly, simulation feigns the existence of reality and 'produces "true" symptoms'. For a simulacrum to produce true symptoms of the real, it follows pre-existing models of reality. As a result, facts lose their own trajectories; instead, they revolve around the model's designs and requisites. Thus, simulation involves the liquidation of the referentials. If ideology is 'a false representation of reality' that distorts truth but nevertheless builds upon the existence of the real, simulation on the other hand empties the substance of the real. It no longer represents but creates perfect, albeit fake, 'truth'. Lastly, simulation constitutes a self-induced and non-dialectical circuit of power. The operation of simulation is no longer 'specular and discursive' but 'nuclear and genetic'. The system created by simulation is a monolithic and self-induced circuit where signs are 'exchanged against each other rather than against the real'.[65]

By utilising Baudrillard's theory of simulation, I address the question regarding the nature of Chongqing's Red culture campaign. I will try to convince the readers that Chongqing's Red culture campaign was not a *real* Maoist mass campaign but demonstrated critical features of simulation. Because of such nature of the campaign, the relationship between the political programme and its participants display dissociative features which entail critical social and political consequences.

Tactics and strategy

According to Michel de Certeau's theory of everyday practice, tactics are procedures of practices that are dispersed, opaque, and quiet, yet capable of deflecting imposing systems and dominant institutions. These practices, such as talking, reading, cooking, and shopping, constitute an infinite number of small changes that are almost invisible but pervasive. The success of a tactic depends on its users' creativity and, most importantly, their ability to catch fleeting opportunities. Moreover,

26   *Red culture campaign in perspective*

a tactic does not seek to escape the space where its practitioner is constrained by the existing order and institution but poaches, and diverts, in an artful way, within the territory of the more powerful. The locale of everyday life, therefore, is where the 'weak' triumphs over the 'strong'. Tactics constitute 'a hidden production', insinuated into the locale of everyday life. By using de Certeau's notion of tactics, I wish to avoid the tendency in the existing literature on Chinese society to identify agency only in cases of resistance and to focus on the subalterns where the power of everyday life is concerned. I wish to emphasise that such actions of tactics are not undertaken only by those who are severely marginalised, or those who have so many grievances that they have chosen to resist the authorities, but rather are common practices that can be observed in the everyday life of ordinary people.

The practice of tactics presupposes a powerful counterpart for its actors. This counterpart can be characterised by 'strategy', the concept that contrasts with tactics. *Strategy* is conceptualised by de Certeau as the established, rationalised, expansionist, centralised, and dominating rules employed by 'a subject of will and power', on the basis of which 'objective' political, scientific, and economic models are built. A strategy circumscribes its own 'proper' place and generates relations that are isolable and extractable from the environment. It constructs grand narratives of history and holds the 'power of knowledge'. The strategic system is often gigantic, tightly-woven, prescribing, and repressive.[66] The Red culture campaign was the effect of an *interaction* between the strategies of the official programme and the tactical nature of the practices themselves.

By utilising de Certeau's theory on the practices of everyday life, I share de Certeau's concern with 'the individual subject in political life'.[67] As discussed, the practitioners of tactics in everyday life, often deemed to be weak, silent, and docile, are able secretly to direct the trajectory of life according to their own interests and rules without issuing an open challenge to the dominators. Individuals can exercise creativity in deflecting the structural constraints of modern life through reinscribing and rereading the texts of the social world. The actors of the tactics are thus 'unrecognized producers, poets of their own acts, silent discoverers of their own paths in the jungle of functionalist rationality'. A significant implication for studying tactics, according the Certeau, is to open up an additional imaginary landscape for the study of the 'problematics of repression'. Research that focuses on the institutional apparatuses of repression largely ignores the fact that practices assumed to be dominated by an oppressive mechanism are, in fact, heterogeneous and flexible. Such practices, hiding under the appearance of constant metamorphosis, constitute a social reality that is both 'fleeting and permanent'. Research that works within this imaginary landscape of the tactics explores social reality at a deeper and less traversed level.[68]

By drawing upon de Certeau's concept of tactics, I address the nature of the participants' practice. I analyse the strategic nature of the official programme and the tactical nature of the participant's practice. Here I attempt to amend the weaknesses inherent in Baudrillard's concept of simulation and establish the associative relationship between the political power and the individuals. In the following sections, I explore such an associative relationship in the forms of exchange and framing.

Exchange

A critical form of relationship that underpins the interaction between the Red culture campaign and the practices of its participants is that of *exchange*. Discussion of the sociological significance of exchange can be traced back to the works of Georg Simmel, who regards exchange as a fundamental social form, championing it as 'the purest and most concentrated form of all human interactions'. Most consequentially, exchange is a productive and creative social form. It is a fundamental process that gives birth to 'something new', that is, the value of an object. Value is not a 'ready-made' quality of objects but attained through a process of 'objective valuation' during exchange. Exchange, according to Simmel, is not only a significant social form but a 'primary one', a 'sociological structure *sui generis*'.[69] The concept of 'social exchange' was further developed in the mid-20th century by scholars such as Blau and Homans and primarily used as an analytic concept for understanding social behaviour, particularly how individuals make choices and decisions. This application was based on the feature of *reciprocity*, that is, people's expectation of a return when they perform certain social actions.[70] During the last few decades of the 20th century, social exchange theory has been primarily associated with the analytic paradigm of the rational choice model, predicated on the assumption that the actors within an exchange are purposive, rational, and calculative.[71]

Both the behaviourist and microeconomic approaches to exchange have been duly criticised by social theorists for failing to account for the complexity and subjectivity of social life. They point out that social exchanges are often based on trust and an expectation of a long-term relationship instead of immediate returns. In fact, the concept of exchange has been used by social theorists to understand group solidarity,[72] identity construction,[73] and social networks.[74] In this research project, exchange is a social form that characterised the interaction between the official programme of the Red culture campaign and the practices of its participants. Evoking this concept is useful in accounting for the interdependence of the two, despite the huge discrepancies in terms of their political power. It captures the process of interaction whereby creative and value-engendering practices are possible.

Framing processes

The interaction between the political programme of the Red culture campaign and its participants concerns not only practices but also how both sides frame the event and its meanings. Frame analysis is often carried out to understand how actors make sense of the world and evaluate alternative options of behaviour. In this research, frame analysis will be centered on two main questions: how frames are constructed in the narratives of the Red culture campaign by both the government and the participants and how frames can be contested among different actors of a collective activity.

Drawing upon Garfinkel's idea that there exist multiple realities of the world, Goffman takes a situational perspective to map out how individuals could adopt

28 *Red culture campaign in perspective*

different views of a common situation in which they find themselves. Goffman argues that social members constantly reread the happenings around them, and these rereadings are vulnerable. He therefore sets out the task to search for the basic frameworks upon which individuals draw to make sense of the social world they live in. According to Goffman, ' "frames" are principles of organizations which govern events – at least social ones – and our subjective involvement in them'.[75] Multiple frameworks can be applied by one individual at any given moment during a social action. 'Frames of activities' refer to the 'organizational principles' according to which individuals not only perceive the meanings of the social world but also adjust their behaviours in light of such understandings. 'Primary frameworks', 'keyings', and 'fabrications' are such frames of activities.

'Primary framework' provides an original meaning to social events and thus enables the readers of the events to decide 'what it is that is going on'.[76] The primary framework used by a particular social group is an important element of its culture. 'Keying', a critical term used by Goffman to describe the processes of social transcription, refers to the transformation of primary meaning carried out by individuals to decide 'what it is we think is really going on'.[77] For example, an act of 'fighting' (primary meaning) can be reinterpreted as a form of 'play' as a result of the observer's excise of 'keying'.[78] Like other forms of meaning making, keyings are susceptible to mistakes and re-keyings. Goffman sees this as critical evidence that human activities are vulnerable and, more importantly, changeable. In addition to the keying processes, another major way to transform the meaning of an action is that of 'fabrication', which refers to an 'intentional effort of one or more individuals to manage activity so that a party of one or more others will be induced to have a false belief about what it is that is going on'.[79] Like keying, fabrication is built upon the foundation of 'primary frameworks', meaning that it only acts upon events that are already 'meaningful' in their own right. Keying and fabrication constitute the two major forms of how the meanings of social activities can be transformed.

Goffman's term 'framing' originally applied to how individuals construct reality for themselves, but in the social movement tradition that grew out of his work, scholars have focused on how movements frame specific grievances with collective action frames that dignify claims, connect them to others, and help produce a collective identity. Unlike Goffman's cognitive approach to framing, I will follow the traditions of social movement theories to focus more on the social aspect of both the construction and contentions of the frames.

David Snow applies and modifies Erving Goffman's concept of 'frame' in his theory to account for the process where people bring shared meanings to their actions. Snow defines 'framing' as 'conscious strategic efforts by groups of people to fashion shared understandings of the world and of themselves that legitimate and motivate collective action'.[80] The issue of framing is brought to the front of analytical focus as an attempt to rebel against the previously dominant framework of the resources mobilisation theory, which according to its critics, bluntly ignores the importance of ideas and emotions during social movements. Subsequent scholars on social movement, such as Smelser, Melucci, and Touraine, also

Red culture campaign in perspective 29

take the issues of meaning and identity central to their analysis of social movements. Cultural elements, in particular, 'the sources and functions of meaning and identity', become the central elements in analysis of new social movements.[81]

One of the key areas of research on the framing process is to investigate the contending efforts of narrating the significance of the collective action among the actors of the movement themselves or between actors and their 'enemies', during which alternative routes, values, and goals are debated. Frames are 'the specific metaphors, symbolic representations, and cognitive cues used to render or cast behaviour and events in an evaluative mode and to suggest alternative modes of action'.[82] They are shared meanings that define problems and suggest solutions to the problem. Therefore, frames contain both diagnostic and prognostic elements.[83] Compared with ideologies, frames are often much less sophisticated or systematic. Frames can be quite fragmented; they are not necessarily as logical as ideologies. Although Chongqing's Red culture campaign is not a social movement, as argued previously in this chapter, it nevertheless exhibits sufficient characteristics of mass action to warrant a treatment of framing analysis similar to that of social movement studies.

Summary

This chapter facilitates the understanding of Chongqing's Red culture campaign by discussing the framework for studying social movements in China. Although Chongqing's Red culture campaign was not a typical social movement, nevertheless the analysis of the campaign can draw on inspirations from the existing literature. What underlies the study of social movements in China is a discussion of the 'state-society' relationship. What underlies the study of the 'state-society' relationship is a series of questions on issues of domination and resistance. Thus, the study of the Red culture campaign is indeed about unfolding the power relations that underpin it. In this chapter, simulation, tactics, strategy, exchange, and framing are theoretical concepts introduced to unfold such power relationships between the political programme of the Red culture campaign and the participants' practices.

Notes

1 William A. Gamson and David S. Meyer, 'Framing Political Opportunities', in *Comparative Perspectives on Social Movements: Political Opportunities, Mobilizing Structures, and Cultural Framings*, ed. by Doug McAdam, John D. McCarthy & Mayer N. Zald (Cambridge: Cambridge University Press, 1996), p. 283.
2 Zhou Xuanguang, 'Unorganized Interests and Collective Action in Communist China', *American Sociological Review*, 58 (1993), 54–73.
3 Walder 1986, quoted in Zhou, 'Unorganized Interests and Collective Action in Communist China', p. 55.
4 Doug McAdam, 'The Framing Function of Movement Tactics: Strategic Dramaturgy in the American Civil Rights Movement', in *Comparative Perspectives on Social Movements: Political Opportunities, Mobilizing Structures, and Cultural Framings*, ed. by Doug McAdam, John D. McCarthy & Mayer N. Zald (Cambridge: Cambridge University Press, 1996).

30 *Red culture campaign in perspective*

5 Gamson and Myer, 'Framing Political Opportunities'.

6 Vivienne Shue, *The Reach of the State: Sketches of the Chinese Body Politic* (Stanford, CA: Stanford University Press, 1990).

7 Lynn White, *Policies of Chaos: The Organizational Causes of Violence in China's Cultural Revolution* (Princeton: Princeton University Press, 1989).

8 Elizabeth Perry and Li Xun, *Proletarian Power: Shanghai in the Cultural Revolution* (Oxford: Westview Press, 1997).

9 Guobin Yang, 'Achieving Emotions in Collective Action: Emotional Processes and Movement Mobilization in the 1989 Chinese Student Movement', *The Sociological Quarterly*, 41 (2000), 593–614.

10 Steven Pfaff and Guobin Yang, 'Double-edged Rituals and the Symbolic Resources of Collective Action: Political Commemorations and the Mobilization of Protest in 1989', *Theory and Society*, 30 (2001), 539–89.

11 Shaoguang Wang, *Failure of Charisma: The Cultural Revolution in Wuhan* (Oxford: Oxford University Press, 1995).

12 Hongbiao Yin, *Shizongzhe de zuji, wenhua da geming qijian de qiangnian sichao* (Footprints of the Missing: Trends of Thought of Young People During the Cultural Revolution) (Hong Kong: The Hong Kong Chinese University Press, 2009).

13 Shue, *The Reach of the State*.

14 Elizabeth Perry, 'Trends in the Study of Chinese Politics: State-Society Relations', *China Quarterly*, 139 (1994), 704–13.

15 Fayong Shi and Yongshun Cai, 'Disaggregating the State: Networks and Collective Resistance in Shanghai', *The China Quarterly*, 186 (2006), 314–32.

16 Jennifer Y. J. Hsu and Reza Hasmath, 'The Changing Faces of State Corporatism', in *The Chinese Corporatist State: Adaptation, Survival and Resistance*, ed. by Jennifer Y. J. Hsu and Reza Hasmath (London: Routledge, 2013), pp. 1–9.

17 Joel S. Migdal, *State in Society: Studying How States and Societies Transform and Constitute One Another* (Cambridge: Cambridge University Press, 2001).

18 Peter B. Evans, Dietrich Rueschemyer, and Theda Skocpol, *Bringing in the State Back In* (New York: Cambridge University Press, 1985).

19 Rachel Stern and Kevin O'Brien, 'Politics at the Boundary: Mixed Signals and the Chinese State', *Modern China*, 38 (2012), 174–98.

20 Jessica Teets, 'Post-Earthquake Relief and Reconstruction Efforts: The Emergence of Civil Society in China?', *China Quarterly*, 198 (2009), 330–47.

21 Joseph Cheng, Kinglun Ngok, and Wenjia Zhuang, 'The Survival and Development Space for China's Labor NGO: Informal Politics and Its Uncertainty', *Asian Survey*, 50 (2010), 1082–106.

22 C. Hsu, 'Beyond Civil Society: An Organizational Perspective on State-NGO Relations in the People's Republic of China', *Journal of Civil Society*, 6 (2010), 259–77.

23 Michael Keane, 'Broadcasting Policy, Creative Compliance and the Myth of Civil Society in China', *Media Culture & Society*, 23 (2001), 783–98.

24 Jennifer Hsu and Reza Hasmath, 'The Local Corporatist State and NGO Relations in China', *Journal of Contemporary China*, 23 (2013), 516–534.

25 Yong Gui, Weihong Ma & Klaus Mühlhahn, 'Grassroots Transformation in Contemporary China', *Journal of Contemporary Asia*, 39 (2009), 400–23.

26 I describe the personal fate of Bo in the epilogue of this book.

27 John Scott, *Power* (Cambridge: Polity, 2001), p. 16.

28 Scott, *Power*, pp. 13–5.

29 Seymour Martin Lipset, quoted in Baogang Guo, 'Political Legitimacy in China's Transition: Toward a Market Economy', in *China's Deep Reform: Domestic Politics in Transition*, ed. by Lowell Dittmer and Guoli Liu (Oxford: Rowman & Littlefield Publisher, INC, 2006), p. 149.

30 Joseph Fewsmith, 'Elite Politics', in *The Paradox of China's Post-Mao Reforms*, ed. by Merle Goldman and Roderick MacFarquhar (London: Harvard University Press, 1999), pp. 54–6.

31 Sophie Richardson, 'Self-Reform within Authoritarian Regimes: Reallocations of Power in Contemporary China', in *Political Civilization and Modernization in China*, ed. by Yang Zhong and Shiping Hua (London: World Scientific, 2006), pp. 149–74 (p. 150).

32 Baogang Guo, 'From Conflicts to Convergence: Modernity and the Changing Chinese Political Culture', in *Political Civilization and Modernization in China*, ed. by Yang Zhong and Shiping Hua (London: World Scientific, 2006), pp. 79–80.

33 Guo, 'Political Legitimacy in China's Transition', p. 150.

34 Robert Weatherley, *Politics in China since 1949: Legitimizing Authoritarian Rule* (London: Routledge, 2006), p. 4.

35 Elizabeth J. Perry offers a counterargument to this common observation that China's revolutionary campaigns have been replaced by rational-bureaucratic methods of governance. She argues that the tradition of political campaigns remains important in the Reform era, although it has morphed from a form of mass mobilisation to what Perry calls 'managed' campaigns, which rely more on grass-roots officials than the ordinary people. See Elizabeth J. Perry, 'From Mass Campaigns to Managed Campaigns: "Constructing a New Socialist Countryside"', in *Mao's Invisible Hand: The Political Foundations of Adaptive Governance in China*, ed. by Sebastian Helimann and Elizabeth J. Perry (London: Harvard University Asia Center, 2011), pp. 30–61.

36 Weatherley, *Politics in China Since 1949*, pp. 5–12.

37 Anna L. Ahlers and Gunter Schubert, ' "Adaptive Authoritarianism" in Contemporary China: Identifying Zones of Legitimacy Building', in *Reviving Legitimacy: Lessons for and From China*, ed. by Deng Zhenglai and Sujian Guo (Plymouth: Lexington Books, 2011), pp. 61–82; Sebastian Helimann and Elizabeth J. Perry, 'Embracing Uncertainty: Guerrilla Policy Style and Adaptive Governance in China', in *Mao's Invisible Hand: The Political Foundations of Adaptive Governance in China*, ed. by Sebastian Helimann and Elizabeth J. Perry (London: Harvard University Asia Center, 2011), pp. 1–29.

38 Fewsmith, 'Elite Politics', pp. 54–6.

39 Andre Laliberte and Marc Lanteigne, 'The Issue of Challenges to the Legitimacy of CCP Rule', in *The Chinese Party-State in the 21st Century: Adaptation and the Reinvention of Legitimacy*, ed. by Andre Laiberte and Marc Lanteigne (Oxon: Routledge, 2008), pp. 1–21.

40 Gordon White, *Riding the Tiger: The Politics of Economic Reform in Post-Mao China* (London: Macmillan, 1993).

41 Xinmin Pei, 'Microfoundations of State-Socialism and Patterns of Economic Transformation', *Communist and Post-Communist Studies*, 29 (1996), 131–45.

42 Jean C. Oi, *Rural China Takes Off: Institutional Foundations of Economic Reform* (Berkeley: University of California Press, 1999).

43 Victor Nee, Sonja Opper & Sonia M. L. Wong, 'Politicized Capitalism: Developmental State and the Firm in China', in Victor Nee & Richard Swedberg, eds, *On Capitalism* (Stanford, Stanford University Press, 2007), pp. 93–127

44 Dazhi Yao, 'Good Governance: Another Kind of Legitimacy?', in *China's Search for Good Governance*, ed. by Zhenglai Deng and Sujian Guo (New York: Palgrave Macmillan, 2011), pp. 23–34.

45 Yuchao Zhu, ' "Performance Legitimacy" and China's Political Adaptation Strategy', in *The Chinese Party-State in the 21st Century: Adaptation and the Reinvention of Legitimacy*, ed. by Andre Laiberte and Marc Lanteigne (Oxon: Routledge, 2008), pp. 175–94.

46 Jamie P. Horsley, 'Public Participation and the Democratization of Chinese Governance', in *Political Civilization and Modernization in China*, ed. by Yang Zhong and Shiping Hua (London: World Scientific, 2006), pp. 207–50.

47 Feng Xu, 'New Modes of Urban Governance: Building Community/shequ in Post-danwei China', in *The Chinese Party-State in the 21st Century: Adaptation and the Reinvention of Legitimacy*, ed. by Andre Laiberte and Marc Lanteigne (Oxon: Routledge, 2008), pp. 22–38.

32 *Red culture campaign in perspective*

48 Scott, *Power*, pp. 4, 25–6.
49 Yongshun Cai, 'Power Structure and Regime Resilience', *British Journal of Political Science*, 38 (2008), 411–32.
50 Zheng, 'China in 2011'.
51 Kevin J. O'Brien and Lianjiang Li, *Rightful Resistance in Rural China* (Cambridge: Cambridge University Press, 2006).
52 Guo, 'From Conflicts to Convergence', p. 89.
53 Ching Kwang Lee, 'Is Labour a Political Force in China?', in *Grassroots Political Reform in Contemporary China*, ed. by Elizabeth J. Perry and Merle Goldman (London: Harvard University Press, 2007), p. 229.
54 Lee, 'Is Labour a Political Force in China?', p. 244.
55 Jianrong Yu, *Contentious Politics: Fundamental Issues in Chinese Political Sociology* (Beijing: *Renmin Chubanshe*, 2010).
56 Yongshun Cai, *Collective Resistance in China: Why Popular Protests Succeed or Fail* (Stanford, CA: Stanford University Press, 2010).
57 Lee, 'Is Labour a Political Force in China?', p. 250.
58 Alan P. L. Liu, *Mass Politics in the People's Republic: State and Society in Contemporary China* (Oxford: Westview Press, 1996).
59 Lee, 'Is Labour a Political Force in China?', p. 250.
60 Xi Chen, 'Between Defiance and Obedience: Protest Opportunism in China', in *Grassroots Political Reform in Contemporary China*, ed. Elizabeth J. Perry and Merle Goldman (London: Harvard University Press, 2007), p. 280.
61 James C. Scott, *Weapons of the Weak: Everyday Forms of Peasant Resistance* (New Haven: Yale University Press, 2008).
62 James C. Scott, *Domination and the Art of Resistance* (New Haven: Yale University, 1990).
63 Wanning Sun, '"Just Looking": Domestic Workers' Consumption Practices and a Latent Geography of Beijing', *Gender, Place and Culture*, 15 (2008), 475–88.
64 Sylvere Lotringer, 'Exterminating Angel: Introduction to Forget Foucault', in *Forget Foucault* (Los Angeles, CA: Semiotext(e), 2007), pp. 7–25.
65 Jean Baudrillard, *Symbolic Exchange and Death* (London: Sage, 1993), p. 6.
66 De Certeau, *The Practice of Everyday Life* (Berkeley and Los Angeles, CA: University of California Press, 1984), p. 36.
67 De Certeau, *The Practice of Everyday Life*, p. xiii.
68 De Certeau, *The Practice of Everyday Life*, p. 41.
69 Georg Simmel, 'Exchange', in *On Individuality and Social Forms*, ed. by Donald N. Levine (Chicago: The University of Chicago Press, 1971), pp. 43, 57, 68.
70 P. Blau, *Exchange and Power in Social Life* (New York: Wiley, 1964); George C. Homans, 'Social Behavior as Exchange', *American Journal of Sociology*, 63 (May 1958), 597–606; Edwin Uehara, 'Dural Exchange Theory, Social Networks, and Informal Social Support', *American Journal of Sociology*, 96 (1990), 523–4.
71 For example, see J. Coleman, 'A Rational Choice Perspective on Economic Sociology', in *The Handbook of Economic Sociology*, ed. by N. Smelser and R. Swedberg (Princeton: Princeton University Press, 1994); Milan Zafirovski, 'Social Exchange Theory Under Scrutiny: A Positive Critique of Its Economic-Behaviorist Formulations', *Electronic Journal of Sociology*, 7 (2005), 3.
72 For example, see M. Mauss, *The Gift: Forms and Functions of Exchange in Archaic Societies* (New York: Norton, 1967); Mary R. Gilmore, 'Implications of Generalized versus Restricted Exchange', in *Social Exchange Theory*, ed. by Karen S. Cook (Newbury Park, CA: Sage, 1987).
73 For example, see P. Burke, 'An Identity Model for Network Exchange', *American Sociological Review*, 62 (1997), 134–50.
74 For example, see Richard M. Emerson, 'Social Exchange Theory', *Annual Review of Sociology*, 2 (1976), 335–62.

75 Erving Goffman, *Frame Analysis: An Essay on the Organization of Experience* (Boston: Northeastern University Press, 1986).
76 Goffman, *Frame Analysis*, p. 25.
77 Goffman, *Frame Analysis*, p. 43–5.
78 Goffman, *Frame Analysis*, p. 45–6.
79 Goffman, *Frame Analysis*, p. 83.
80 Doug McAdam, John D. McCarthy & Mayer N. Zald, 'Introduction', in *Comparative Perspectives on Social Movements: Political Opportunities, Mobilizing Structures, and Cultural Framings*, ed. by Doug McAdam, John D. McCarthy & Mayer N. Zald (Cambridge: Cambridge University Press, 1996), p. 6.
81 McAdam, 'Introduction', p. 5.
82 Mayer N. Zald, 'Culture, Ideology, and Strategic Framing', in *Comparative Perspectives on Social Movements: Political Opportunities, Mobilizing Structures, and Cultural Framings*, ed. by Doug McAdam, John D. McCarthy & Mayer N. Zald (Cambridge: Cambridge University Press, 1996), p. 262.
83 John D. McCarthy, Jackie Smith & Mayer N. Zald, 'Accessing Public, Media, Electoral, and Governmental Agendas', in *Comparative Perspectives on Social Movements: Political Opportunities, Mobilizing Structures, and Cultural Framings*, ed. by Doug McAdam John D. McCarthy & Mayer N. Zald (Cambridge: Cambridge University Press, 1996), p. 291.

Bibliography

Ahlers, Anna L. and Gunter Schubert, '"Adaptive Authoritarianism" in Contemporary China: Identifying Zones of Legitimacy Building', in Deng Zhenglai and Sujian Guo, eds, *Reviving Legitimacy: Lessons for and From China* (Plymouth: Lexington Books, 2011), pp. 61–82

Baudrillard, Jean, *Symbolic Exchange and Death* (London: Sage, 1993)

Blau, P., *Exchange and Power in Social Life* (New York: Wiley, 1964)

Burke, P., 'An Identity Model for Network Exchange', *American Sociological Review*, 62 (1997), 134–50

Cai, Yongshun, *Collective Resistance in China: Why Popular Protests Succeed or Fail* (Stanford, CA: Stanford University Press, 2010)

——— 'Power Structure and Regime Resilience', *British Journal of Political Science*, 38 (2008), 411–32

Certeau, Michel de, *The Practice of Everyday Life* (Berkeley and Los Angeles, CA: University of California Press, 1984)

Chen, Xi, 'Between Defiance and Obedience: Protest Opportunism in China', in Elizabeth J. Perry and Merle Goldman, eds, *Grassroots Political Reform in Contemporary China* (London: Harvard University Press, 2007), pp. 253–81

Cheng, Joseph, Kinglun Ngok, and Wenjia Zhuang, 'The Survival and Development Space for China's Labor NGO: Informal Politics and Its Uncertainty', *Asian Survey*, 50 (2010), 1082–106

Coleman, J., 'A Rational Choice Perspective on Economic Sociology', in Neil Smelser and Richard Swedberg, eds, *Handbook of Economic Sociology* (Princeton: Princeton University Press, 1994)

Emerson, Richard M., 'Social Exchange Theory', *Annual Review of Sociology*, 2 (1976), n.p.

Evans, Peter B., Dietrich Rueschemyer, and Theda Skocpol, *Bringing in the State Back In* (New York: Cambridge University Press, 1985)

Fewsmith, Joseph, 'Elite Politics', in Merle Goldman Roderick MacFarquhar, eds, *The Paradox of China's Post-Maro Reforms* (London: Harvard University Press, 1999), pp. 47–75

34   *Red culture campaign in perspective*

Gamson William A. and David D. Meyer, 'Framing Political Opportunity', in Doug McAdam, John D. McCarthy & Mayer N. Zald, eds, *Comparative Perspectives on Social Movements: Political Opportunities, Mobilizing Structures, and Cultural Framings* (Cambridge: Cambridge University Press, 1996), pp. 275–90

Gilmore, Mary R. 'Implications of Generalized versus Restricted Exchange', in Karen S. Cook, ed., *Social Exchange Theory* (Newbury Park, CA: Sage, 1987)

Goffman, Erving, *Frame Analysis: An Essay on the Organization of Experience* (Boston: Northeastern University Press, 1986)

Gui, Yong, Weihong Ma, and Klaus Mühlhahn, 'Grassroots Transformation in Contemporary China', *Journal of Contemporary Asia*, 39 (2009), 400–23

Guo, Baogang, 'From Conflicts to Convergence: Modernity and the Changing Chinese Political Culture', in Yang Zhong and Shiping Hua, ed., *Political Civilization and Modernization in China* (London: World Scientific, 2006), pp. 79–80

——— 'Political Legitimacy in China's Transition: Toward a Market Economy', in Lowell Dittmer and Guoli Liu, eds, *China's Deep Reform: Domestic Politics in Transition* (Oxford: Rowman & Littlefield Publisher, INC, 2006), pp. 147–76

Helimann, Sebastian and Elizabeth J. Perry, 'Embracing Uncertainty: Guerrilla Policy Style and Adaptive Governance in China', in Sebastian Helimann and Elizabeth J. Perry, eds, *Mao's Invisible Hand: The Political Foundations of Adaptive Governance in China* (London: Harvard University Asia Center, 2011), pp. 1–29

Homans, George C., 'Social Behavior as Exchange', *American Journal of Sociology*, 63 (May 1958), 597–606

Horsley, Jamie P., 'Public Participation and the Democratization of Chinese Governance', in Yang Zhong and Shiping Hua, ed., *Political Civilization and Modernization in China* (London: World Scientific, 2006), pp. 207–50

Hsu, Carolyn, 'Beyond Civil Society: An Organizational Perspective on State-NGO Relations in the People's Republic of China', *Journal of Civil Society*, 6 (2010), 259–77

Hsu, Jennifer and Reza Hasmath, 'The Changing Faces of State Corporatism', in Jennifer Hsu and Reza Hasmath, eds, *The Chinese Corporatist State: Adaptation, Survival and Resistance* (London: Routledge, 2013), pp. 1–9

——— 'The Local Corporatist State and NGO Relations in China', *Journal of Contemporary China*, 23 (2013), 516–534

Keane, Michael, 'Broadcasting Policy, Creative Compliance and the Myth of Civil Society in China', *Media Culture & Society*, 23 (2001), 783–98

Laliberte, Andre and Marc Lanteigne, 'The Issue of Challenges to the Legitimacy of CCP Rule', in Andre Laiberte and Marc Lanteigne, eds, *The Chinese Party-State in the 21st Century: Adaptation and the Reinvention of Legitimacy* (Oxon: Routledge, 2008), pp. 1–21

Lee, Ching Kwang, 'Is Labour a Political Force in China?', in Elizabeth J. Perry and Merle Goldman, eds, *Grassroots Political Reform in Contemporary China* (London: Harvard University Press, 2007), p. 228–52

Liu, Alan P. L., *Mass Politics in the People's Republic: State and Society in Contemporary China* (Oxford: Westview Press, 1996)

Lotringer, Sylvere, 'Exterminating Angel: Introduction to Forget Foucault', in *Forget Foucault* (Los Angeles, CA: Semiotext(e), 2007), pp. 7–25

McAdam, Doug, 'The Framing Function of Movement Tactics: Strategic Dramaturgy in the American Civil Rights Movement', in Doug McAdam, John D. McCarthy & Mayer N. Zald, eds, *Comparative Perspectives on Social Movements: Political Opportunities, Mobilizing Structures, and Cultural Framings* (Cambridge: Cambridge University Press, 1996), pp. 337–56

McAdam, Doug, McCarthy, John D., and Mayer N. Zald, 'Introduction: Opportunities, Mobilizing Structures, and Framing Processes – Toward a Synthetic, Comparative Perspective on Social Movement', in Doug McAdam, John D. McCarthy & Mayer N. Zald, eds, *Comparative Perspectives on Social Movements: Political Opportunities, Mobilizing Structures, and Cultural Framings* (Cambridge: Cambridge University Press, 1996), pp. 1–22

McCarthy, John D., Jackie Smith, and Mayer N. Zald, 'Accessing Public, Media, Electoral, and Governmental Agendas', in Doug McAdam, John D. McCarthy & Mayer N. Zald, eds, *Comparative Perspectives on Social Movements: Political Opportunities, Mobilizing Structures, and Cultural Framings* (Cambridge: Cambridge University Press, 1996), pp. 275–90

Mauss, M., *The Gift: Forms and Functions of Exchange in Archaic Societies* (New York: Norton, 1967)

Migdal, Joel S., *State in Society: Studying How States and Societies Transform and Constitute One Another* (Cambridge: Cambridge University Press, 2001)

Nee, Victor, Sonja Opper & Sonia M.L. Wong, 'Politicized Capitalism: Developmental State and the Firm in China', in Victor Nee & Richard Swedberg, eds, *On Capitalism* (Stanford, Stanford University Press, 2007), pp. 93–127

Oi, Jean C., *Rural China Takes Off: Institutional Foundations of Economic Reform* (Berkeley: University of California Press, 1999)

Pei, Xinmin, 'Microfoundations of State-Socialism and Patterns of Economic Transformation', *Communist and Post-Communist Studies*, 29 (1996), 131–45

Perry, Elizabeth, 'From Mass Campaigns to Managed Campaigns: "Constructing a New Socialist Countryside" ', in Sebastian Helimann and Elizabeth J. Perry, eds, *Mao's Invisible Hand: The Political Foundations of Adaptive Governance in China* (London: Harvard University Asia Center, 2011), pp. 30–61

———— 'Trends in the Study of Chinese Politics: State-Society Relations', *China Quarterly* (1994), 704–13

Perry, Elizabeth and Li Xun, *Proletarian Power: Shanghai in the Cultural Revolution* (Oxford: Westview Press, 1997)

Pfaff, Steven and Guobin Yang, 'Double-edged Rituals and the Symbolic Resources of Collective Action: Political Commemorations and the Mobilization of Protest in 1989', *Theory and Society*, 30 (2001), 539–89

Richardson, Sophie, 'Self-Reform within Authoritarian Regimes: Reallocations of Power in Contemporary China', in Yang Zhong and Shiping Hua, eds, *Political Civilization and Modernization in China* (London: World Scientific, 2006), pp. 149–74

Scott, James C., *Domination and the Art of Resistance* (New Haven: Yale University, 1990)

———— *Weapons of the Weak: Everyday Forms of Peasant Resistance* (New Haven: Yale University Press, 2008)

Scott, John, *Power* (Cambridge: Polity, 2001)

Shi, Fayong and Yongshun Cai, 'Disaggregating the State: Networks and Collective Resistance in Shanghai', *China Quarterly*, 186 (2006), 314–32

Shue, Vivienne, *The Reach of the State: Sketches of the Chinese Body Politic* (Stanford, CA: Stanford University Press, 1990)

Simmel, Georg, 'Exchange', in Donald N. Levine, ed., *On Individuality and Social Forms* (Chicago: The University of Chicago Press, 1971)

Stern, Rachel and Kevin O'Brien, 'Politics at the Boundary: Mixed Signals and the Chinese State', *Modern China*, 38 (2012), 174–98

Sun, Wanning, ' "Just Looking": Domestic Workers' Consumption Practices and a Latent Geography of Beijing', *Gender, Place and Culture*, 15 (2008), 475–88

36 *Red culture campaign in perspective*

Teets, Jessica, 'Post-Earthquake Relief and Reconstruction Efforts: The Emergence of Civil Society in China?' *China Quarterly*, 198 (2009), 330–47

Uehara, Edwin, 'Dural Exchange Theory, Social Networks, and Informal Social Support', *American Journal of Sociology*, 96 (1990), 521–57

Wang, Shaoguang, *Failure of Charisma: The Cultural Revolution in Wuhan* (Oxford: Oxford University Press, 1995)

Weatherley, Robert, *Politics in China Since 1949: Legitimizing Authoritarian Rule* (London: Routledge, 2006)

Weber, Max, *Max Weber: On Charisma and Institution Building*, S. N. Eisenstadt, ed. (London: The University of Chicago Press, 1968)

White, Gordon, *Riding the Tiger: The Politics of Economic Reform in Post-Mao China* (London: Macmillan, 1993)

White, Lynn, *Policies of Chaos: The Organizational Causes of Violence in China's Cultural Revolution* (Princeton: Princeton University Press, 1989)

Xu, Feng, 'New Modes of Urban Governance: Building Community/shequ in Post-danwei China', in Andre Laiberte and Marc Lanteigne, eds, *The Chinese Party-State in the 21st Century: Adaptation and the Reinvention of Legitimacy* (Oxon: Routledge, 2008), pp. 22–38

Yang, Guobin, 'Achieving Emotions in Collective Action: Emotional Processes and Movement Mobilization in the 1989 Chinese Student Movement', *Sociological Quarterly*, 41 (2000), 593–614

————— 'The Liminal Effects of Social Movements: Red Guard and the Transformation of Identity', *Sociological Forum*, 15 (2000), 379–406

Yao, Dazhi, 'Good Governance: Another Kind of Legitimacy?', in Zhenglai Deng and Sujian Guo, eds, *China's Search for Good Governance* (New York: Palgrave Macmillan, 2011), pp. 23–34

Yin, Hongbiao, *Shizongzhe de Zuji, Wenhua Da Geming Qijian de Qiangnian Sichao* (Footprints of the Missing: Trends of Thought of Young People During the Cultural Revolution) (Hong Kong: The Hong Kong Chinese University Press, 2009)

Yu, Jianrong, *Contentious Politics: Fundamental Issues in Chinese Political Sociology* (Beijing: Renmin Chubanshe, 2010)

Zafirovski, Milan, 'Social Exchange Theory Under Scrutiny: A Positive Critique of Its Economic-Behaviorist Formulations', *Electronic Journal of Sociology*, 7 (2005), 1–40

Zald, Mayer N. 'Culture, Ideology, and Strategic Framing', in Doug McAdam, John D. McCarthy & Mayer N. Zald, eds, *Comparative Perspectives on Social Movements: Political Opportunities, Mobilizing Structures, and Cultural Framings* (Cambridge: Cambridge University Press, 1996), pp. 261–274

Zhou, Xueguang, 'Unorganized Interests and Collective Action in Communist China', *American Sociological Review*, 58 (1993), 54–73

Zhu, Yuchao, '"Performance Legitimacy" and China's Political Adaptation Strategy', in Deng Zhenglai and Sujian Guo, eds, *Reviving Legitimacy: Lessons for and from China* (Plymouth: Lexington Books, 2011), pp. 175–94

3 Chongqing's Red culture campaign as simulation

Now I draw on Baudrillard's concept of simulation to answer the question: was Chongqing's Red culture campaign a *real* mass campaign? I argue that Chongqing's Red culture campaign was not a *real* Maoist mass campaign but demonstrated critical features of simulation. Baudrillard devises a theory of simulation as a radical critique of the capital, which he believes has 'cancelled the *principle of reality*' and had a particularly hallowing effect on modern life.[1] It should be pointed out that the fact that Chongqing's Red culture campaign exhibits features of simulation does not mean that Chinese society has entered an 'era of simulation', as Baudrillard describes the late capitalist society. Nevertheless, Baudrillard's theory of simulation is useful in this case for it facilitates a better understanding of the nature of both the Red culture campaign and political power that supported and sustained the programme.

Simulation

Baudrillard's theory of simulation concerns a specific kind of power and its organization in modern society. As explained in Chapter 2, simulation is a process during which models of reality are produced. Simulation artificially generates systems of signs that are used to substitute the representations of reality. To qualify as *simulation*, Chongqing's Red culture campaign firstly had to display the true symptoms of a Maoist mass campaign. To produce true symptoms of the mass campaign, it must follow a pre-existing model. Secondly, simulation involves the liquidation of the referentials. Facts lose their own trajectories but revolve around the model's designs and requisites. Simulation empties the substance of the real. Lastly, simulation constitutes a self-induced and non-dialectical circuit of power, where signs are exchanged within a monolithic and self-induced system of itself. I will explain each of the features of simulation exhibited by Chongqing's Red culture campaign.

The production of true symptoms

A classic Chinese mass campaign, according to White, involves the following components: the proposition of a radical goal, the privileging of collective

38 *Red culture campaign as simulation*

benefits over personal choices, and a strenuous effort to mobilise the masses towards conformity.[2] A campaign usually starts with talks given by the Party leaders. After they articulate a specific idea, the idea is officialised in the form of a directive, circulars, or some format of official document. Mass campaigns, when carried out, usually contain three main features. Firstly, they often evoke highly performative political actions and enforcement. Mass campaigns rely on flamboyant public spectacles as a critical means to communicate political messages to the people as well as an effective way to demonstrate the political prowess of the ruling party. For example, as part of the campaign to introduce the culture of the new ruling Party in the early founding years of the People's Republic of China (PRC), a *yangge* performance could involve as many as 250 dancers. Red flags and five-pointed stars were the ostentatious decoration employed during such shows. The targeted audiences included the highest-level leaders, such as Mao Zedong and Zhou Enlai, as well as thousands of ordinary spectators when some of the performances were held outdoors in Tiananmen Square.[3] In political campaigns, such as the suppression of counter-revolutionaries, 'the masses' were routinely involved in 'heavily staged political theatre'. The masses attended exhibitions, accusation meetings, and public trials. Their 'chorus-like participation' served to reaffirm the state's popular legitimacy. One noteworthy characteristic of the public drama of political campaigns was that strenuous effort was devoted to stage-managing an appearance of spontaneity. During the mass accusation meetings (*kong su hui* 控诉会) held during the campaign to suppress counter-revolutionaries, for example, the local cadres had to make long preparations for both the accusations of the counter-revolutionaries and the responses of the masses.[4] The success of a campaign was dependent on not only adopting an 'extraordinary, revolutionary political technique' that can successfully mobilise people but also effective 'organization, planning, and repetition'.[5]

Secondly, a mass campaign is usually underpinned by specific ideological doctrines. Ideology here refers to a systematic propagation of specific ideas and beliefs that would normatively justify specific social, economic, or political conditions and structures.[6] It is believed to exercise an explicit or implicit influence on encouraging, or prohibiting, certain political actions. Ideology is a critical source of political power and an indispensable element in orchestrating successful mass campaigns. For example, the 'mass-line' doctrine was considered a key component of Mao Zedong's thought and used in many of the campaigns as the 'correct' political line. This strategy was underpinned by a specific way of articulating the role of the masses in history. In the early 1940s of the Yan'an era, Mao formulated the idea for the Chinese Communists that the success of the revolution would not come from above but had to rely on the masses.[7] The famous dictum – 'from the masses, to the masses' (*cong qunzhong zhong lai, dao qunzhong zhong qu* 从群众中来，到群众中去) – has been identified as the essence of the 'mass line'. In 1943, Mao articulated the meaning of this revolutionary truism in the directive – 'Some Questions Concerning Methods of Leadership' (*guanyu lingdao fangfa de ruogan wenti* 《关于领导方法的若干问题》). The 'mass-line' strategy emphasised that everything the Party did needed to be for the benefit of the masses, and also everything the Party did had to rely on the masses. It was an effort for the Party to build close, positive relations with the masses. Since Mao's formulation, the idea of relying on the masses has been included in many political campaigns, including the Red Guard movement. To disseminate specific ideas to mobilise the people, political campaigns were often preceded by extensive work by the propaganda machine. In China's anti-Confucian campaign (1973–1974), implemented during the later stage of the Cultural Revolution (CR), for instance, a large number of newspaper articles were produced to attack Confucianism and support the Legalistic tradition. Historical analogy was used as a justification and weapon in the later political attacks and fractional struggles.[8]

Thirdly, a mass campaign normally aims to generate certain actions that will facilitate the implementation of specific policies or help achieve political goals. Despite following the Leninist tradition in using mass campaigns as a revolutionary strategy, China's formidable leader, Mao Zedong, left his unique and profound personal mark on the Chinese style of mass campaigns. Mass campaigns were adopted as not only a tool for political mobilisation but also a critical method for implementing key policies.[9] In the years of regime consolidation after the founding of the new nation, numerous political campaigns were executed to solve specific problems as the CCP attempted to Legalistic tradition rebuild the state and its institutions. Political campaigns constituted the 'primary vehicle' for the newly-established Party-state to deal with challenges such as an urgent need to consolidate the central state control over the existing bureaucratic organization, fight the remaining political enemies, and tame the powerful social groups.[10] Conducted by the administrative organizations of the Party-state, the campaigns stirred up popular participation to strike real or perceived enemies of the state, such as spies and counter-revolutionaries.[11] During the Red Guard Movement, for example, Mao chose to mobilise the masses to challenge the Party establishment and government bureaucracies. Young students from universities and middle schools, in particular, were mobilised 'to expose our dark aspect openly, in an all-round way, and from below'.[12] The active participation of the masses resulted in the collapse of the political structure in cities and the overthrow of most of the Party leadership at all levels of the bureaucracy during the period from May 1966 to April 1969.[13]

As described, the classic model of a mass campaign contained highly performative political actions and evoked specific ideological doctrines. Chongqing's Red culture campaign displayed the 'true' symptoms of a mass campaign. It contained a series of regular and frequent operations that built up the momentum of a campaign that was grand in scale and influential in effect. Like most of the CCP campaigns, the Red culture campaign was preceded by a talk by Bo Xilai during his trip to Bashu primary school on 31 May 2008. He articulated the significance of singing classic Red songs for the first time in public:

> (To primary school students) . . . You need to learn more good songs, such as 'ge chang zuguo' (Ode to the Motherland 《歌唱祖国》, 'wo men shi gongchanzhuyi jiebanren' (We Are the Heir to Communism 《我们是共产主义接班人》), 'baowei huanghe' （Defend the Yellow River 《保卫黄河》),

40 *Red culture campaign as simulation*

and so on . . . for a nation to be strong, we should foster a high morale and health spirits among the young people.[14]

Following Bo's remarks, the Red culture campaign was officially launched in June 2008, accompanied by a large staged performance 'Ode to the Dear Party – Singing Contest in Commemoration of "July 1st".' The participants were employees of the municipality's government bureaucracies. In the aftermath of the event, the Party Committee and the municipal government jointly issued the 'Directive on the Launching of Singing Red Classic Songs Activities' (*Guanyu guangfan kaizhan hongse jingdian gequ chuanchang huodong de yijian* 《关于广泛开展红色经典歌曲传唱活动的意见》[15]) to encourage lower levels of government, bureaucratic organs in the municipal government, social groups, large enterprises, and higher education institutions to follow the example and be diligent in organizing singing activities in Chongqing. Attempting to expand both the scale and content of the program, the municipal Party Committee issued another directive, 'Decision on Promoting Vigorous Development and Prosperity of Culture' (*Zhonggong Chongqing shiwei guanyu tuidong wenhua dafazhan dafanrong de jueding* 《中共重庆市委关于推动文化大发展大繁荣的决定》) in June 2009 to promote a Red cultural campaign with four elements – 'Singing Red, Reading Classics, Telling Stories, and Spreading Mottos' (*chang du jiang chuan* 唱读讲传).

The Red culture campaign was listed at the top of the nine cultural events promised by the municipality government in the year 2009.[16] The Propaganda Department subsequently nominated 405 Red culture bases in Chongqing, including all levels of government agencies, schools, and universities as well as the PLA troops based in Chongqing. By the end of 2010, it was reported that 148, 000 'Singing Red' performances had been carried out with an aggregate attendance of more than 87.3 million. Activities of 'Reading Classics' amounted to 44, 000, with an aggregate attendance of 17.6 million. There had been 86,000 'Telling Stories' gatherings and 0.17 billion 'Red Motto' messages sent out through mobile phone text messages or shared on China's most popular social media, such as QQ.com.[17] The spectacle of the Red culture campaign reached its most explosive scale and effects in the few months leading to the 90th anniversary of the founding of CCP in July 2011. A series of mass activities featuring the theme of 'Love the Party, Love the Nation, Love the Hometown' were produced at a dazzling frequency and intensity, including Daily Red Songs, Red Song Singer Competition, May 1st Labour Day Gala' and the First Youth Chorus Singing Competition, only to list a few. In June, the Chongqing delegation went to Beijing to join the national celebration of the Party's birthday in the capital. In addition to performing at the Beijing Cultural Palace Grand Theatre at the open ceremony of the special programme named 'The Fragrance of Hundred Flowers – Holding High the Banner of the Party', the Chongqing delegation brought their Red programme to the PLA Second Artillery Force, Beijing's Chaoyang District, Tsinghua University, the National Committee of the Chinese People's Consultative Conference, and the Central Party School during its tour the Beijing. Between 28 June and 1 July, the second China's Red Song Gala (*zhonghua honggehui* 中华红歌会) amassed 108 choruses and 8,000 performers coming from all over China. A series of performances that claimed an attendance of greater than 800,000 participants concluded the spectacular Red season in Chongqing. By July 2011, the campaign claimed an aggregate participation of more than 100 million people in all varieties of activities. By January 2012, it was reported, for the last time on record, more than 250,000 performances of the Red culture programme had been staged in Chongqing.[18] The accuracy of these breathtaking numbers of activities and attendance was difficult to verify. But accuracy was the not the main issue here. The key point was that Chongqing passionately painted and rigorously pursued an image of an immensely contagious campaign that was fully embraced by the people.

Moreover, like most of the Chinese Communist Party's (CCP's) ideological campaigns, music was used as one of the most popular tools in mobilising the participation of the local people. For as long as the CCP has existed, art has been utilised as a political and symbolic tool for orchestrating ideology campaigns and transmitting revolutionary and cultural ideals. A wide variety of art forms, such as singing, storytelling, and dancing have been employed by the CCP as useful mechanisms for constructing its own narrative of history as well as portrayals of the socialist ideals after the Communist regime was founded.[19] Since the 1920s, 'revolutionary' songs, which were mostly adapted from the melodies of folk songs, started to emerge as an educational tool in China's revolution. These songs usually adopted themes of anti-imperialism and patriotism and were performed in the style of mass choral singing.[20] In 'The Memories of the Red Army Long March' (*hongjun changzheng ji* 《红军长征记》), published in 1937, Red songs were collected alongside 100 essays written by the Red Army's Long Marcher on their recollections of the journey.[21] During the CR, music education was largely mass oriented and focused on promoting revolutionary spirits.[22] Amateur musicians were encouraged to compose and perform songs that were closely related to the life of the proletariat, whereas professionals were urged or forced to labour with the workers or farmers for re-education and self-reform. Most notable was also the dominance of the cultural scene by the genre of 'eight model dramas', promoted and popularised by Jiang Qing during the CR. Moreover, a five-volume anthology named the 'New Songs of the Battlefield' (*zhan di xin ge* 《战地新歌》)[23] was compiled and introduced to the public. The 556 songs in the anthology could be classified according to six themes: 'CCP classics', 'praise, battle and political campaigns', 'ethnic nationality', 'workers, peasants and soldiers', and 'youth and children'.[24] These songs were mostly based on traditional folk melodies; they were simple enough for common people to sing along. As Ouyang points out, the repetition of simplified slogans and lyrics 'fostered a sense of unity and a sense of belonging'.[25] During this period, a strong emphasis on choral singing developed. Music was heavily imbued with moral conviction and political teaching.[26] As shown, music, particularly Red songs, has always been an essential part of the revolutionary culture of the CCP. During Chongqing's Red culture campaign, singing Red was evidently the most popular form of mass activities for local residents in Chongqing. In many cases, 'singing Red' was representative of the whole programme. The images of the mass singing of Red songs were most often cited

42 *Red culture campaign as simulation*

as evidence of both the success and horror of the campaign, depending on the side of debate one stands by. Singing Red was the core and symbol of Chongqing's Red culture campaign.

However, despite producing symptoms of a mass campaign as shown, the Red culture campaign exhibited critical features of a simulacrum. The Red culture campaign seemed far less interested in generating meaningful social and political action by selling a systematic representation of the world, that is, an ideology, rather than appearing to be doing so. There are three pieces of evidence supporting this argument, that is, the procession of a model for the campaign, the liquidation of the referential by the campaign, and the campaign as a self-induced circuit.

The procession of a model

The first piece of evidence was that the campaign prioritised the emulation of the revolutionary 'mass campaign' model over making sure the policies and activities were designed to tackle real issues and problems of the current society. The operation of the campaign was preceded by an established model of the mass campaign. As a result, facts were organized to fit the rationale and structures of the campaign rather than actively directing the trajectories of the programme. It was evident that in the implementation processes of the campaign, great effort was made to arrange the events and performances in a way that they would testify to the idea of the centrality of 'the masses'.

Take the Chongqing satellite channel's star programme 'Daily Red Song' as an example. The 'mass-line' approach was strenuously pursued by an *organized performance* of the 'mass-line' approach. The 'Daily Red Song' show was launched in 2011 on Chongqing's satellite channel as both a showcase for the success of the programme in amassing support and participation from the local people and part of the mobilisation effort to engage the TV audience in the campaign. The programme initially consisted of chorus singing performed by teams of students, nurses, bureaucrats, police officers, employees of state-owned enterprises (SOEs), and so on. In November the same year, the 'Daily Red Song' show was redesigned to incorporate a section called the 'Red Song Star', which was devoted to inviting individuals who were passionate about singing Red songs to participate in the show. The introduction of the section was claimed to be answering the 'ardent requests' of the public. Typically, there were ten contenders each day. These amateur singers came from all walks of life – students, teachers, farmers, retirees, cadres, soldiers, and so on. There were also 50 judges selected from the audience to decide on the winner of the 'Red Song Star' competition. From the outlook, it was a typical mass event that was introduced upon the initiative of the people, participated in by the people, and judged by the people.

A close examination of the details of the programme, however, reveals a 'mass-line' approach that was carefully performed. First, the performers in the section of 'Red Song Star' wore very casual clothes. The government admitted that it 'requested' the performers not dress in uniformity. The amateur singers were asked to dress casually as if they had been singing offstage in everyday life. This was an important indication of two 'facts'. The first was that the participants were *ordinary* people who were passionate about singing Red instead of professional actors or actresses. The second message was that these Red culture activities were voluntary gatherings of the people to sing and dance, just like those in public squares that one could expect to run into every day. It was a carefully crafted image of casualness and spontaneity, which was critical for sustaining the narrative of a genuine mass campaign that relied on the initiative of the ordinary people.

Secondly, an interesting alteration of the ways the individual singers entered the stage was revealing. When the section of the 'Red Song Star' was first introduced to the programme, the singers entered from the side of the stage. Starting from January 2012, the singers entered the stage from the middle of the crowd of the audience. It was a perfect illustration of how the show was trying to present the nature of this singing competition, that it was literally 'coming from the masses' (*cong qunzhong zhong lai* 从群众中来) – the first half of the central theme of the 'mass-line' strategy. The other half, 'going to the masses' (*dao qunzhong zhong qu* 到群众中去) was demonstrated by the fact that the 'Daily Red Song' show went to every one of the 38 districts in the Chongqing municipality to engage the local people, despite much of Chongqing's territory being remote, mountainous areas.

Thirdly, the individuals' 'spontaneous' engagement in the 'Red Song Star' contest was also the result of careful organization. Take the 'Tongnan Week' of the 'Daily Red Song' show (2 January 2012–8 January 2012) as an example, 18 chorus teams and 65 amateur singers participated in the show. Among the 65 individuals who participated in the section of the 'Red Song Star' contest, 37 were in fact affiliated with the same institutions or organizations (schools, companies, bureaucratic divisions, etc.) of the chorus teams. Among the remaining 28 people who did not belong to any of the chorus teams, 11 were from the same institutions or organizations with at least one other participant who participated in the same contest. Only 17 seemed to be 'individual' participants. Among these 17 people, eight were teachers or students, eight were employees or former employees in the public sector or state-owned or centrally controlled enterprises. Only one was an entrepreneur. The fact that the majority of the 'individual' participants were actually from the same institution or organization of the chorus, and the fact that a considerable percentage of the remaining ones had colleagues with them participating the programme, indicated a high probability that the spontaneous participation of individual participants was prearranged. It was also notable that the remaining few who did not fit these two categories were predominantly from schools and state-owned companies, which were convenient targets when mobilising participants. This pattern was highly consistent in the larger sample of the 'Daily Red Song' shows. Chongqing's Red culture campaign made an admirably arduous effort to meet expectations of what a mass campaign should look like. Every effort was made to make sure the 'facts' of the programme fit into the model of 'the people's campaign'.

Liquidation of the referential

Despite appearing like a classic mass campaign, Chongqing's Red culture campaign nevertheless displayed the critical features of simulation. One of them demonstrated in the case of the Red culture campaign concerned the process of

44 *Red culture campaign as simulation*

'liquidating the referential'. As discussed in previous chapters, Red songs traditionally referred to the 'propaganda songs of China's socialist revolution'[27] and served the function of mobilising the masses and disseminating the ideologies of socialism and communism. They connote passion, rebellion, sacrifice, and glory. The CCP has a long history of using the Red songs as political and symbolic tools to disseminate ideologies and ignite popular support at the height of political campaigns. At first glance, the Red culture campaign seemed to be doing the same thing – using music to spread a particular set of values and ideological convictions. If one looks closer, however, there was a qualitative difference between the notion of *Red* in the previous mass campaigns and Chongqing's Red culture programme. 'Red' used to be a concept that *represented*. 'Red' used to represent the great sacrifices made to fight the national enemies and win the civil war against the Kuomintang; it represented a CCP that was the legitimate ruling party of the newly-founded nation; it represented the leadership of Chairman Mao, who urged people to join the Great Proletarian Revolution. In Chongqing's Red culture campaign, however, the definition of Red was expanded to include everything that was 'positive' and 'healthy'. As a consequence of this expansion of the definition of Red, one could no longer pinpoint exactly what was being referred to in the official narrative of the Red culture programme and what effect on the public the reference to Red was designed to achieve. The definition of Red was devoid of much of its political substance and ceased to function as an ideological tool. The notion of Red was reduced to a sign that exists only to attest its own existence. It did not represent. It simulated. It simulated to conceal the fact that the spirit of the revolution no longer existed, that the masses who believed in sacrifice for the collective good no longer existed, and that the Party that fought for the interests of the workers and peasants no longer existed.

The self-induced circuit

The second feature of simulation demonstrated by Chongqing's Red culture programme is that of a self-induced, inwardly-enfolded, and non-dialectical power circuit. This feature was linked with a particular type of performativity that was based on a form of exchange not between the immediate actors and viewers but within the internal territory of a singular political power. Jeffrey Alexander argues that the key to a successful performance is its capacity to establish a mutual understanding of the 'authenticity' of both the intent and content of the performance between the observers and actors. The actors may not be true believers of the message conveyed by the performance, but the critical thing is to convince the audience that the symbolic meaning conveyed through the performance is valid.[28] Interestingly, Chongqing's Red culture campaign seemed to be a performance predicated not on a mutual understanding of the significance of the programme between the actors and the audience but on an exchange of the signs and meanings within the structures of the political power itself.

The first sign of the Red culture programme being a self-induced circuit was that it did not need the audience. Traditional Maoist mass political campaigns needed

Red culture campaign as simulation 45

the audience. For example, in the 'Campaign to Suppress Counter-revolutionaries and Regime Consolidation' (1950–1953), a number of social groups were actively and intentionally targeted as the 'audience'. Besides suspected counter-revolutionaries and their supporters, the campaign also targeted the 'wavering urbanities and "middle elements"', who had not fully committed to the new regime, the 'hard core activists and "regular cadres"', and the 'leading local cadres and Party committees' in the urban areas. Targeting these social groups as audiences of the campaign helped the Party to achieve specific political goals – that is, strengthen popular patriotism, comfort the activists who felt entitled to more fruits of the revolution, and provide moral incentives to the lower stratum of the people of the state.[29]

Chongqing's Red culture campaign needed the audience in the sense that it needed people to *act* as the audience. It did *not* need a *real* audience because the ultimate goal was not to convince people about the ideas that underpinned the legitimacy of its existence. It should be acknowledged here that this argument lacks direct evidence from the testimonies of the leaders of the programme about their original intentions for the campaign. Nevertheless, observations on the following aspects of the programme were likely to support this argument. Firstly, tickets to the Red-themed shows were not normally sold to the public. The audience was composed of students, elderly people, civil servants, soldiers, and so on who were organized to attend the shows. In some cases, the audience included the actors themselves. It might be that the Red culture shows were too 'decent' to adopt a commercial logic or that selling tickets was simply not the goal. One employee who worked for a private advertising company argued that a major 'deficiency' of the Red-themed shows was that they were always in an overly simplistic and extremely boring format. Her company worked on dozens of cases for the local district governments to launch their Red culture programmes. Working in the advertising industry, she was trained to be creative. Singing Red programmes, however, did not require new ideas to make the shows fashionable. Whenever extra designs, such as a more interactive approach, were proposed to the local governments, they were inevitably dropped. 'The only thing needed was for a number of choruses to go on stage and sing and, if possible, have the audience sing along. There is no need for commercial elements or creativity. You just do it basic and easy'.[30] The result was:

> Because it was so formal, people would not hold it dear to their hearts. The only thing it meant to people was that 'my mom went to sing Red songs today' and nothing more. We'll skip the political implications, but it was indeed too boring and simple.[31]

She seemed deeply baffled about why commercial logic and techniques could not be incorporated into the production of Red-themed shows, why it had to be in the form of chorus singing but not karaoke, which was more popular during people's leisure activities, and why the competition unit of the show could not be adapted to the genre of those talent shows, such as 'Super Girl' (*chaoji nvsheng* 超级女声), so that more audience members could be attracted.

46 *Red culture campaign as simulation*

It might be that Chongqing's Red culture programme was not meant to be attractive or interesting in the first place. It might be that the whole idea of singing Red was not about teaching people to sing Red songs or selling them ideas about the value of these songs. There was a disconnection between the foreground scripts of the performance, that is, a narrative of the significance of the 'Red' culture, and the background symbols of political power, meaning the fact that Bo was willing and capable of carrying out a mass campaign in the name of the CCP as a revolutionary party. As a result, the success of the Red culture campaign did not depend on whether the actors of the performance successfully conveyed the significance of the Red culture to the audience so that the two could reach a mutual understanding of the narrative.[32] Instead the success of the campaign as performance was subject to the implicit rules of power struggles at the top of the political elites of the CCP. It was performance that exchanged signs with the political power in Beijing, not with the audience in Chongqing. To some extent, this was a game within the circle of political elites. There was indeed a political message that must be pushed through here – the campaign adhered to the traditions of the CCP. This political message was critical at a time when the CCP's political elites were contending and negotiating for the top jobs in the impending restructuring of China's political landscape in late 2012 (the 18th Party Congress) and early 2013 (the People's Congress). It was a show put on in Chongqing but for the audience in Beijing. The real audience was not the audience sitting watching the singing performance but political elites who would have to interpret the messages behind Bo's display of political muscle and ideological commitment. Clearly, there were exchanges of signs and meanings during the 'performances', but these happened within the enclosed power circuit of CCP politics. The connections between the revolutionary ideals and the masses were faked.

Moreover, Chongqing's Red culture campaign did not mobilise the masses to accomplish action that would help to substantiate the concrete ideas expressed in its propaganda. The examples of the Red Guard movement and the Campaign to Suppress Counter-revolutionaries, mentioned earlier, illustrate how real mass campaigns mobilised people to induce relevant political action. There was a real connection and consistency between the political ideology of the 'mass-line' and the political action of relying on the masses to challenge the existing political establishment.[33] In the case of the Red culture campaign, it mobilised people to sing Red songs, but this singing did not accomplish any tangible political goal that was intrinsically related to the ideological underpinnings of the political programme itself. It confirmed the idea of the 'centrality' of the masses, but they were mobilised not to act on any concrete policies, except for demonstrating and re-enforcing the masses-oriented nature of the campaign. It was a *circular* movement, during which the meaning and significance of the campaign existed only to confirm the existence of each other. It might therefore be useful to perceive the Red culture campaign as a self-induced, inwardly-enfolded, and non-dialectical circuit that effects exchanges within itself. The project of the Red culture campaign, therefore, operated not as a dialogue between the political power and the masses but was a reference to the political power itself and only for itself. It was 'non-dialectical'.[34]

Implications of Chongqing's Red culture campaign as simulation

There are several critical implications concerning the kind of political power observed in the case of the Red culture campaign. There is a particular type of danger that is associated with the 'murderous capacity' of simulation. As Baudrillard argues, traditionally, power dissimulates itself, pretending that it is not there when it truly exists. In late modern capitalist society, capital destroys the dichotomies between 'true and false, good and evil'.[35] Power, therefore, has to reply on its ability to *simulate* – to pretend it is there when it actually is not. Power simulates to salvage the relevance of the fundamental principles of modern life, such as rationality and morality. It does not matter whether power is judged to be rational or irrational, moral or immoral. What really matters is that it is still being judged within the paradigm of modern values. In fact, contradictory terms and values have become commutable and exchangeable. One can no longer tell the distinctions between the beautiful and the ugly, left and right, true and false. The world is now governed by indeterminacy and reversibility instead of linearity, rationality, or absolute truth. This is exactly what Baudrillard calls the 'murderous capacity' of the simulacrum and exactly why Baudrillard claims that 'simulation is infinitely more dangerous' than distorted truth. In the case of Chongqing's Red culture campaign, the liquidation of the references to the real, that is, the concept of Red, also had the potential to threaten the distinction between right and wrong, true and false. Thus, the real danger of such campaigns taking place in today's China is not that the actors and audiences, under certain pressure, go along to sing Red songs. The real danger neither is a return to the CR. It is far more worrying that people learn to suspend their judgment because they know that the campaign, and the political power behind it, had long since stopped concerning what it appears to be dealing with – good and evil, right and wrong, true and false. A disillusioned, cynical population is no less disturbing than a passionately mobilised one.

The second implication concerns Baudrillard's argument that extreme power cannot last. 'Every system that approaches perfect operativity simultaneously approaches its downfall',[36] argued Baudrillard. At the tipping point of absolute power, power becomes so fragile and absurd that any action could be subversive and causes the irrevocable breakdown of the perfect system.[37] If power can stage its own death to recover a spark of its own existence, does it mean that the political power indicated in the case of Chongqing's Red culture campaign, which exchanges signs within itself and is capable of carrying out meticulously operated campaigns, is approaching the tipping point of its inevitable downfall? It might have been good evidence indicating the collapse of the political power had the Red culture campaign been carried out as an all-out simulation. But it was not. Chongqing's Red culture campaign had a rather ambiguous relation with the central leadership in Beijing throughout its course. When Bo was sacked from his position in March 2012, the campaign gradually faded out of people's lives. The central political leadership of the CCP in Beijing played a significant role in determining the fate of the Red culture campaign. The leadership apparently is still genuinely interested in selling ideas to the public. The failures of the CR, the

48 *Red culture campaign as simulation*

success of the post-CR reform policies, patriotism, and the latest 'Chinese dream' are all ideas that the Party communicates with the people and hopes the people will truly buy into. Thus, Chongqing's Red culture campaign is perceived as an isolated instance of simulation. It does not imply that the general ideological work of the CCP has entered the phase of simulation.

The relationship between Chongqing's Red culture campaign and the cultural-ideological agenda of the CCP's central leadership was complex. On the one hand, one should note that the popularisation of Red songs and the Red culture is far from a unique invention of Bo. In fact, it did not differ significantly from the waves of Red culture campaigns implemented in China during the reform era. For example, in the early 1990s, widespread 'Mao fever' was instigated as the country commemorated the 50th anniversary of Mao Zedong's *Yan'an* talk in 1991 and Mao's 100th birthday in 1993. Since then, there has been an official effort to promote a specific genre of cultural production, called the 'mainstream melody' (*zhuxuanlü* 主旋律), which glorifies the ruling party and adopts the major themes of patriotism and nationalism. In 2011, as the CCP celebrates its 90th anniversary, singing Red was one of the most popular events in which popular participation was encouraged nationwide. In fact, there was a considerable overlap between the Red songs promoted in Chongqing and those promoted by the central government's Department of Propaganda.[38]

On the other hand, based on a description in Steen's detailed account of the evolution of the Red culture in China, one can point to two possible differences between Chongqing's Red culture campaign and other projects of the 'mainstream melody' on the national scale. Although the incorporation of 'new Red songs' was observed in the promotion of Red songs in other national campaigns, this seemed a more genuine effort to 'increase their appeal and ensure widespread participation, especially of younger audiences'.[39] The CCP as the ruling party obviously had a far greater stake in selling an ideological system to its people and convincing them of its ideological legitimacy than any possible concern on the part of Bo Xilai about whether the local people in Chongqing truly believed in the glorious culture of humanity. The CCP has been far more open to genres of music and performance that are attractive, flexible, and market friendly than the Chongqing government under the leadership of Bo. The popularisation of the Red culture at the national level included commercial endeavours, such as Red tourism and TV programmes that adopted successful business models, and were much more open to elements of entertainment and popular culture, such as a programme produced by the Jiangxi Satellite TV – 'China Red Song Concert' (*zhongguo hongge hui* 中国红歌会).[40] Bo's determination to cancel commercial advertising on Chongqing's satellite TV, for example, seemed to conflict with the CCP's blueprint and principles for future cultural reforms in China, which emphasised the critical role of the market. This evidence seems to suggest that the CCP's effort to popularise the mainstream culture was a genuine culture campaign, rather than a simulation, as in the case of Chongqing's Red culture campaign.

It is therefore understandable that Chongqing's Red culture campaign had a relatively ambiguous relationship with the central leadership in Beijing throughout the course of its development. It seemed that there had been considerable division among the top leadership regarding the practices and meanings of the 'Chongqing Model'.[41] During Bo's tenure in Chongqing, seven of the nine members of the Standing Committee not only visited Chongqing but praised many of the policies implemented there by Bo. Noticeably, the then-general Party secretary, Hu Jintao, never visited Chongqing nor showed any support for Bo's 'Chongqing Model', whereas the premier, Wen Jiabao, remained an outspoken critic of the 'Chongqing Model' and publically voiced his concern over what Bo's policies could have implied for the future of China's political reforms. Instead, both Hu and Wen seemed to be leaning towards Bo's political rival at the time, Wang Yang, and his policies in Guangdong Province, who were friendlier towards the market economy and civil society. In the end, the central political leadership of the CCP's decision to prosecute Bo brought an end to the Red culture campaign. In comprehending the fate of the Red culture campaign, it is important to understand that there were multiple layers of political power involved in the programme, and one should avoid conflating these different levels of political power of the CCP. The CCP is a heterogeneous, fractioned, and complex political organization and power matrix. Power is constantly divided, contested, and reorganized within the party among individuals as well as the different levels of bureaucracy.

The problematic of characterising Chongqing's Red culture campaign as simulation

Baudrillard's concept of simulation as a self-induced and non-dialectical power circuit is ingenious but incomplete. The image of a power that perpetuates by only exchanging within itself rarely exists in the empirical world. Although political power exchanges signs of power within its own sphere, the masses were able to leave their own imprints on the campaign. This is because, on the one hand, the campaign had to be *practiced*; songs had to be sung; shows had to be organized; books had to be read. During this process, there exist flows of resources among all parties involved, which enable practices of tactics on the part of ordinary people who do not strictly follow the plans of the official programme. On the other hand, the participants are capable of framing the meaning and significance of the campaign by themselves, on the basis of which disagreements, dissents, and changes can be imagined and become possible when top-down plans are executed in the realm of actual life. The process of social practices in the space of the multidimensional society was not only underpinned by the economic and political structures but also deeply embedded in the complexity and contingencies of the everyday life. This is exactly what has been missing in Baudrillard's theory and the problematic of applying Baudrillard's concept of simulation to the Chongqing's Red culture campaign. Thus, the interaction between the political programme of the Red culture campaign and the practices of the participants have both elements of *disassociation* as the result of the campaign being simulated as well as *association* as the result of it being practiced in the everyday lives of its participants. In the following four chapters, I will introduce the forms of practice by participants

50   *Red culture campaign as simulation*

of the Red culture campaign and describe the interactive relationships in forms of exchange and framing.

Notes

1 Sylvere Lotringer, 'Exterminating Angel: Introduction to Forget Foucault', in *Forget Foucault* (Los Angeles, CA: Semiotext(e), 2007), pp. 7–25.
2 Tyrene White, *China's Longest Campaign: Birth Planning in the People's Republic, 1949–2005* (London: Cornell University Press, 2006), p. 3.
3 Chang-tai Huang, 'The Dance of Revolution: *Yangge* in Beijing in the Early 1950s', *China Quarterly*, 181 (2005), 82–99.
4 Julia C. Strauss, 'Paternalist Terror: The Campaign to Suppress Counterrevolutionaries and Regime Consolidation in the People's Republic of China, 1950–1953', *Comparative Study of Society and History*, 44 (January, 2002), 95–7.
5 White, *China's Longest Campaign*, p. 7.
6 Jan Pakulski, 'Poland: Ideology, Legitimacy and Political Domination', in *Dominant Ideologies*, ed. by Nicholas Abercrombie, Stephen Hill and Bryan S. Turner (London: Unwin Hyman, 1990), p. 58.
7 Josef Gregory Mahoney, 'Ideology, Telos, and the "Communist Vanguard" From Mao Zedong to Hu Jintao', *Journal of Chinese Political Science* 14 (2009), 135–66.
8 Merle Goldman, 'China's Anti-Confucius Campaign, 1973–74', *China Quarterly*, 63 (1975), 435–62.
9 Robert Weatherley, *Politics in China since 1949: Legitimizing Authoritarian Rule* (London: Routledge, 2006).
10 Strauss, 'Paternalist Terror', p. 80.
11 Strauss, 'Paternalist Terror', p. 95.
12 Harry Harding, 'The Chinese State in Crisis, 1966–1969', in *The Politics of China: the Eras of Mao and Deng*, 3rd edition, ed. by Roderick MacFarquhar (Cambridge: Cambridge University Press, 1997), p. 229.
13 Harding, p. 229; Michel Bonnin, 'The "Lost Generation": Its Definition and Its Role in Today's Chinese Elite Politics', *Social Research*, 73 (2006), 247.
14 'Bo Xilai: Yao peiyang haizi yangyang jiankang jingqishen' (Bo Xilai: To Cultivate Children's Spirit), *Chongqing Daily*, May 31, 2008.
15 11 July 2008.
16 '*Bo Xilai: Chang xiang zhuxuanlu, ningju jingqishen*' (Bo Xilai: Sing Aloud and Spirit Up), Chongqing Daily, June 23, 2009.
17 '*Renmin ribao zhuanfang He Shizhong: "changdujiangchuan" tizhen shehui 'jingqishen*' (The People's Daily Interviewing He Shizhong: 'changdujiangchuan' Raises of the Social Spirit), *Chongqing Daily*, 4 December, 2010.
18 Statistics accessed at Chongqing government's website: www.cq.gov.cn/today/news/376959.htm.
19 Huang, 'The Dance of Revolution', 2005, pp. 82, 87, 98.
20 Andrea Steen, ' "Voices of the Mainstream": Red Songs and Revolutionary Identities in the People's Republic of China', in *Vocal Music and Contemporary Identities: Unlimited Voices in East Asia and the West*, ed. by Christian Utz and Frederick Lau (London: Routledge, 2013), pp. 225–47.
21 Hua Gao, '*Hongjun Changzheng de Lishi Xushu Shi Zenyang Xingcheng de*' (How Was the Historical Narrative of the Red Army's Long March Constructed), in *Geming Niandai* (*The Era of Revolution*) (Guangdong: Guangdong *renmin chubanshe*, 2010), pp. 139–149.
22 Wai-chuang Ho and Wing-Wah Law, 'Values, Music and Education in China', in *Music Education Research*, 6 (July 2004), 151.
23 Published between 1971 and 1974.

24 Bryant Lei Ouyang, 'Music, Memory, and Nostalgia: Collective Memories of Cultural Revolution Songs in Contemporary China', *The China Review*, 5 (Fall 2005), 151–175.
25 Bryant, 'Music, Memory, and Nostalgia', p. 164.
26 Ho and Law, 'Values, Music and Education in China'.
27 Steen, ' "Voices of the Mainstream" '.
28 Jeffrey Alexander, *Performance and Power* (Cambridge: Polity Press, 2011), 25–8.
29 Strauss, 'Paternalist Terror', pp. 86–7.
30 Interview with GZ45.
31 Interview with GZ45.
32 Alexander, pp. 29–32.
33 What exactly happened during the campaign on the ground was quite another story. The mobilisation of the masses unfortunately created deep divisions within the society and led to widespread social chaos.
34 Jean Baudrillard, *Forget Foucault* (Los Angeles, CA: Semiotext(e), 2007).
35 Baudrillard, *Symbolic Exchange and Death* (London: Sage, 1993), pp. 43, 46.
36 Baudrillard, *Symbolic Exchange*, p. 4.
37 Baudrillard, *Symbolic Exchange*.
38 See Appendix IV and V.
39 Steen, ' "Voices of the Mainstream" ', p. 238.
40 Steen, ' "Voices of the Mainstream" ', p. 236.
41 Zheng, 'China in 2012'.

Bibliography

Alexander, Jeffrey, *Performance and Power* (Cambridge: Polity Press, 2011)
Baudrillard, Jean, *Forget Foucault* (Los Angeles, CA: Semiotext(e), 2007)
Bonnin, Michel, 'The "Lost Generation": Its Definition and Its Role in Today's Chinese Elite Politics', *Social Research*, 73 (2006), 245–74
'*Bo Xilai: chang xiang zhuxuanlu, ningju jingqishen*' (Bo Xilai: Sing Aloud and Spirit Up), *Chongqing Daily*, 23 June 2009
'*Bo Xilai: yao peiyang haizi angyang jiankang jingqishen*' (Bo Xilai: To Cultivate Children's Spirit), *Chongqing Daily*, 31 May 2008
Gao, Hua, '*Hongjun Changzheng de Lishi Xushu Shi Zenyang Xingcheng de*' (How Was the Historical Narrative of the Red Army's Long March Constructed), in *Geming Niandai* (*The Era of Revolution*) (Guangdong: Guangdong *renmin chubanshe*, 2010), pp. 139–49
Goldman, Merle, 'China's Anti-Confucius Campaign, 1973–74', *China Quarterly*, 63 (1975), 435–62
Harding, Harry, 'The Chinese State in Crisis, 1966–1969', in Roderick MacFarquhar, ed., *The Politics of China: The Eras of Mao and Deng*, 3rd edition (Cambridge: Cambridge University Press, 1997), pp. 147–245
Ho, Wai-chuang and Wing-Wah Law, 'Values, Music and Education in China', *Music Education Research*, 6 (July 2004), 149–67
Huang, Chang-tai, 'The Dance of Revolution: *Yangge* in Beijing in the Early 1950s', *China Quarterly*, 181 (2005), 82–99
Lotringer, Sylvere, 'Exterminating Angel: Introduction to Forget Foucault', in *Forget Foucault* (Los Angeles, CA: Semiotext(e), 2007), pp. 7–25
Mahoney, Josef Gregory, 'Ideology, Telos, and the "Communist Vanguard" From Mao Zedong to Hu Jintao', *Journal of Chinese Political Science*, 14 (2009), 135–66
Ouyang, Bryant Lei, 'Music, Memory, and Nostalgia: Collective Memories of Cultural Revolution Songs in Contemporary China', *China Review*, 5 (Fall 2005), 151–75

52   Red culture campaign as simulation

Pakulski, Jan, 'Poland: Ideology, Legitimacy and Political Domination', in Nicholas Abercrombie, Stephen Hill, and Bryan S. Turner, eds, *Dominant Ideologies* (London: Unwin Hyman, 1990), pp. 38–63

'*Renmin ribao zhuanfang He Shizhong: 'changdujiangchuan' tizhen shehui 'jingqishen*' (The People's Daily Interviewing He Shizhong: 'changdujiangchuan' Raises of the Social Spirit), *Chongqing Daily*, 4 December 2010

Steen, Andreas, ' "Voices of the Mainstream": Red Songs and Revolutionary Identities in the People's Republic of China', in Christian Utz and Frederick Lau, eds, *Vocal Music and Contemporary Identities: Unlimited Voices in East Asia and the West* (London: Routledge, 2013), pp. 225–47

Strauss, Julia C., 'Paternalist Terror: The Campaign to Suppress Counterrevolutionaries and Regime Consolidation in the People's Republic of China, 1950–1953', *Comparative Study of Society and History*, 44 (January, 2002), 80–105

Weatherley, Robert, *Politics in China Since 1949: Legitimizing Authoritarian Rule* (London: Routledge, 2006)

White, Tyrene, *China's Longest Campaign: Birth Planning in the People's Republic, 1949–2005* (London: Cornell University Press, 2006)

Zheng, Yongnian, 'China in 2012: Troubled Elite, Frustrated Society', *Asian Survey*, 53 (2013), 162–75

4 Who were the participants in Chongqing's Red culture campaign?

In July 2011, official statistics released by the Chongqing government claimed that an aggregate population of more than 100 million people participated in all varieties of activities during the Red culture campaign. The population of Chongqing was 30 million. This means that if the official statistics were right, each resident of the municipality would have participated in the campaign at least three times on average during the time span of less than four years. The official statistics might be largely inflated[1]; it was true, however, that the campaign was rather inclusive and recruited participants from all age groups with various occupational backgrounds, such as government bureaucracies, schools and universities, the PLA troops, and retirees. This chapter mainly focuses on the sample of participants interviewed for this project. There were three major groups of interviewees: retirees, university students, and employees of the government bureaucracy and state-owned and private enterprises. They were typical examples of the local people who participated in the Red culture campaign. In this chapter, I offer a detailed account of the generational differences in terms of socio-economic status, life stage, and values among the three social groups. The mobilisation of such a large and diverse population of participants also depended on the specific institutional conditions in China, which will be described in the last section of this chapter.

The participants in the campaign

A total of 74 participants in the Red culture campaign were interviewed for this research project. Twenty-three of them were retirees, 25 university students, and 26 employees. The university students included both undergraduate and graduate students. The term 'employee' here refers to people in the workforce. They were employees of the government bureaucracy, state-owned enterprises (SOEs), and private companies. The interviewees were recruited if they fitted into these three specific social groups under investigation. Unfortunately, no reliable statistical data were available about the Red culture campaign that could be used to guide the sampling procedures. I did not attempt to generate a representative sample for the purpose of the research is to obtain an in-depth understanding of the participants' subjective experiences as well as the process of meaning making during their participation. Nevertheless, variation was attempted. Shared and differing patterns of practices were sought within and across different groups of participants. While

54   *Participants in Red culture campaign*

recruiting interviewees for these groups, the snowballing technique was used. The interviewees were encouraged to recommend other candidates with similar experiences to the researcher.

Retirees

The retirees consisted of members of community art groups, that is, choir and dancing groups, and those who voluntarily formed singing groups in public parks and squares. Four such community groups (Spring Breeze in Shapingba District; White Cloud and Autumn Moon, both in Nan'an District; and Blue Heaven in Yuzhong District),[2] three parks (Shaping Park in Shapingba District, Bijin Park in Yubei District, and Eling Park in Yuzhong District), and a public square (in Nan'an District) were selected as the major locales for the interviews and observations.

The four art groups represented four different types of communities that support their activities. Spring Breeze had 34 members who had retired from working at the same SOE, most of whom were in their 50s and 60s, with a very few in their 70s. White Cloud recruited those who had been 'educated youths' (*zhiqing*) who were sent to the rural villages during the Cultural Revolution (CR). The team was supervised by an 'educated youths' association funded by donations from successful entrepreneurs who were once 'educated youths' themselves. The singing group had 50 to 60 members, of whom more than half were active. Autumn Moon was associated with the residential community where it was located. Its membership fluctuated between 80 and 100. Founded in the 1990s, the team was quite famous in the district. Blue Heaven was affiliated with an artistic organization with a government background. It was founded in 2007 and had 60 members.

The three parks selected hosted a variety of different activities. For example, in E'ling Park, there was a well-equipped karaoke spot funded by the park's administrative office. In Shaping Park, on the other hand, singing spots were organized by voluntary groups of amateur musicians playing *Erhu* (a traditional Chinese musical instrument), keyboards, and so on. In Bijin Park, Red song singing lessons were taught every morning. In Hongsheng Square, karaoke booths were set up every evening at which the local residents sang.

University students

The university students came from two major universities in central Chongqing. Five studied at University A, a predominantly social science university. The remainder studied, or used to study, at University B, a comprehensive university that traditionally excels in teaching natural sciences and engineering. The majority of the university student interviewees were undergraduates, and only two were graduates.

Employees

There were two subgroups of participants within the social group of employees. The first subgroup (type I) consisted of participants in Red-themed activities who were organized by their employers or the government. They worked either in state-owned companies or public institutions and represented their work units in Red-themed activities. The second subgroup (type II) consisted of nine participants whose work was intrinsically related to the Red culture programme. The population of the first category came from very diverse career backgrounds, yet their experience of participating in the Red culture campaign was similar. The population of the second category all worked in the area of cultural production, but their experiences of participating in the campaign differed considerably.

Different generations of participants

Generation was a critical factor that affected how the different social groups attached values and meanings to, and ultimately made a judgment about, both their own experiences of the Red culture campaign and the campaign as a broader political project. Karl Mannheim sees the sociological problem of generation as one of social location. A generation, from a sociological perspective, differs from a concrete community in which the members have to know each other or an organization which is purposefully set up to achieve certain goals. People belong to the same generation because they share 'a common location in the social and historical processes'. They are subject to 'a specific range of potential experience . . . a certain characteristic mode of thought and experiences, and a characteristic type of historically relevant action' within these social and historical processes.[3] People who belong to the same generation should be in such a shared position that they are likely to experience an event in very similar ways, especially during their formative years. The formation of generations, therefore, is closely tied to 'the movement of social change'.[4] Within the same generation, there are different generational units. The members of a generational unit share concrete, close bonds as well as an active identity. This identity is underpinned by the 'fundamental integrative attitudes and formative principles' shared by members of this generational unit. This active identity is believed to be able to facilitate certain 'continuing practices'.[5]

The concept of generation has often been used to explain the social and political behaviour of a particular social group. Schuman and Scott make a valuable contribution to the literature on the relationship between generation and behaviour by emphasising the role of collective memories in bridging the two variables. Their research supports the argument that collective memories of historical events differ according to generational cohorts. Moreover, the political and social changes that occur in their adolescence and early adulthood have the most profound impact on the memories of a particular generation.[6] The result supports a widely-adopted method that is used to define generation. That is, generation can be defined by the historical movements that occurred during people's formative years. Some researchers have suggested the time bracket to be between 17 and 25 years old.[7]

The participants in the Red culture campaign who were interviewed for this research project belong to different generations. The categorisation of the generations was based on the historical periods which corresponded to the interviewees' formative years. It is worth noting here that the historical events experienced by

56 *Participants in Red culture campaign*

the interviewees not only determined what kind of collective memories they possessed but also impacted on the interviewees' current life conditions and positions in the social strata. The categorisation of the generations differs slightly from the categories of social groups used in other chapters (i.e., retirees, university students, and employees). The existing literature has identified four distinctive historical periods that constitute the formative experience of today's Chinese people. They are 'the Great Leap Forward', the CR, the beginning of the economic reform in 1978, and 'the societal transition' since 1992.[8] Based on the historical periods that they experienced during their formative years, the interviewees in this research project are categorised as the CR generation, the generation of youth, and middle-aged employees.

Firstly, the retirees identified themselves as the generation that 'grew up under the Red flag'.[9] In fact, most of them belonged to the CR generation described in scholarly work.[10] This so-called lost generation, or generation of the CR, has been a popular research subject.[11] Based on his extensive research on the CR, particularly the movement of sending 'educated youth' (*zhiqing* 知青) to the countryside, Bonnin defines China's lost generation as 'all those people whose formative years were affected by the "revolutionary" period of the Cultural Revolution or by the ensuing policy of "revolution in education" '.[12] It roughly includes those born between 1947 and 1960.[13] Within the broad generation of the CR, there are multiple generation units. Those in their mid-50s were typically born after the founding of the People's Republic of China (PRC); they were former 'educated youth' during the CR and had gone through the painful mass lay-off during the SOE restructuring in the 1990s. Some of the employees, now in their 50s and approaching retirement, were likely to be former educated youth and shared many collective memories of the pre-reform era with the younger retirees. Therefore, the senior employees and the younger retirees belonged to the same generational unit. Those in their 60s were more likely to be '*laosanjie*',[14] who experienced both the Red Guard and the Educated Youth movements. They were sent out to the countryside, far from home. Many endured very harsh circumstances during the movement. The other unit of *zhiqing*, who were born between 1954 and 1960, did not participate in the Red Guard movement and were mainly sent to the suburbs of their native cities in the late 1970s. They usually had less dramatic experiences than the '*laosanjie*'.[15]

University students, on the other hand, were typically born at the end of the 1980s and in the early 1990s. They grew up in the reform era, when China's economy began to grow rapidly. The portion of employees who were born in the 1980s belonged to the same generation as the university students. They experienced the same social and historical processes as China underwent its post-1992 accelerated economic liberalisation during childhood and adolescence. This generation was exposed to consumerism and globalisation, and constituted the dominant group of 'netizens' in China. Research on the variation of values among the different generations in China has shown that there are substantial gaps between the generations in this regard. The younger generation, who experienced the societal transition during their formative years, placed significantly more value on their self-development, individualism, and the freedom to choose a lifestyle.[16] As Liu observes in her research on Chinese urban youth, the young people in today's China exhibit 'double-qualities' in their representation of the self. They are

> simultaneously materialistic and idealistic, instrumental and expressive . . . apolitical but nationalistic, modern and traditional, blessed with material prosperity and under greater pressure to strive for greater material wealth, and exposed to an unprecedented range of choices and yet lacking a sense of security.[17]

The young people are caught between being free consumers in the market economy and compliant political subjects under the one-Party rule authoritarian regime. They are subjected to a profound process of social fragmentation and individualisation in the absence of a welfare state. As a result, the Chinese urban youth, in seeking freedom of self-expression, often quickly become 'dismal pragmatists' as they grow up.[18]

The group of employees who are in their late 30s and 40s occupied positions in life that differ from those of the university students, retirees, and their more senior work colleagues. These people were typically born during the last phase, or in the aftermath, of the CR. Compared to the participants in their 20s, these employees are more likely to be sympathetic to the revolutionary culture of China's past as it was passed down by their parents' generation. Currently, this group of employees is in a highly pressurised stage of adulthood, and are typically making a living and running a household of their own. They have to deal with multiple issues related to their career advancement, children's education, and care of their elderly parents simultaneously.

Institutional conditions

The Residents' Committee

The Residents' Committee was a very important factor that played an intermediary role in mobilising the retirees to participate in the campaign. The retiree choruses relied heavily on the Residents' Committee to provide them with rehearsal rooms and basic logistic help. For example, Autumn Moon had a particularly close relationship with its associated neighbourhood committee. In addition to a well-furnished rehearsal room, equipped with a piano, the committee also paid for the costumes, transportation costs, and meals related to the performances. The Residents' Committee's heavy involvement in the organization and mobilisation of the Red culture campaign was rooted in the particular governance structure of China's urban cities.

'Community-building' was an important governance technique, adopted by the Chinese government to counter the negative effect of social fragmentation resulting from the dissolution of the work units and the planned economy. It was initiated in the mid-1980s and has been increasingly strengthened since the 1990s.

58 *Participants in Red culture campaign*

The community, as the basic unit of China's urban system, has had an ambiguous political status. On the one hand, the Residents' Committee is supposed to be a self-governing mass organization; on the other hand, it is directly supervised by the district office, the lowest level of government in Chinese cities. A Residents' Committee is obliged to rely on its own resources to carry out the main functions of the organization. At the same time, it is led and controlled by the cadres of the Chinese Communist Party (CCP). Since 2000, the Residents' Committee has been entrusted by the government with a wider range of responsibilities, including providing social welfare services for the residents, managing health care and sanitation, organizing educational and cultural activities, and so on. Among these tasks, providing services for senior citizens forms a central task of community work.[19]

Understanding the unique role and function of the Residents' Committee helps explain the popularity of community art groups during the Red culture campaign and the durability of these activities. Because the local neighbourhood committee was supervised and controlled by the government, they had the political responsibility for organizing Red culture activities. For example, the 'Daily Red Songs' show, produced by Chongqing's satellite channel, required each of Chongqing's 40 districts[20] to prepare programmes for TV broadcast over a whole week. The task was distributed from the city to the districts and then from the districts to the Residents' Committees. When Autumn Moon was preparing to participate in the 'Daily Red Songs' TV programme, an employer of the Residents' Committee came to speak at each rehearsal about the details and requirements of the programme he/she had received from above. He/she was also in charge of providing costumes and props for the performances. On the other hand, because promoting community-level artistic groups and providing cultural services for the elderly had always been part of the routine work of the Residents' Committees (only later appropriated as part of the Red-themed activities during the campaign), the Residents' Committees were unlikely completely to withdraw their support after the Red culture campaign terminated. They played an extremely significant role in sustaining the retirees' singing activities.

Universities and the Youth League Committee

For university students, they participated in the Red culture campaign primarily through the organizational efforts of their universities. The involvement of the universities in the Red culture campaign cannot be fully comprehended unless some political and institutional background about higher-level education in China is provided. Historically, the Party has always exercised strong control over the universities. In the aftermath of the founding of the PRC, the control over China's universities by the Party-state was tightened as the Chinese People's Congress (CPC) approved the setting up of political organs within the universities' administration.[21] The universities' administrations are closely intertwined with politics as the Party secretaries of the universities have more power than the presidents, who nominally head the university administration. Although there has been a tendency to decentralise governance in universities in recent decades, as the state lessens control over more specific administrative tasks such as admission standards, degree examinations, curricular development, and so on, the Party has never given up its 'macro-control' over China's higher education, and continues to direct universities by retaining the power to appoint university presidents and Party secretaries.[22] To date, Chinese universities maintain the transmission of the Party values as a major component of their educational goals. Students are required to attend a number of ideological modules in addition to their academic programmes.[23] In the areas of teaching and research, teachers and researchers continue to feel pressure when selecting research topics that are considered politically sensitive. Positions for political staff at universities remain reserved for Party members, whose tasks include recruiting students for Party membership, organizing extracurricular campus activities, and so on.[24]

It is important to note that the Chinese universities are under both the vertical control of the Ministry of Education and the horizontal control of the local provincial governments.[25] In fact, the lower levels of government in recent years have played increasingly important roles in supervising and managing China's higher education. Since the universities are under the control of the local governments, it is understandable that participating in the Red culture campaign, a signature project of the municipality government of Chongqing, was therefore an important political task for the universities in the city to fulfill. The control of the universities by the Party is usually realised through the Party's Committee and the Youth League Committee, built into the education institutions. The students' societies, for example, are supervised by the Party's Youth League Committee. During the Red culture campaign in China, the Youth League Committees played a particularly salient role in organizing Red-themed activities on campus. The student choruses, for example, were under close supervision by the officials of the Youth League Committee, who not only passed down assignments to the students but also monitored the content and quality of the programmes. The Party's Youth League Committees exercised a huge impact on the scope of the campaign taking place on campus.

For example, a drama society in University B benefited from the Red culture campaign and produced a successful Red-themed play, which won various prizes in municipality-level and national drama competitions. In the aftermath of the success of this play, however, the society ceased to flourish. In an attempt to revitalise itself, the society decided to restage the play for the fresh intake of undergraduate students in 2011. The drama society was very disappointed when the Youth League Committee at their school apparently showed no sympathy for their endeavour and failed to approve the 10,000 *yuan* ($\approx$£1,000) budget needed for the play to be brought back to the stage.[26] A member of the drama society argued that this was because the student drama society and the committee had very different priorities. The society wanted to perform the play to promote itself and attract new members, whereas the committee was uninterested because 'the school officials have already seen the play',[27] so there was no point in investing in it further. The author of the play also speculated that the committee was uninterested this time because they had already reaped the gains this prize-winning, Red-themed play could bring to the school. As the case of this drama society

60 *Participants in Red culture campaign*

shows, the Red culture campaign offered opportunities for many student societies to prosper, often not by directing channeling resources into the societies but by activating the universities to support them as part of their political obligation to the municipal government. For students or teachers who understood how to 'go with the flow', it was a good chance to secure monetary, institutional, and political support. However, the support from the university was conditional. In this example, without the financial support of the university, the drama society could not even manage to revive the drama on stage at their school, not to mention win honours at the municipal or even national level. The example of the drama society illustrates that during the process of exchange between students and the campaign, there was collaboration as well as moments of tension between the university and the student society which directly influenced the durability of the practices of 'creative compliance' on the part of the students.

The state-owned and private enterprises

The most important mediator between the employees and the Red culture campaign was the employers. The level of importance attached to specific performances by the leadership of the companies had a direct effect on whether professional teachers were hired, how long the rehearsals lasted, as well as how sophisticated the costumes and set would be on the day of the performance. To understand the role played by the enterprises, some background information on the relationship between the Party-state and companies, whether state-owned or private, was in order. During the economic reforms carried out in China since 1978, a central task of the state was to transform the SOEs into modern companies. As a result, the SOEs gained substantial managerial autonomy from the state administration. A series of drastic SOE reforms were implemented since the mid-1980s, including the introduction of the 'contract responsibility system' in 1988, in an attempt to cure the persistent ills of low efficiency and productivity. When these reforms faltered, the leadership of the CCP turned to other routes. Backed up by Deng Xiaoping, some 'capitalist methods' were introduced into the reform. Efforts were made to build a shareholding system for the enterprises. Until the late 1990s, many large and medium-sized SOEs had been corporatised; their ownership was diversified. During this process, the ideological doctrines of socialism, for example, the 'predominance of public ownership of the means of production' and the 'leadership of the ruling Communist Party' continued to shape the law-making processes and institutional reforms.[28] Thus, even in the reform era, the state played a particularly crucial role in the construction of the market economy in China, including establishing an institutional framework and enforcing market rules.[29]

In the case of the privately-owned enterprises, studies have shown that direct state involvement in corporate government has a positive effect on the economic performance of newly-incorporated firms.[30] Although the exact relationship between the political connections and financial performance of corporations is still open to debate,[31] many studies support the argument that affiliation with the ruling CCP has a beneficial effect on the performance of private companies.[32]

Participants in Red culture campaign 61

Other research has found that the importance of political connections for entrepreneurs has been increasing since the Chinese state officially legitimised private business. The legitimisation fosters the interpenetration and coalition between entrepreneurs and the Party-state cadres and officials.[33] As the research indicates, the entrepreneurs' participation in politics is partly determined by how developed the markets and market-supporting institutions are. The more developed the markets and their institutions, the less likely it is for entrepreneurs to enter politics. When markets fail, the entrepreneurs tend to seek political participation to help with their business operations.[34] As a result, it has been observed that the importance of Party membership and political connections is stronger in regions where the market institutions and legal protection are weaker, such as China.[35] The value of political capital, therefore, is particularly salient in the institutional domains of the market economy, where the government has the power to regulate the market.[36] After decades of market reform, the local party committees and government still had tremendous power over the decision-making processes regarding the local economic activities.[37]

All in all, even in the era of the market economy, the Party-state continues to exercise paramount influence on the economic performance of both the SOEs and private companies. Because the individuals' material well-being is significantly correlated with their occupations and the specific types of enterprise they work for,[38] the Party-state therefore has both a direct and indirect effect on the livelihoods of the employees. Enjoying a monopolistic grip on resources, the Party effectively shapes people's interests. As Gore argues, the Party 'continues its practice of penetrating, organizing, mobilizing, shaping, and channeling the population'.[39]

The enterprises, whether state-owned or private, were willing to invest resources in the campaign. Participation in the most popular political programme of the time was both an administrative responsibility that they could not refuse and a gesture paying tribute to the authority of the Party committee and its leadership. This explains why many of the SOEs were involved in the Red culture campaign in the first place. On the other hand, as many of the SOEs have been corporatised and are owned by a diversity of shareholders, the companies had to face competition in the market. Most of them nowadays enjoy a certain level of managerial autonomy have and placed profit making as the priority of their enterprises. It was therefore unsurprising that no enterprise interviewed in this project had, or was willing, to compromise their normal working routines or economic performance while participating in the Red culture campaign. When they had to, however, the activities usually took the form of extracurricular activities during the employees' spare time that could help boost work morale and build a corporate culture. When the task was demanding, for example, involving the first level of participation, the companies tended to pick junior staff or those working in marginalised departments. One employee, who was a department manager of an SOE, explained:

> We are a company trying to run a business. Doing business in recent years hasn't been easy, so we haven't devoted too much (to the campaign). Just a little bit, as a response to the call of the government.[40]

62 *Participants in Red culture campaign*

In the case of the privately owned companies, some appeared to be even more active than the SOEs in trying to get involved in the Red-themed shows. Without the normative pressure of the 'administrative task', they still chose to take seriously the political significance of the campaign. This makes a lot of sense if one understands how vital it is for privately owned companies to maintain a good relationship with the local government and its officials in China. Because the market institutions and legal protection remain very weak in China, this relationship could determine the private companies' survival and prospect of prospering. The relationship between the companies and the local party committees and governments, who had a lot of influence over the local economic activities, became a critical factor in deciding the extent to which the company employees were involved in the Red culture campaign. As the campaign drew to a close in early 2012, the Red-themed activities carried out within enterprises duly died away.

Summary

This chapter introduced the sample of participants interviewed for this research project. They were not representative of the whole population of participants in Chongqing municipality, yet their experiences provided a microcosm from which we can get a glimpse of what was happening on the ground during the Red culture campaign. This chapter, by introducing the different generations to which the participants belonged and mapping out the institutional conditions under which the participants were recruited and encouraged to take part in the campaign, provides a prelude to the detailed description of their experiences presented in the next three chapters of this book. The three groups of participants, that is, the retirees, the university students, and the employees, belonged to different generations, which would ultimately condition how they attached generation-specific values and meaning to their involvement in the political programme. Thus, generation constitutes an important explanatory factor for analysing the experiences of the participants. The other critical factor is the institutional conditions. For each group of participants, the Residents' Committee, the universities and the Youth League Committee, and the state-owned and private enterprises, played significant roles, respectively, in mobilising the participants and conditioning their experiences of the campaign. The core to understanding such institutional influence on the practices of the participants is to understand the relation between the Party and local institutions.

Notes

1 An official of the local Propaganda Department described to the researcher how the numbers of attendance were produced. It was quite likely that the local offices of all levels of governments, who were responsible for organizing Red-themed activities, over-reported the number of participants to their higher-ups.
2 All names of organizations and individuals mentioned in the book are pseudonyms.
3 Karl Mannheim, 'The Problem of Generations', in *Essays on the Sociology of Knowledge*, ed. by Paul Kecskemeti (London: Routledge & Kegan Paul LTD, 1952), pp. 288, 291.

Participants in Red culture campaign 63

4 Michel Bonnin, 'The "Lost Generation": Its Definition and Its Role in Today's Chinese Elite Politics', *Social Research*, 73 (2006), 247.
5 Mannheim, 'The Problem of Generations', pp. 304–5.
6 Howard Schuman and Jacqueline Scott, 'Generations and Collective Memories', *American Sociological Review*, 54 (1989), 359–60, 379.
7 Bonnin, 'The "Lost Generation"', p. 247.
8 Bonnin, 'The "Lost Generation"', p. 247.
9 Interview with A03.
10 There was one interviewee, age 70, who would fall out of Bonnin's definition of the CR generation. The formative experiences for this interviewee would be years preceding the CR.
11 Bonnin, 'The "Lost Generation"', p. 246.
12 Bonnin, 'The "Lost Generation"', p. 251. The policy of 'revolution in education' was abandoned in 1978.
13 Bonnin, 'The "Lost Generation"', p. 253.
14 Middle school and high school graduates of 1966 to 1968.
15 Bonnin, 'The "Lost Generation"', p. 256.
16 Jiaming Sun and Xun Wang, 'Value Differences between Generations in China: A Study in Shanghai', *Journal of Youth Studies*, 13 (2010), 65–81.
17 Fengshu Liu, *Urban Youth in China: Modernity, the Internet and the Self* (London: Routledge, 2010), pp. 182–3.
18 Liu, *Urban Youth in China*, pp. 188–9.
19 David Bray, 'Building "Community": New Strategies of Governance in Urban China', in *China's Governmentalities: Governing Change, Changing Government*, ed. by Elaine Jeffreys (Oxon: Routledge, 2009), pp. 88–106
20 In October 2011, the 40 districts in Chongqing were reduced to 38.
21 Wang Li, 'Higher Education Governance and University Autonomy in China', *Globalisation, Societies and Education*, 8 (2010), 477–95.
22 Li, 'Higher Education Governance'.
23 Rui Yang et al., '"Dancing in a Cage": Changing Autonomy in Chinese Higher Education', *Higher Education*, 54 (2007), 589.
24 Sun-Yan Pan, 'Intertwining of Academia and Officialdom and University Autonomy: Experience from Tsinghua University in China', *Higher Education Policy*, 20 (2007), 121–44.
25 Li, 'Higher Education Governance', p. 489; Yang, '"Dancing in a Cage"', p. 577.
26 Another member stated that the budget was downgraded to 6000 to 7000 *yuan* (≈ £600–700) later but still failed to gain approval.
27 Interview with XS24.
28 Chao Xi, 'Transforming Chinese Enterprises: Ideology, Efficiency and Instrumentalism in the Process of Reform', in *Asian Socialism and Legal Change: The Dynamics of Vietnamese and Chinese Reform*, ed. by John Gillespie, Pip Nicholson, and Penelope Nicholson (Canberra: The Australian National University, 2005), pp. 91–114.
29 Victor Nee, 'The Role of the State in Making a Market Economy', *Journal of Institutional and Theoretical Economy*, 156 (2000), 64–88.
30 Victor Nee, Sonja Opper, and Sonia Wong, 'Developmental State and Corporate Governance in China', *Management and Organization Review*, 3 (2007), 19–53.
31 For example, Fan et al. show that the political ties of CEOs have a negative effect on the post-IPO performance of China's new partially-privatized firms. See Joseph Fan, T. J. Wong & Tianyu Zhang, 'Politically Connected CEOs, Corporate Government, and Post-IPO performance of China's Newly Partially Privatized Firms', *Journal of Financial Economics*, 84 (2007), 330–57.
32 Hongbin Li, L. Meng, Q. Wang & L. A. Zhou, 'Political Connections, Financing and Firm Performance: Evidence from Chinese Private Firms', *Journal of Development Economics*, 87 (2008), 283–99.

64 *Participants in Red culture campaign*

33 Eun Kyong Choi and Kate Xiao Zhou, 'Entrepreneurs and Politics in the Chinese Transitional Economy: Political Connections and Rent-seeking', *China Review*, 1 (2001), 111–35.
34 Hongbin Li, Lingsheng Meng, and Junsen Zhang, 'Why Do Entrepreneurs Enter Politics? Evidence from China', *Economic Inquiry*, 44 (2006), 559–78.
35 Li et al., 'Political Connections, Financing and Firm Performance'.
36 Victor Nee and Sonja Opper, 'Political Capital in a Market Economy', *Social Forces*, 88 (5), 2105–32.
37 Sonja Opper, Sonia Wong, and Ruyin Hu, 'Party Power, Markets and Private Power: CCP persistence in China's listed Companies', *Research in Social Stratification and Mobility*, 19 (2002), 105–38.
38 Donald J. Adamchak, Shuo Chen, and Jiangtao Li, 'Occupations, Work Units and Work Rewards in Urban China', *International Sociology*, 14 (1999), 423–41.
39 Lance Gore, *The Chinese Communist Party and China's Capitalist Revolution: The Political Impact of the Market* (London: Routledge, 2011), p. 20.
40 Interview with GZ29.

Bibliography

Adamchak, Donald J., Shuo Chen & Jiangtao Li, 'Occupations, Work Units and Work Rewards in Urban China', *International Sociology*, 14 (1999), 423–41
Bonnin, Michel, 'The "Lost Generation": Its Definition and Its Role in Today's Chinese Elite Politics', *Social Research*, 73 (2006), 245–74
Bray, David, 'Building "Community": New Strategies of Governance in Urban China', in Elaine Jeffreys, ed., *China's Governmentalities: Governing Change, Changing Government* (Oxon: Routledge, 2009), pp. 88–106
Choi, Eun Kyong and Kate Xiao Zhou, 'Entrepreneurs and Politics in the Chinese Transitional Economy: Political Connections and Rent-seeking', *China Review*, 1 (2001), 111–35
Fan, Joseph, T.J. Wong, and Tianyu Zhang, 'Politically Connected CEOs, Corporate Government, and Post-IPO Performance of China's Newly Partially Privatized Firms', *Journal of Financial Economics*, 84 (2007), 330–57
Gore, Lance, *The Chinese Communist Party and China's Capitalist Revolution: The Political Impact of the Market* (London: Routledge, 2011)
Li, Hongbin, Lingsheng Meng, Qian Wang, and Li-An Zhou, 'Political Connections, Financing and Firm Performance: Evidence From Chinese Private Firms', *Journal of Development Economics*, 87 (2008), 283–99
Li, Hongbin, Lingsheng Meng, and Junsen Zhang, 'Why Do Entrepreneurs Enter Politics? Evidence from China', *Economic Inquiry*, 44 (2006), 559–78
Li, Wang, 'Higher Education Governance and University Autonomy in China', *Globalisation, Societies and Education*, 8 (2010), 477–95
Liu, Fengshu, *Urban Youth in China: Modernity, the Internet and the Self* (London: Routledge, 2010)
Mannheim, Karl, 'The Problem of Generations', in Paul Kecskemeti, ed., *Essays on the Sociology of Knowledge* (London: Routledge & Kegan Paul LTD, 1952), pp. 286–92
Nee, Victor 'The Role of the State in Making a Market Economy', *Journal of Institutional and Theoretical Economy*, 156 (2000), 64–88
Nee, Victor and Sonja Opper, 'Political Capital in a Market Economy', *Social Forces*, 88 (2010), 2105–32
Nee, Victor, Sonja Opper, and Sonia Wong, 'Developmental State and Corporate Governance in China', *Management and Organization Review*, 3 (2007), 19–53

Nee, Victor, Sonja Opper & Sonia Wong, 'Politicized Capitalism: Developmental State and the Firm in China', in Victor Nee & Richard Swedberg eds., On Capitalism (Stanford, Stanford University Press, 2007), 93–127

Opper, Sonja, Sonia M.L. Wong, and Hu Ruyin, 'Party Power, Markets and Private Power: CCP Persistence in China's Listed Companies', *Research in Social Stratification and Mobility*, 19 (2002), 105–38

Pan, Sun-Yan, 'Intertwining of Academia and Officialdom and University Autonomy: Experience from Tsinghua University in China', *Higher Education Policy*, 20 (2007), 121–44

Schuman, Howard and Jacqueline Scott, 'Generations and Collective Memories', *American Sociological Review*, 54 (1989), 359–81

Sun, Jiaming and Xun Wang, 'Value Differences between Generations in China: A Study in Shanghai', *Journal of Youth Studies*, 13 (2010), 65–81

Xi, Chao, 'Transforming Chinese Enterprises: Ideology, Efficiency and Instrumentalism in the Process of Reform', in John Gillespie, Pip Nicholson, and Penelope Nicholson, eds, *Asian Socialism and Legal Change: The Dynamics of Vietnamese and Chinese Reform* (Canberra: The Australian National University, 2005), pp. 91–114

Yang, Rui, Lesley Vidovich, and Jan Currie, '"Dancing in a Cage": Changing Autonomy in Chinese Higher Education', *Higher Education*, 54 (2007), 575–92

5 Experiencing the campaign

Patterns of practices by the local people in Chongqing

The patterns of participation among the participants of the Red culture campaign can be categorised into three levels according to three factors: the level of the organization, the quality of the performance, and the amount of publicity given to the performance. The first level of participation was highly organized. The performance was of a relatively high quality and subject to a large amount of publicity. Participation that was organized by the district or municipal-level government and performances for local TV programmes were typical examples of the first level of participation. The second level of participation was organized within the communities, schools, or companies of the participants. The organizational effort was of a lesser scale. The quality of performance was lower than the first level, and the effect of the activities was mainly contained within the organizing units themselves. For example, participation at school- or faculty-level, and extracurricular activities organized within companies belonged to this type of participation. The third level of participation consisted of voluntary practices of Red-themed activities. There was no formal organization or explicit requirement regarding the quality of the performance. This level of participation was mainly practiced for self-entertainment.

First level of participation

Retirees

Retirees participated in the Red culture campaign at the first level by joining prestigious community art groups. Team Blue Heaven, for example, participated in more than 20 high-profile Red-themed performances in Chongqing in 2011. Thanks to their affiliation with the municipal culture centre, their performance of Red songs was recorded as an example for other participating chorus teams in Chongqing. They performed a variety of Red songs, including 'The Song of the Yangtze River' (*changjiang zhi ge* 《长江之歌》) and 'Praise for the Red Plum Blossom' (*hong mei zan* 《红梅赞》), both considered to match well the history of Chongqing. Team Spring Breeze, on the other hand, was busy preparing for a dancing competition that was organized by the Yuzhong District in October 2011. They danced to two tunes: 'Harmonious China' (*hexie zhongguo* 《和谐中国》)

and 'My Motherland' (*wo de zuguo* 《我的祖国》). The first was chosen by the organizing committee for all contestants, whereas the second was chosen by the team itself. As the date of the competition approached, they practiced twice weekly. There was a selection process before anyone was admitted to the team. Team Autumn Moon, another renowned chorus team in Nan'an District, was invited to participate in a TV programme called 'Daily Red Songs' (*tiantian hongge hui* 天天红歌会) in March 2012. They prepared two songs: 'Revival' (*zou xiang fuxing* 《走向复兴》) and 'The Country' (*jiangshan* 《江山》), both of which were written in the 21st century and were typical examples of 'new' Red songs. Whereas the first song praised the revival of the Chinese nation during the reform era, the second reinforced the 'mass-line' approach of the Chinese Communist Party's (CCP's) mission as the ruling Party in modern China. Team Autumn Moon represented their district in this programme and performed alongside other choruses, whose membership ranged from primary school students to government bureaucrats. In the previous year, the programme 'Daily Red Songs' was recorded live, and the sound quality proved rather unsatisfactory. As a result, in 2012, the choruses were asked to record their singing in advance of the actual production of the TV programme. The chorus was also instructed to be more sophisticated in terms of their choreography and make better use of props. Rehearsals took place twice weekly in the month preceding the performance. When the team met again after the recording session, further instructions regarding the performance was given to the members. 'We have to be serious when we are performing so that the audience cannot tell we are playing a tape', said the teacher. The official from the Residents' Committee issued a similar instruction, with a hint of philosophical sophistication: 'the key thing is to mix the real with the fake so well that the fake seems more real than real. You have to perform real on the day so that it is properly faked'.[1]

University students

The university students who were involved at this level of the campaign participated through their student societies or art groups. For instance, one student chorus organized by the Communist Youth League of University A was a favourite, frequent performer in a series of municipality-level performances, including the Third Chongqing University Artistic Performance exhibition, Chongqing's Singing Red Rally, the Singing Red tour to Beijing, and so on. The conductor had been with the team for almost 10 years and had good connections within the music community in Chongqing. The team had a membership of 70 students, among which 40 to 50 were core members. The students in the chorus had usually had an interest in singing before joining the team and possessed a basic level of singing competence as they needed to pass an entrance test. On occasions when a larger team was required, more students were temporarily 'borrowed' from different faculties. The conductor of the chorus claimed that they participated in more than 80 performances in 2011. Although a difficult song would take months to rehearse before the team could perform it in public, the invitation to participate in performances

68 *Experiencing the campaign*

sometimes arrived merely days before the performance. The conductor and students took great pains to fulfill the tasks. They sung many Red songs, such as 'On Top of Taihang Mountain' (*taihang shan shang* 《太行山上》), 'Moon over Xijiang' (*xijiang yue* 《西江月》), 'Young People, Chinese Heart' (*qingnian ren, zhongguo xin* 《青年人，中国心》), 'The Country' (*jiang shan* 《江山》), 'Me and My Country' (*wo he wo de zuguo* 《我和我的祖国》), 'Song of the Anti-Japanese Military and Political University' (*kang ri jun zheng daxue xiaoge* 《抗日军政大学校歌》), and so on.

In other cases, students from different societies could be recruited to participate in a programme, for example, the recitation of 'Quotations for Clean Governance' (*lian zheng yu lu* 廉政语录).[2] It was a signature programme which contributed to the 'Reading Classics' section of the Red culture programme. The recitation contained a selection of famous quotes approved by Bo Xilai but was choreographed by the students themselves. The quotations selected ranged from ancient political philosophy about the art of politics to how to be a good cadre in today's political system. It was a successful and popular recitation that was invited to be performed repeatedly at the Red-themed shows whenever 'important people', such as high-level cadres from Beijing or leaders from overseas, visited Chongqing. According to one of the key performers of this programme, they were asked to perform at least once a week during the busiest season. The rehearsals were frequent and demanding not only because there were frequent performances but also due to the high level of turnover within the team. New students were constantly being recruited, and the rehearsals had to start from the beginning again.

Employees – type I

Employees participated in the municipal-level participation by joining the chorus of their company. This usually involved a relatively experienced conductor, who had good connections with the Propaganda Department, TV station, cultural organizations, and so on, being employed by the chorus. Junior staff members at SOEs were often the favourite candidates for tasks like this. Participating in municipal-level participation was time-consuming. It required a lot of rehearsals, which usually took place outside the working hours. It was also considerably energy consuming, especially when the team was on performance tour outside Chongqing. Although these employees were chosen by their supervisors or managers at work, mostly for reasons unconnected with their artistic capabilities, they nevertheless had to possess a basic level of singing competence to be able to engage in the high-level performance. The young employees participated in many public performances, including quite a few at the Chongqing Theatre on important holidays. One member of a chorus, which performed in Beijing and Hong Kong with the Chongqing delegation, recounted the many Red songs she had sung with her team, such as 'Ode to the Motherland' (*zuguo song* 《祖国颂》), 'On the Hopeful Land' (*zai xiwang de tianye shang* 《在希望的田野上》), 'Defending the Yellow River' (*baowei huanghe* 《保卫黄河》), 'The Story of Spring' (*chuntian de gushi* 《春天的故事》), and so on. The amount of rehearsal required to perform these songs was related to their levels of difficulty. If a song was particularly difficult, it could be rehearsed as frequently as five times a week, with each session lasting at least two hours (and sometimes extending to three or four hours). Typically, rehearsals took place from 6 to 9 p.m., after work. The performance of the Red songs, however, did not always take place outside working hours, in which case the employees would have to work overtime on other days as their workload was rarely reduced because of their obligation to perform at Red-themed shows.

Second level of participation

Retirees

Not everyone made it to the Chongqing People's Hall or the Chongqing Theatre. Some of the retired people's chorus teams participated in the Red culture campaign by singing within their own communities. Team White Cloud of the Zhiqing Association, for example, practiced two songs – 'Revival' (*zou xiang fuxing* 《走向复兴》) and 'The Most Beautiful Song for the Mother' (*zui mei de ge'er xian gei mama* 《最美的歌儿献给妈妈》) – for the 2012 Spring Festival Gala organized for the members of the association. Moreover, the association also organized 'revisiting the countryside' trips during which they performed Red songs for local villagers. During one of these trips, 360 members of the Zhiqing Association returned to Zhongxian in Chongqing, where some of them had been sent as educated youth more than 30 years ago. People sang the classic Red song – 'Without the CCP, There Will Be No New China' (*meiyou gongchandang, jiu meiyou xin zhongguo* 《没有共产党，就没有新中国》) – while boarding the ferryboat that took them back to their youthful years. They were warmly welcomed by the local government and gave a staged performance featuring Red songs and dances.

University students

Many students participated in the Red culture campaign through school-level organized performances on important legal and traditional holidays. For example, University B put up a grand Red-themed show to commemorate the 90th anniversary of the founding of the CCP on 1 July 2012. Each faculty contributed one programme, and each class within a faculty would contribute four or five students to form the faculty team. A huge stage was set up on the main campus. The university took the show very seriously. Two consecutive dress rehearsals were held prior to the actual performance. The atmosphere was formal and ceremonious. Red-themed programmes included a variety of traditional dancing, the singing of 'The Yellow River Cantata' (*huanghe da hechang* 《黄河大合唱》), and the recitation of 'Praise for the Red Plum Blossom' (*hongmei zan* 《红梅赞》), and so on. One student who participated in the chorus that sang 'Farewell to the Red Army' (*shi song hongjun* 《十送红军》) had rehearsed for about a month before stepping onto the stage. Another student, who performed in a dancing programme – 'The Army and the People United as a Family' (*junmin tuanjie*

70 *Experiencing the campaign*

yijia qin 《军民团结一家亲》) – had also received training from a professional dancing teacher once a fortnight for a couple of months prior to the performance.

In addition, students also participated in faculty-level activities that were often organized by their university's Youth League Committee or faculty tutors. In some cases, singing activities were organized as a special session of the 'Youth League Day' that was held at least once or twice per term by the Youth League branches. Often everyone in the class participated. According to one student, the song selected by her class was 'My Country' (*wo de zuguo* 《我的祖国》). They rehearsed a few times after class before the activity, and there was no teacher to train them. On the day of the competition, they performed for students from other classes within the same faculty. Sometimes, a competition was set up between different classes. One student remembered that a singing contest had been organized by the faculty tutor among the 10 classes in his college. His class won first prize in the competition for singing 'Ode to the Motherland' (*gechang zuguo* 《歌唱祖国》). The tutor who organized the contest was considered very 'Red' by the students because of his orthodox Marxist beliefs. 'Perhaps it was because of his age. Every time he held a meeting with us, it was as if he wanted to brainwash us', commented the student. There was no professional teacher to train the team. One of the student cadres in the class was good at singing, so she took responsibility for leading the rehearsal. The song was chosen by the students themselves. 'But there were not many to choose from, anyway', he added.[3] At this level, the performance was significantly less serious or formal compared to the first level.

A number of students also participated in several periphery Red-themed activities, such as speech contests or essay competitions. For example, one student participated in an essay composition competition themed 'Singing Praises to the Party'. Although she found it difficult to write such an essay, she decided to participate in the competition because she reckoned that 'it was okay to participate once in a while, and there were small prizes, after all'.[4] In the end, she produced a 1,000-word essay recounting the ways in which her grandmother's belief in and membership of the Communist Party had influenced her. Similarly, another student participated in a speech contest organized by her faculty. She said that she entered the competition mainly because she liked making speeches. As a fresher, the common wisdom passed down from the senior students was to try to take part in a variety of activities. 'And it did not take me long, anyway', claimed the interviewee. She heard about the competition in the morning, had written the script by noon, and went straight into the contest that afternoon, winning second prize. Her speech was titled 'Happy Birthday, My Party'.

Employees – type I

For employees who participated at this level of performance, Red-themed activities were often organized within their own company. Most such performances were organized in late June 2011 to commemorate the 90th anniversary of the founding of the CCP. The other occasions for putting on Red-themed shows were the various kinds of holidays and festivals throughout the year. Rehearsals were usually held in the afternoons after working hours. They might also start slightly earlier to make use of the final bit of the working hours. The preparation period lasted from two to three weeks to two to three months, depending on the level of importance attached to the performance, which was dictated by whether or not the company management would participate in the performances and how seriously they took them. Some companies hired professional teachers to teach the performers basic singing techniques and give advice on costumes, whereas others relied on talents within the company.

For SOEs, when the higher system (*xitong* 系统) to which they belonged was organizing a large-scale performance, they were obliged to respond to the 'executive order' (*xingzheng renwu* 行政任务). When a large show was in preparation, a notice was sent to each department within the enterprise, which would then prepare one or two programmes. The show normally took the form of a contest between the different departments of the company. Usually, the Party members within each department were active participants. One employee of a state-owned company recalled that his department sang two songs – 'Unity Is Power' (*tuanjie jiushi liliang* 《团结就是力量》) and 'Bless the Motherland' (*zhufu zuguo* 《祝福祖国》). In another state-owned company, one team chose two songs – 'Ode to the Heroes' (*yingxiong zange* 《英雄赞歌》) and 'Play the Drum and Sing the Song' (*da qi shougu chang qi ge* 《打起手鼓唱起歌》). Although most of the songs selected tended to be conventional choices, there was considerable flexibility with regard to the songs selected for performances within the company. For example, 'Play the Drum and Sing the Song', an old ethnic folk song, was reappropriated by a Hong Kong pop singer, Mo Wenwei, in 2009. 'It was the version of Mo Wenwei's song that we chose', the participants claimed with pride.[5] In another case, a departmental director from an SOE, who was in his 50s, chose two songs for his department's chorus – 'The Sun Is the Reddest, Chairman Mao Is the Dearest' (*taiyang zuihong, mao zhuxi zui qin* 《太阳最红，毛主席最亲》), and 'Sailing the Sea Depends on the Helmsman' (*dahai hangxing kao duoshou* 《大海航行靠舵手》). These two songs, very popular during the Cultural Revolution (CR), were not on the list of officially-recommended Red songs and probably would never have been included in municipality-level shows, yet they were chosen by individual cadres and performed within the company. 'It was just for fun. They were so distant but so familiar at the same time. They were funny', said the interviewee who selected these two songs for his team to perform.[6]

Some private companies also organized Sing Red activities. A private media technology company hired a professional conductor to teach their employees to sing Red songs. Every Thursday, after work, teaching sessions were held, lasting about an hour. About 70 employees from various departments of the company participated. Both the general manager and the vice general manager of the company stated that they disliked the Red culture campaign that was taking place in the city. Nevertheless, singing helped to boost morale in the workplace:

I do not like what Bo is doing here in Chongqing, probably because of my own family history but, as a company, what we want is straightforward. We want to build a corporate culture. When singing, the employees, you know,

72 *Experiencing the campaign*

joke with each other, or whatever. This feeling of solidarity is good for the company. If everyone sings Red songs in China, no one will be afraid to help an elderly person who falls in the street. If you are a member of the company, you have to accept our culture.[7]

Nonetheless, the private enterprises that took the trouble to build a singing team usually aimed at more than self-education. They obviously did not want to be left out of the most popular event sweeping the city. The general manager of the company explicitly told the hired teacher that their aim was 'to participate in some of the performances organized by the Yuzhong District', despite his claim that he disliked the Red culture campaign. One employee who worked in the municipal government's Propaganda Department also confirmed that many private companies sent demos to their office, hoping to be selected as performers in the government's shows.[8]

Third level of participation – exclusively for retirees

The singing Red activities that were observed in many parks in Chongqing belonged to the third level of participation. These activities were far less organized than the other two types and were mainly for 'self-entertainment'. The quality of performance required was the lowest. In Shaping Park, Bijin Park, and Eling Park, a variety of singing Red activities were observed.

Shaping Park

Built in the 1950s, Shaping Park was one of the oldest and most famous parks in Chongqing. An oval-shaped lake, surrounded by thick greenery, lay at its centre. Most days, at least three to five singing groups could be observed in the park. The largest group in Shaping Park consisted of a dozen amateur musicians. A wide variety of musical instruments were played, including seven *Erhu* (a traditional Chinese music instrument), a lute, a violin, and a keyboard. The musicians were former colleagues, old friends, or simply music lovers. The favourite songs sung in this spot included 'Blooming Azalea All Over the Mountain' (*man shan kai bian yingshanhong* 《满山开遍映山红》), 'Entering a New Era' (*zou jin xin shidai* 《走进新时代》), 'There the Peach Blossom in Full Bloom' (*zai na taohua shengkai de difang* 《在那桃花盛开的地方》), 'Playing My Beloved Pipa' (*tanqi wo xinai de tupipa* 《弹起我心爱的土琵琶》), 'At a Distant Place' (*zai na yaoyuan de difang* 《在那遥远的地方》), 'A Good Day Today' (*jintian shi ge hao rizi* 《今天是个好日子》), and 'We Soldiers' (*dangbing de ren* 《当兵的人》). The singers comprised seven or eight regular participants, but there could be as many as 50 spectators or more.

Another major singing spot was run by a retired nursery teacher, Hong, who had been playing keyboard for it daily for the past three years. This group was far smaller than the previous one. Its core members consisted of only a dozen frequent attendees. Some of the others only came to listen to others singing. Hong

Experiencing the campaign 73

received one *yuan* (≈£0.10) from each person for each song she played for them. Attendees could sing as much as they wished once their payment exceeded the maximum charge of five *yuan* (≈£0.50). A typical day started from 2:30 p.m. for Hong. Weather permitting, Hong sometimes worked until 9 p.m. Every day she brought seven piles of song sheets with her, and she said that she had to learn a lot of songs, including new ones. If someone requested a song that she could not play because she did not know it, that person would never return. She also brought a trolley with her containing a bunch of plastic flowers. Sometimes the flowers were offered to someone who had successfully entertained the crowd and later returned to the trolley to await the next performance. The participants won applause as well as friendship. One participant in his 70s would bring a bottle of *baijiu* (Chinese spirit) to share with the friends he had made at this singing spot. When someone who was expected failed to appear, people would wonder if something had happened. When a frequent singer at the spot heard that Hong's wrist was hurting due to the long hours spent playing the keyboard, he brought her two plasters the following day, a small but touching gesture that expressed his care and friendship.

Bijin Park

In Bijin Park, free Red song teaching sessions were held every morning. The participants were all retirees who lived nearby. About 30 participants would attend the singing session from 8:30 to 10:30 a.m. on a typical day, after which two thirds of them stayed for a dancing session that lasted for about another hour. The songs they practiced included 'Good Things about the Tibetan Plateau' (*qingzang gaoyuan haochu duo* 《青藏高原好处多》), 'Songs for the Dabie Mountain' (*gechang dabieshan* 《歌唱大别山》), 'Loving the People' (*qingxi renmin* 《情系人民》), 'Why Is the East So Red?' (*dongfang weishenme hong* 《东方为什么红?》), and 'Beautiful South Lake in Mengzi County' (*mentzi nanhu mei you mei* 《蒙自南湖美又美》). The singing session ended with a song named 'I Don't Want to Say Goodbye' (*wo bu xiang shuo zaijian* 《我不想说再见》). After this song, there was an additional ritual of chanting slogans:

> 'To sing Red songs together, the more we sing, the louder we are; to sing Red songs together, the more we sing, the healthier we are; to sing Red songs together, the more we sing, the more we love to sing' (*hongge dajia chang, yue chang yue xiangliang; hongge dajia chang, yue chang yue jiankang; hongge dajia chang, yue chang yue xiang chang* 红歌大家唱，越唱越响亮；红歌大家唱，越唱越健康；红歌大家唱，越唱越想唱).

Public square

The volunteer keyboard player for Team White Cloud, Fang,[9] had another 'job' in the evening. When I met her during a Team White Cloud rehearsal, she invited me to visit her in the public square to 'see how the poor, who belong to the lowest

74 *Experiencing the campaign*

stratum of society, sing Red songs'. She ran a karaoke booth in a public square every night from 7 to 10 p.m. At about 6:45 p.m., she would arrive in the square with two big trolleys carrying her keyboard and two big loudspeakers. Her sister helped her set up the booth and charge each singer a fee. Each song cost two *yuan* (≈£0.2). Fang told me that it had cost her 2,000 *yuan* (≈£200) to learn how to play the keyboard after she retired from work. For the most part, however, she insisted that she actually taught herself how to play the hundreds of songs she has now mastered. There were three or four karaoke booths in the square competing for the attention of passers-by. Fang explained the tricks of the trade: 'Whoever has the best loudspeaker attracts the biggest crowd'.[10] The size of the crowd varied from a dozen people to hundreds, depending on the weather. The number of people who actually paid to sing, however, was far smaller. On good days, there might be around 20 people; on bad days, there was only a handful. Fang and her sister usually sang a few songs to warm up the crowd. 'Let's sing Red songs together! Red songs make you happy!' Fang, who had an extremely outgoing and lively character, often chanted these slogans to attract clients. 'The people who come to sing at my booth live at the bottom of society. . . . This is their only entertainment', she explained. Although Fang loved to call her booth a 'Singing Red' spot for the poor, in fact, a wide variety of songs were sung at her booth, including typically old songs, such as 'The Waves of Honghu Lake' (*hong hu shui, lang da lang* 《洪湖水, 浪打浪》), 'Singing a Folk Song for the Party' (*chang zhi shange gei dang ting* 《唱支山歌给党听》), and popular love songs such as 'Give Me a Cup of Forget-You-Syrup' (*gei wo yibei wang qing shui* 《给我一杯忘情水》).

Eling Park

The activities observed in Eling Park fell somewhere between the second and third levels of participation. On the one hand, there was a well-equipped karaoke spot set up by the park's administrative office. Therefore, the Sing Red activities in this park were semi-organized. The booth was operated from 9:30 to 11:30 a.m. and 2:30 to 5 p.m. by the park staff. There was a quota of 30 songs per session. The booth was so popular that the quota was usually filled within half an hour of it opening. On the other hand, the practice of singing Red songs was entirely voluntary. The participants were mainly elderly people and a few unemployed young people. Some of the recently retirees dressed up to sing at the booth, as if they were still going to work. The loudspeakers were so powerful that they drove other singing spots away from the 'official' ones. Popular songs included 'Today Is Your Birthday' (*jintian shi ni de shengri* 《今天是你的生日》), 'Meeting at Aobao' (*ao bao xiang hui* 《敖包相会》), 'Waiting for You' (*wei ni dengdai* 《为你等待》), 'Singing Folk Songs for the Party' (*zai chang shange gei dang ting* 《再唱山歌给党听》), 'Flowery Woman' (*nv ren hua* 《女人花》), 'A Beautiful Legend' (*meili de chuanshuo* 《美丽的传说》), 'Song for the Prairie' (*caoyuan zhi ge* 《草原之歌》), and so on. There were no requirements laid down regarding the quality of the singing or the competency of the participants.

Levels of participation, organization, and quality of performance

In general, higher levels of participation entailed higher levels of organization. The performances of the first level required sophisticated organizational work that involved coordinating a large network of actors, including the government bureaucracy, media, artistic organizations, audiences (including high-level officials, at times), and so on. In the case of the second level of performances, the organizational work was on a smaller scale but still concerned a number of players and involved various institutions and individuals, such as the university administration, the faculties, the Youth Leagues, the student cadres, and the student performers. The third level of participation consisted of voluntary singing in public spaces. It therefore entailed the least amount of organizational work on the part of the government and public institutions. Nevertheless, this is not to say that the voluntary singing did not require organization. As shown, these practices usually relied on a few very active participants to take the initiative in bringing retirees together.

Among the three different social groups of participants, the university students and retirees were relatively easy to organize and manage. University students were physically concentrated on campus and had relatively flexible timetables. The schools and teachers remained respected authorities in student life. The retirees, meanwhile, had free time and, above all, a commitment to their singing groups. The employees, in comparison, were more difficult to manage because they were likely to be more mature and occupy social positions with far more power and prestige than university students and retirees. The problem with the employees, according to one chorus conductor, was not that their behaviour was unruly but that they simply did not care about the rehearsals or performances as much as the other groups of participants. Even when the employees participated in the activities, they were likely to be in pursuit of more than mere artistic appreciation. The advantage of managing an employees' chorus, on the other hand, was that it was likely to have more financial resources at its disposal than the choruses consisting of students or retirees.

Higher levels of participation also meant higher requirements regarding the quality of the performances. The quality of the performances was conditioned upon the level of cultural competence and the amount of financial and human resources invested in preparing for them. The level of cultural competence required was positively related to the level of performance. The higher the level of the participation, the higher the level of cultural competence required of these performers. For those who participated in the first level of participation, passing an entry test was often required.[11] If there was no entry test for joining the chorus, there was usually a selection process for members who actually went to perform on important occasions. Participating at the second level of participation required a lower level of cultural competence. The requirement of cultural competence was minimal for the third level of participants. For the retired people, frequent and durable involvement occurred at both the first level of formal performances and second level of community-based performances. Moreover, retirees were the only ones who

76 *Experiencing the campaign*

participated in the third level of participation. This meant that they had the widest opportunity to enter into the Red culture campaign. As long as the retirees were willing to participate, they could almost always find a way to become part of the campaign. On the other hand, although university students also had a variety of choices among the first and second level of participation, if they wished to become involved in the campaign, and apparently singing at the college or class level required a low level of singing competency, these activities were largely ad hoc and did not amount to frequent involvement. Similarly, the employees participated in both the first and second levels of performances. Participation was to a large extent contingent upon a variety of conditions, such as the government's directives and the attitudes of the companies' management, which were not intrinsically linked to the participants' personal interests. Whereas the level of cultural competence conditioned the level of participation for all three social groups, it played a less restrictive role for retirees than for the other two groups of participants.

Investment in financial and human resources was critical for ensuring the quality of the performances. The Propaganda Department of the municipality government, which was in charge of the campaign, in most cases did not directly fund the activities of the participants. In the case of the community teams, most of them collected an annual membership fee from their members. They received help from the residence committees, corporations, and art organizations. It is unsurprising that putting on a high-level performance of good quality demanded considerable investment. Even the third level of participation, that is, voluntary activities in public spaces initiated by ordinary people themselves, required a sustainable cycle of financing, however meager the financial resources were. For example, the performers had to pay a small fee to the keyboard player for the singing spots to continue. They also had to cover the fees for copying the singing materials used by the singing groups. In the case of the university students and employees, their activities relied exclusively on funding by their universities or employers. Moreover, given that monetary rewards were never a key factor in sustaining such activities, emotional attachment (an important aspect of human resources) was particularly effective in mobilising activities at this level. This factor will be further discussed in the next chapter.

The relationship between the level of participation and the amount of publicity, on the other hand, was less straightforward. Normally, only the first level of participation was able to be publicised regularly in the official media, for example, local newspapers and TV channels. Activities belonging to the second level received the least public exposure because they took place within their respective institutions and organizations. The retired people's third level of participation was the least 'official' in nature but was in fact highly visible. This was because most of the activities at this level took place in public spaces, that is, parks and squares. Therefore, despite the lack of publicity through the official media, these activities contributed significantly to the dissemination of information about the Red culture campaign.

A final point that is worth mentioning is that the teachers and conductors played key roles in defining the quality of the singing activities of the retirees. In the public parks, there were no requirements for the teachers to be qualified. For example, the lady who volunteered to coach the singing group in Bijin Park was a retired language teacher with a self-proclaimed lifelong interest in music. The task of the teacher was to lead the singing and ensure that everyone was engaged and happy. There was little technical coaching offered as the group did not aspire to perform on formal occasions or enter any organized competitions. The community teams, on the other hand, took matters more seriously and hired teachers. Choices were made based on a combination of factors: social networks, professional suitability, commuting convenience, and budget. Team White Cloud was forced to hire a new teacher when the previous one resigned due to the unbearably long commuting hours. The new teacher/conductor was a former professional singer but not a music teacher. The team members complained behind her back that she was not a 'proper' teacher and that without a 'proper' teacher, the team was 'like a heap of loose sand'.[12] By contrast, the Blue Heaven team took great pride in their teacher, who was 'very professional'. The teacher, who was also the conductor of the chorus, was in her early 30s and had a master's degree from a music college. She charged as much as 300 *yuan* (≈£30) per teaching session, much more than the teacher of Autumn Moon, a retired middle school music teacher who charged only an average of 25 *yuan* (≈£2.5) per teaching session. The teacher of Autumn Moon was willing to accept such a low payment as a gesture of goodwill towards the team that she had been coaching for more than eight years. Whereas Autumn Moon was invited to attend district-level activities, Blue Heaven often represented Chongqing at the national contests. The quality of teaching varied significantly among the community choruses in Chongqing and had an evident impact on the singing experience of the retired people.

Working as participating – employees type II

Employees belonging to this subgroup had jobs either related to the Party's thought work or in industries related to cultural production. Some worked on the production side of the Red culture campaign, such as the producers and writers of Red culture TV programmes, whereas others worked in the implementation process, such as the organizers of Red-themed shows. There were no general patterns in such participants' experiences of the Red culture campaign. These were unique according to the specific work they did. Instead of summarising the patterns of experience, the following section will present examples of how the participants experienced the Red culture campaign through their work.

As a participant in the production process of the Red culture campaign, a former employee of the Chongqing Broadcasting Group (CBG) worked from 2009 to 2010 on the production side of a Red-themed TV programme. The programme was classified under the 'Reading Classics' section of the Red culture campaign and produced under the initiative of the Propaganda Department. Bo Xilai, adopting his carefully-crafted colloquial style, compared reading classics with taking vitamins in the preface of the series 'Reading Classics' – 'if you take even one pill per day, it will benefit your health' (*sui meiri yili, yike yangshen*

78 *Experiencing the campaign*

虽每日一粒，亦可养身). The programme was supposed to be an illustrative example of Bo's exposition of the importance of reading classics. The programme went into production under considerable time pressure in 2009. The first edition was a three-minute programme focused on poetry appreciation, which was broadcasted every day. Later it was developed into a 20-minute, new version, dedicated to introducing 'worthy' literary works to the public. The 'worthy' works referred to were those of high literary quality and political appropriateness. A substantial part of the work being appreciated in the programme was 'Red', ranging from Mao's poetry to Russian revolutionary literature. Classic poetry and essays were also safe choices. Regular sessions were dedicated to the appreciation of poetry by the famous poets, such as Nalan Rongruo (Qing Dynasty), Li Qingzhao (song Dynasty), and Du Mu and Meng Haoran (Tang Dynasty). Contemporary works were included as well, such as essays by Shi Tiesheng and Yang Jiang. Foreign literary masters, such as O. Henry and Shakespeare, also made to the list. Once the topics and relevant poems had been selected by the editors of the TV programme, assignments were sent out to a group of writers, mainly teachers and university literature students who would write the narratives for the programmes. A lot of editorial work followed to prepare the narrators, mainly involving checking the pronunciation and definition of the many difficult characters contained in the ancient poems and prose.

When the programme was launched, the interviewee, who was the producer of this programme, often had to work overtime. There was a lot of pressure for she had to oversee both the content and political implications of this programme. Because it was intended to 'educate' people, the information had to be accurate, and she could not afford to make mistakes. Extra care was needed to safeguard the appropriateness of the content:

> Usually the programmes passed the review process fairly easily but sometimes we picked the wrong poems out of ignorance. For example, once, we picked a poem by Mao Zedong, which turned out to be a love poem to his wife, Jiang Qing, so it couldn't be used for the programme.[13]

Another piece on an author with links to an anti-CCP newspaper in Hong Kong was rejected as well. The difficulty with this kind of programme, according to her, was that it was 'hyper-political', so one had to pay particular attention to the 'direction' of the content.[14]

Another interviewee worked for a major local newspaper and was 'borrowed' to work at a special, temporary '*changdujiangchuan*' (唱读讲传) office set up within the Propaganda Department. The office oversaw the organization of Red-themed activities at the municipality level and, according the interviewee, organized 50 to 60 performances annually. The interviewee worked in the office for six months, and its members were mostly borrowed from other work units within the culture system (*wenhua xitong* 文化系统). The office was dismantled in early March when the Red culture campaign was drawing to a close. During his placement in the office, his work mainly concerned the coordination of the different parties involved in the Red-themed performances and activities. When a performance was assigned to the office for important holidays or festivals, the main task was to organize the different programs into a coherent show. Because almost every show was similar in content and style, it was not challenging work as long as one was familiar with the routines. There was also a relatively stable pool of regular programmes on which the office could draw. The main task, therefore, was to make telephone calls to participants, ensuring that they had the correct details about the performances. Because the plans for the performances changed a lot, sometimes as many as four times a day, multiple rounds of phone calls had to be made to all concerned performers. The length of the preparation period fluctuated a lot, from a few days to a few weeks. When a Red-themed show was required at short notice, a lot of work was compressed into a very limited time span. Sometimes, the interviewee worked until 2 or 3 a.m. The interviewee also participated in the organization of the Chongqing delegation's Hong Kong tour. As a member of the organization team, he had to fly to Hong Kong a few days prior to the performances. 'There was a lot of work due to the different systems between Hong Kong and mainland China'.[15]

In contrast to other employees who worked in the government-controlled cultural system, employees of the private advertising companies were also involved in the production of Red culture programmes. In this case, the interviewee worked for a medium-sized private advertising company. During the Red culture campaign, it had many clients who were district-level governments and commercial work units that had a 'need' to put on a staged performance of Red-themed programmes. According to the interviewee, the busiest time for organizing Red-themed performances was the first few months of 2011. The assignment was to design specific themes and decorate the stages for the performances in accordance with the requirements of the clients. Although the general idea was always to 'sing Red', different clients had different demands. The levels of sophistication and delicacy regarding the stage design, which dictated the fees charged by the company, varied considerably among clients. A package of the highest standard could cost more than a million *yuan* (≈£100,000), whereas a far smaller scale one could get by with 50,000 to 100,000 *yuan* (≈£5,000–£10,000).[16] Inviting famous singers would entail considerable additional expenses. The programs were normally assembled by the clients themselves, and there was no need for commercial advertising for this kind of performance. The advertising company's point of contact in the local government was the Propaganda Department. There was fierce competition among the private advertising companies to bid for these projects. The key criteria included the actual quality of the project proposals, the relationship between the company's boss with the government, and the proposed fees charged for the projects. The employee commented on the wisdom of charging fees for such projects:

> It is not about charging the lowest level of fees. Not at all, if your client is a government. The critical thing is that you have a good reason for charging high fees. It is about being able to pinpoint what exactly the local government

80 *Experiencing the campaign*

wants to get out of such shows. For example, if the district level government was putting on a show, they would want to invite their superiors in the municipality government to come and watch it. You've got to have something that will impress their superiors. That was what they really cared about. Not if the expenses were high or low.[17]

The interviewee gave an example of a launch ceremony that she had worked on for a local government. The local government wanted to launch a series of Red-themed activities. The theme chosen was 'The Red July'. The most important element of the whole project, explained the interviewee, was the launch ceremony. This was the time when the cadres at the municipality level (one always invited the cadres one level higher than oneself) would be invited to attend the ceremony. This was when creativity mattered because the rest of the performances would be more or less the same everywhere. The launch ceremony was the only chance for this particular series of activities to stand out and make an impression. One proposal for this project, for example, was to have a huge LED screen in the shape of the national flag on the stage. At the launch ceremony, the distinguished guests, that is, the invited cadres, would each insert a piece of metal, shaped like a star, onto the flag, which would instantly light up the LED screen with a floating Red colour. At the same time, music would accompany a monologue praising the national flag. If the ceremonies were held outdoors, fireworks were another essential element that could highlight them. 'They care about these things, whether the fireworks were sufficiently electrifying, and whether the crowds were sufficiently animated. They care very, very much about these things'.[18] After the ceremony, it was 'business as usual':

Schools would sing Red songs, followed by hospitals, followed by work units. In the end, there was a scoring system. If there were children, they would be among the first tier of three prizes; if there were retired cadres, they would be among the first three; the others would be moved behind. It was all about formalism.[19]

The level of the quality of such programs all depended on how serious the senior cadres of this particular client government or work unit were. If they were serious, the advertising company might hire professional teachers to train the performers and add a few special arrangements; if they were not that serious, things could be really simple – 'all you need to do is to hire some costumes, choose a song, and sing'.[20]

Summary

All three social groups participated in the first level of participation, which required strenuous rehearsals and good connections with the organizing bodies, such as the Propaganda Department, the TV station, and so on. All three social groups participated in the second level of participation. The organization of second level participation was highly dependent on the initiative and commitment of the organizations to which the participants belonged. In the case of the Zhiqing Association, it organized activities for its members because these activities suited their interests and fulfilled the retirees' need for entertainment. In the case of the universities and SOEs, they organized Red-themed performances, typically on important holidays and anniversaries, to pay tribute to the most popular political events in the municipality. It was part of their demonstration of political commitment to the ruling party and the signature project of their Party secretary Bo Xilai. Nevertheless, because the effect of such activities was mainly restricted within the organizing communities, there tended to be more freedom when choosing songs for such performances in comparison with the activities at a higher level. Whereas the official performances had to present an image of being inclusive, that is, selecting both revolutionary and new Red songs, while actively avoiding songs that had been popular during the CR, the songs chosen for the second level of activities were usually related to the personal preferences of the organizers. With regard to the third level of participation, only the social group of retirees participated at this level. There was no restriction about which songs could be sung on these occasions. Voluntary participation in the campaign meant that a high level of genuine interest was taken in the activities. Yet the investment in terms of time and energy varied significantly among the participants at this level. Some retirees were committed to the daily practice of singing Red in the parks, while others participated in a far more haphazard manner.

Notes

1 Fieldwork 1 March 2013, with Team Autumn Moon in Nan'an District.
2 University A.
3 Interview with B23.
4 Interview with B09.
5 Interview with C05.
6 Interview with C24.
7 Fieldwork notes taken at a private company.
8 Interview with C17.
9 The name has been changed to protect the identity of the interviewee.
10 Fieldwork notes 2 March 2012.
11 These tests were often not very strict, especially in the case of retirees. Nevertheless, there was a strong sense of 'not everyone can get in' with regard to these choruses. One needed to possess a basic level of competence at singing.
12 Fieldwork notes 10 January 2012.
13 Interview with C15.
14 Interview with C15.
15 Interview with C17.
16 Interview with C20.
17 Interview with C20.
18 Interview with C20.
19 Interview with C20.
20 Interview with C20.

6 How the official programme interacted with the practices of the local participants

Exchange[1]

The fact that Chongqing's Red culture campaign was not a real Maoist mass campaign, but exhibited symptoms of simulation, implies specific forms of relationship between the political programme and the practices of its participants. As argued in Chapter 3, on the one hand, the Red culture campaign displayed symptoms of being a self-induced, inwardly-enfolded, and non-dialectical circuit that exchanged within itself. On the other hand, the Red culture campaign also exchanged critical resources with the participants. In this chapter, I examine the exchange of resources between the official programme and its participants. I draw on de Certeau's concepts of strategy and tactics to characterise the official programme and the practices of the participants, respectively.

The official programme as strategy

The official Red culture programme resembled what de Certeau would call a *strategy*. Strategy consists of established, expansionist, and dominating rules that are enforced by a strong power. It draws out its own territory, constructs narratives of history, and tends to be prescribing and repressive. In the case of the Red culture campaign, to forcefully circumscribe its place within the Party's political landscape, a large amount of resources had to be utilised. Firstly, executive power allowed the campaign to mobilise all levels of governments in Chongqing to pour an incredible amount of monetary and human resources into sustaining a wide range of Red-themed activities all year around, as has been illustrated in the previous chapter. The leadership urged every department and unit to incorporate the Red culture programme into their regular Party work and study tasks. The fact that the number of activities organized by the local governments was regularly reported and evaluated made it a 'political commitment' for the local cadres to promote the programme. Under pressure to commit to the political programme, different sectors of society poured in a variety of resources, including financial investment and the participants' time and energy.

Secondly, Bo Xilai, an experienced, astute politician, and a prominent member of the 'princeling' fraction, possessed formidable political resources within China's ruling stratum. During Bo's tenure, many high-profile Party officials visited

Chongqing and publically praised the Red culture campaign. At the same time, Chongqing's delegates toured Hong Kong and Beijing to showcase the achievements of the Red culture campaign. In June 2011, the Chongqing delegation visited Beijing to attend the national celebration of the Party's birthday in the capital. In addition to performing at the Beijing Cultural Palace Grand Theatre during the opening ceremony – 'The Fragrance of a Hundred Flowers – Holding High the Banner of the Party' – the Chongqing delegation brought their Red programme to the PLA Second Artillery Force, Beijing's Chaoyang District, Tsinghua University, the National Committee of the Chinese People's Consultative Conference, and the Central Party School during its visit to Beijing. The visits by high-profile officials to Chongqing and the Chongqing delegates' tours outside Chongqing were widely interpreted as Bo's effort to lobby for the Red culture campaign and seek endorsement for it by China's political elites. Successfully or not, Bo was using his own influence to promote, or at least add a shield of protection, to his spectacular campaign.

Here may raise the question whether Bo Xilai was a 'charismatic' leader and to what extent his charisma helped mobilising the masses to participate in the campaign. In fact, Bo Xilai can hardly be characterised as a proper 'charismatic leader', if we follow strictly with the Weberian definition of charisma, according to which the charismatic leader holds *other worldly* strength that is beyond the reach of ordinary men. Such charismatic leaders hold no bureaucratic positions but rule solely by the force of personal character. They emerge in times of severe economic, political, or religious crises as the embodiment of supernatural power and call for the absolute obedience of the people as their loyal followers. In fact, charismatic domination is in direct opposition to bureaucratic domination and has no connection with economic practices. The relationship between charismatic leaders with their followers is both personal and irrational.[2] In this regard, so far as Bo Xilai's authority over the local people in Chongqing is concerned, it is fair to say that he was a leader with exceptional capability, but his charismatic authority may have been overestimated. Although his awe-inspiring bearing has been routinely commented as evidence of his personal 'charisma', it is his very position in the bureaucratic establishment and the networks of the CCP's powerful political families which renders him most of the power he proudly and relentlessly wielded. Thus, I will discuss less of his charisma than the office he held as a source of power that initiated and pushed forwards the Red culture campaign in Chongqing.

Thirdly, the Propaganda Department of Chongqing, as the supervisor of the local media, lined up the local newspapers and TV channels as devotees to the programme. The official media were advised to devote valuable pages and hours to promoting the Red culture campaign, including both broadcasting Red-themed shows and live reportage of the campaign. Chongqing's satellite TV channel, for example, launched a number of special programmes from 2008, including 'Zhou Enlai in Chongqing' (*Zhou Enlai zai Chongqing*, 《周恩来在重庆》), 'Sister Jiang' (*Jiang Jie* 《江姐》), 'Faith' (*xinnian* 《信念》), 'Reading' (*pindu* 《品读》),

84 *Official programme: exchange*

'Daily Red Song' (*tiantian hongge hui* 天天红歌会), 'Ten Points about People's Welfare' (*shida minsheng*《十大民生》), 'Roundtable on Common Prosperity' (*gongfu dajiatan*《共富大家谈》), and so on. In 2009, 'China Red' was officially endorsed as the brand for the channel. It was dedicated to promoting mainstream values and fought against the vulgarised entertainment industry.[3] At the end of 2010, the Chongqing Broadcasting Group (CBG) appointed a new president, who under the directives of Chongqing's leadership, implemented more radical changes to TV broadcasting. In January 2011, Chongqing's satellite channel terminated the broadcasting of TV serials at prime time. In March, it cancelled all commercial advertising. As other provincial satellite channels were fighting tooth and nail over how best to entertain the Chinese people, Chongqing's reform of its most profitable channel was regarded as a radical move to assert the cause of its Red culture agenda.

What the Red culture campaign needed from its participants

As powerful as the Red culture campaign was, it nevertheless could not exist without the help of the ordinary people. As shown, the programme operated on an impressive scale and gathered great momentum through its enforcement. Therefore, frequent performances were needed to maintain the political relevance of the programme as well as a certain level of emotional intensity among the participants. This required the performers to invest a large amount of time and energy in the programme, either out of genuine enthusiasm or due to normative pressure. Secondly, for the campaign to pay tribute to the 'mass-line' strategy of the past, the programme needed to mobilise a variety of performers from different age groups and social backgrounds to portray itself as a 'people's campaign'. Thirdly, it had to fight accusations of being linked to the Cultural Revolution (CR). This meant that the campaign needed to be sufficiently inclusive and eclectic in its choice of content and embrace a wide variety of content, including the new Red songs that praised the achievements of the reform policies, to testify that the programme did not oppose the reform policies. Nor was it promoting factionalism and conflicts among the masses, a critical feature of the CR. As a result, the official programme needed a large population of ordinary people to perform its carefully-orchestrated, Red-themed activities. It needed them to sing a variety of old *and* new Red songs and also perform in such a united, happy atmosphere that it could be seen to celebrate the 'harmonious society' that the Chinese Communist Party (CCP) had vowed to build for 21st-century China.

What the participants offered to and received from the Red culture campaign

Retirees

Retirees exchanged their time, enthusiasm, and commitment to the Red culture campaign for performance opportunities, resources to enhance their community building, a channel to release their nostalgic sentiments, values to construct a positive social identity, and increased political strengthen. Firstly, securing performance opportunities was essential for the sustainability and development of an artistic team of retirees. During the Red culture campaign, community art groups were often invited to perform at Red-themed shows that were organized by different levels of the government. If a team participated in competitions and won prizes, the pecuniary rewards constituted an important source of income for covering its daily expenses. When they participated in the public performances organized by various levels of government, they usually received a small stipend as well. Although the amount was usually small, it was important for the activities of the retirees to be sustainable. Moreover, participating in these activities brought fame and credibility to the retirees' teams, which meant they had a better chance of being invited to perform at other private parties or commercial shows, which constituted a major source of income for them. Previously, the retirees' teams relied on performance opportunities at local festivals and private parties. Only the very best could participate in the municipal or even national competitions. During the Red culture campaign, however, the performance opportunities increased in number. Their audience included officials in high positions and sometimes even Bo Xilai himself. In some cases, their performances were even broadcast on Chongqing TV. Thanks to the Red culture campaign, the retirees had an opportunity to take to the best platform in Chongqing to showcase their achievements.

Secondly, for many retirees, joining a singing group brought a sense of community and belonging. They were attracted to the idea of joining a team predominantly because it provided them with an opportunity to make friends. For example, the members of the Spring Breeze team liked to emphasise how well they got along. It was a bustling scene whenever the team took a break during rehearsals. The team members gathered in small groups to chat animatedly, while others sorted out vegetables as if they were at home. A sense of being 'at home' prevailed. One of the members volunteered to bring a rice cooker to the rehearsal room, and a couple of people brought dishes to share for lunch. The friendships extended beyond the rehearsals, and the whole team would gather to celebrate occasions like birthdays, house moves, and weddings. 'We seek every chance to get together',[4] one member told me, and another commented, with some emotion, 'Now, we do not have "*dan wei*" (the company 单位).[5] This feels like we still belong to the "*zu zhi*" (organization 组织)'.[6] Retirees from other teams echoed the view that the best thing about joining a team was that it provided opportunities for people of the same age to get together. Some of the retirees lived alone, calling themselves 'empty nest elderly' (*kong chao laoren* 空巢老人). The team provided them with company and a sense of belonging.

It was also joyful to sing and dance with their friends. 'As long as there is music, I dance to it'.[7] 'We feel younger when we dance',[8] another interviewee claimed. During a Chinese New Year Gala held by White Cloud, the atmosphere was jubilant. People kept singing their favourite songs over dinner, such as 'We Are Living Under the Sunshine' (*women shenghuo zai yangguang xia* 《我们生活在阳光下》), 'It Is a Great Day Today' (*jintian shi ge hao rizi* 《今天是个好

86 *Official programme: exchange*

日子》), 'We'll Meet Again' (*zai xiang hui* 《再相会》), and 'Over the Golden Mountain in Beijing' (*Beijing de jinshan shang* 《北京的金山上》. They sang and danced, just like in the old days, when youth was still something they could afford to squander. They were almost suspiciously too happy, or perhaps they actively chose to be happy on these occasions. One interviewee commented: 'Look at how happy they are, singing and dancing. When this is finished, they have to go home, whether it is a happy one, or not'.[9] The singing team was an emotional hub that allowed many of the retirees to forget, at least temporarily, their worries or dissatisfaction with life. When they had personal problems, some members would share them with and seek the wisdom of the 'brothers and sisters' in their teams.

Thirdly, the Red culture campaign offered an opportunity for the retirees to unleash their nostalgic sentiments. The most common explanation for the fact that the retirees made up the most active group of participants singing Red was that they felt nostalgic for their past youth at a time when today's Red songs were popular. Bryant, in her study of the songs promoted during the CR for propagandistic purposes and mass education, describes the phenomenon of nostalgia for old songs in the contemporary social context. Firstly, music has a distinctive function of evoking people's emotions. People often feel attached to songs that are linked to their personal life experiences. Secondly, a person's age strongly affects his/her emotional connection with the old songs. The CR generation is more likely to construct positive memories about the past because their 'prime period of maturation' corresponded with the most 'emotional and energetic period' in China's recent history. Thirdly, because China has undergone tremendous socio-economic changes, to which the elderly may have difficulty adapting, Bryant observes that the generation of CR youth is more likely to experience confusion and dissatisfaction with regard to current Chinese society. This mentality underpins an individual's political conviction, which explains why many people look back to the past as a refuge and seek comfort in the songs of the old days.[10] Similarly, Guobin Yang, in his study of the nostalgic memories of the former educated youth who were sent out to the countryside during the CR, argued that the rekindling of nostalgic memories in recent years signalled a prevailing discontent with the materialistic, calculative culture that has arisen as a result of the industrialisation and commercialisation of contemporary modern cities.[11]

Nostalgic emotions evidently permeated people's attitudes towards the Red songs. Nostalgia was linked with three particular kinds of social experience. The first one was linked to people's personal experiences of the revolutionary culture and Red songs. Some liked the songs simply because singing reminded them of when they were young. The retirees admitted that they had special emotional ties to the songs of the past because 'we grew up under the Red flag', stated one interviewee.[12] Another interviewee movingly recollected how he joined the Communist Party's army at the age of 15, how he learnt the first song in his life – 'The East Is Red' (*dong fang hong* 《东方红》) – while in the army, and how he sang Red songs in the trenches during the Korean War in 1952. Whenever he encountered difficulties later in life, he would sing. Secondly, singing Red songs also rekindled the retirees' memories of their parents' generation. For example, one of the interviewees confessed that she felt strongly about many of the old revolutionary songs probably because her father had been a Red Army soldier. She considered it important that people pay tribute to her father's generation. Thirdly, nostalgic emotions were also expressed as criticism of the current society, especially by those who had a fonder recollection of the Mao era. One interviewee believed that there were no cancer patients in China during Mao's time because 'people ate well' and there was no pollution.[13] There was less competition over profit and certainly far less greed in society. The cadres of the Communist Party were honest and clean and did actually 'serve the people'. All these attributes of the Mao era had clearly been lost during the 30 years of the reform, which saw China emerge as the second-largest economy in the world but also left many ordinary people suffering as a result of serious social ills. The environment was in a dire condition; people became more aggressive in competing for resources and wealth; corruption was rampant; and justice had disappeared.[14]

Fourthly, participating in the Red culture campaign helped the retirees to construct a positive social identity. As explained, the rekindling of nostalgic memories signalled discontent with the materialistic, calculative culture of today's China. The act of remembering, through the cultural media of biographies, essays, museum exhibitions, and informal social gatherings, helps rearticulate the personal and social identities of a particular generation.[15] In the case of the retirees who participated in Chongqing's Red culture campaign, this identity was built upon social relations that were capable of making them feel properly recognized and respected by the larger society. When the retirees' teams won prizes in competitions or had an opportunity to perform at Chongqing Theatre and the People's Hall of Chongqing, they felt very proud of their achievement. 'When there are performance opportunities, they were all eager to take part. Time to show off, you know'.[16] More importantly, the retirees were particularly excited about the fact that their culture and values, having been deemed outdated for a long time, were now being 'rectified'. 'When the campaign started, I was thrilled! I thought – it's finally the time, the time for us to show the young people what good songs are', recollected one interviewee.[17] Consistent with Yang's argument, a significant number of retirees who were involved in the Red culture campaign felt aggrieved that the culture and values of the past were being abandoned. They felt powerless to reverse this process. It was therefore hardly surprising that, during the Red culture campaign, some of the retirees felt overjoyed that they had been entrusted, finally, with a responsibility to educate today's youth about the traditions and values that were once properly appreciated. In this regard, the retirees evaluated their participation in the Red culture campaign as more than entertaining. It was endowed with social, political, and historical significance.

Finally, the official endorsement of the singing activities could be used as a protection shield for the retirees' leisure activities. Having the good fortune to be openly supported by their government, some self-organized singing groups also actively identified themselves with the singing Red campaign. The following two examples illustrate how identifying with the official programme strengthened the political influence of the social group of retirees. The political influence is here defined as 'the ability of the group to enforce its preferences, even against the

88 *Official programme: exchange*

resistance of other groups'.[18] On one occasion, an intensive dispute broke out in Shaping Park between a group of retirees who were singing and the management team. The retirees at this singing spot were using small microphones, which kept making noises. It happened that those living near the park had complained about the 'noises' made by the singing group, and the police were called to the scene. A member from the park's administrative office confronted the retirees quite aggressively. The retirees in the singing group, on the other hand, did not back off. They avidly argued their case, citing the widespread singing Red campaign in the city and the support of the local government. The bystanders seemed to be more convinced by the retirees' view and began to voice their support of them. When I returned to the park the following week, a wooden sign designated the spot where the retirees gathered to sing as a recognized site for singing Red, and their loudspeakers had increased in size. Clearly, the retirees had won. Although the singing group was thus recognized by the park's administration, there was no restriction placed on which songs were sung at the spot. The retirees organized themselves into a singing group rather than acting on an explicit government decree to participate in the campaign. Nonetheless, when the circumstances demanded, the retirees used the governmental policy as a weapon to defend their habitual social gatherings.

Similarly, in the case of the karaoke booth stationed in the public square, described in the previous chapter, the owner Fang recounted her experience of battling with those living nearby, who complained about the loud noise from the square. At least half a dozen singing booths were erected in the square every evening, hosting singing activities of significantly varying quality. Those living nearby found the singing loud, unpleasant, and increasingly impossible to bear. Many complaints had been made to the police. The police and the administrative office responsible for the public square tried to negotiate between the two parties. Interestingly, although karaoke booths were in theory forbidden from charging fees (according to an administrative office official, who promised to clean up the mess in the square),[19] the booths continued to survive and thrive, with their loudspeakers and the chanting of the slogan – 'Singing Red makes you happier'. Fang did not appear at all concerned about the complaints made against her. She even felt rather proud that a picture of her singing Red in the square had been printed in the newspaper, despite the fact that the title described her territory as a 'howling square'. The people who 'belong to the lowest stratum of the society' surprisingly gained the upper hand in this case and successfully defended their 'only opportunities for entertainment', according to Fang. Perhaps this should not be surprising after all. Who would dare to be held responsible for depriving people of their right to sing Red, given the political climate at the time? In these cases, the political influence of the social group of retirees was strengthened as it successfully enforced its preference in the face of the resistance from other social groups.

University students

The students exchanged their time and involvement in the Red culture campaign for developmental opportunities for student societies and practical benefits such as the development of personal skills, credits for school performances, and the fulfillment of the requirements for their Party membership application. Firstly, many students were involved in the campaign due to their membership of student societies or art groups, such as the drama society and student chorus. Participation in the Red culture campaign provided an excellent opportunity for the student societies to grow. In Chapter 4, we mentioned the example of a Red-themed play produced by a student drama society at University B. The example of this drama society also illustrates how the thriving of a student society was closely tied to its relationship with the Red culture campaign. The drama society produced a Red-themed play based on a real love story between two revolutionary young people. One of them died at the hands of the *Kuomingdang* (the Nationalists) while upholding the communist revolutionary in the twilight of Chongqing's liberation in 1949. The play was produced in 2009 – the year when the 60th anniversary of the founding of the People's Republic of China (PRC), the 60th anniversary of the '11·27 massacre', and the 80th anniversary of the founding of the university were celebrated. Sensing the significance of the timing, the author, a senior university student and president of the student drama society, decided to write a play to commemorate these events. The audience targeted were his fellow students, whom he wished to provoke into considering 'what true love is' and 'what you can do for others'.[20] The author was aware that university students tended to be rather cynical about political teachings on ideals and sacrifice. The romance between two young revolutionaries, therefore, became a unique selling point. The play was well received. When it first debuted at the university, the audience was moved to tears. 'No one commented on the "preaching" of communist ideals', the author proudly claimed.[21] Moreover, the play appeared at an opportune time politically. As Chongqing was deeply submerged in the boisterous Red culture campaign, it could certainly make use of a successful Red play. 'You know, some of the school cadres liked it too', the author confessed. In fact, the success of the play off-campus, including its subsequent collection of a series of honours in Chongqing and at a national competition in 2010, relied on the help of the school's Party Committee and Youth League Committee, which provided essential financial assistance to the society, helped negotiate the conflict between the students' course load and their obligation to the play, and also helped with its promotion outside Chongqing.

Secondly, participating in Red-themed activities could bring very practical benefits. Some university students treated their participation in the campaign as a way to improve their transferable skills, such as their organizational, leadership, and communication skills, all of which were believed to be useful for their later career development. Students who participated in speech contests or essay competitions, as described in Chapter 4, are typical examples of this. One university tutor also confirmed that it was a good strategy to sell these Red-themed activities to students as opportunities for them to acquire valuable skills:

> You can't just say – we are organizing a Red activity, I hope you'll participate. You have to sell it to the students from another perspective, telling them what kind of opportunities they will get. . . . [T]hey have to do research,

90   *Official programme: exchange*

practice, and perform. This will help them with their future career when they go out into the real world. Today's students are very competitive, and willing to take on challenging tasks. To speak and act in front of others is a good chance to challenge oneself.[22]

In many Chinese universities, the competition schemes for scholarships often took into account the students' extracurricular activities. Therefore, some students needed to collect credits from participating in extracurricular activities to boost their prospects of attaining a scholarship. Participating in Red-themed activities that were recognised by the school was a relatively easy and effective way of gaining useful points. For students who were full or probationary members of the Communist Party, there seemed to be a normative pressure for them to participate in these activities. 'Normally, the participants are Party members, because they have to'.[23] In some cases, recruitment was so difficult that in the end, the participants were almost all Communist Party members because 'other students rarely volunteer to participate', recalled one student.[24] For candidates for CCP membership, participation in the Red culture campaign provided good material for their progress reports, based on which they would be assessed for appointment to official membership.[25] In general, many students participated when *asked*. They agreed to participate either due to a sense of obligation or because of the practical benefits that they could reap from participation. These benefits were usually trivial but very effective when framed as relevant to the students' long-term career prospects.

Employees

The employees exchanged their time and involvement for extracurricular activities, career advancement, extra income, and political security. Firstly, many companies, both state-owned and private, organized Red-themed performances *within* their own enterprises, as described in the previous chapter. Singing Red was incorporated into the building of the companies' corporate cultures. The activities organized within a particular company thus fulfilled the double function of serving the popular needs and swimming with the most current political tide. Choral singing was one of the most convenient choices of extracurricular activities, and it could mobilise a large number of employees to accomplish a collaborative task together. Singing usually entailed a much higher participatory rate than other elements of the Red culture programme, such as speech contests, reading groups, or the sending of Red-themed text messages. The managers saw it as an opportunity to enhance employee solidarity, boost work morale, and facilitate communication among different hierarchies of employees. The employees, meanwhile, tended to enjoy all kinds of leisure activities in the highly-pressurised work environment. At least, they did not dislike the activities, especially when they did not take up as much time as the performances on more formal occasions. 'There's a lot of pressure at work, to develop business, so everyone loves extracurricular activities. . . . [I]f there's a performance, everyone wants to participate. . . . You just need to break the routine sometimes'.[26]

Secondly, participating in the Red culture campaign was associated with career advancement, job satisfaction, and the acquisition of professional skills. For one interviewee who worked in the special division office of 'Singing Red, Reading Classics, Telling Stories, Spreading Mottos' in the municipal government, her placement was part of a promotion scheme for young Party cadres. While working in the office, she participated in activities varying from large-scale staged performances, the production of promotional films about the Red culture programme, staging exhibitions for the campaign, and editing the 'Reading Classics' series. Her work revolved around coordinating the various participatory parties and booking venues. She described the experience as eye-opening. Working in this office within the Propaganda Department provided her a high-level platform where she could meet people of high status. It was also a valuable chance for her to enhance her organization and coordination skills. After returning to her old workplace, she was promoted from a division that focused mainly on thought and political work to the more competitive, strategically significant division of marketing and management.

Another employee in the same office, whose work was described in Chapter 4, had particularly fond recollections of his experience of working in the Propaganda Department on the Red culture campaign. 'I learnt a lot, especially about how to organize and coordinate. The work was demanding but I was very happy, I got on really well with my colleagues and we had a very good supervisor'.[27] In fact, he even deemed the six-month temporary assignment at the office to be one of the two most important experiences of his life. The other one was his military service, which had taken place in 'a relatively closed environment'. On being discharged from the military and transferred to a civilian position at his current workplace, he felt he was doing merely repetitive, mundane things. 'But it was different when I worked in the office for the Red culture campaign'.[28] There was probably also a sense of importance and worthiness attached to the job that was associated with the most popular political programme of the time. 'We had a hectic time in the office'.[29]

Working for the Red culture campaign also helped some young people develop knowledge of how to deal with the distinctively Chinese style of government and its officials. For example, the young employee of the private advertising company learnt tricks for dealing with a cadre: 'You have to first take into consideration the person one level higher who directly supervises this one because, 80–90% of the time, your customer is doing this to show to his superior, so you need to know what his superior likes and cares about'.[30] Moreover, when presenting project proposals for government-sponsored activities, it was essential to leave enough room for the government officials to make comments and change the plans.

> Although the government activities mostly needed only a very simple model, you had to propose a far more complex one and create a variety of models for them to choose from. You can't just go to them with the simple model, even if you know with certainty that it is similar to what the final version will be. You have to let them make the final decision'.[31]

92 *Official programme: exchange*

That is, the advertising company had to show its creativity as the trademark of their profession, and the cadres had to show that they were in charge.

Thirdly, people worked for the Red culture campaign for extra income. One young man, who had a degree in literature, freelanced for a Red-themed TV programme called 'Reading'. The first script took him almost a month to finish. As he gradually familiarised himself with the routine and style of such a production, he was able to contribute one or two narratives to the programmes every week. On average, he wrote three to four scripts for the programme every month, from which he earned an extra 1,500 to 2,000 *yuan* (≈£150–200). This was a considerable amount of extra income for the young man, who was saving up to get married. Another group that made money out of the campaign was the artistic directors, chorus conductors, and choreographers who were pursued by the companies to help with rehearsing the Red programmes and singers who were frequently paid to sing for the company choruses at important performances. One interviewee who worked for a culture centre in Chongqing said that she could make 6,000 to 7,000 *yuan* (≈£600–700) annually by occasionally ghosting for choruses. 'Other people made much more, more than 10,000 *yuan* (≈£1000), easily. The conductors and pianists made three or four times that amount'.[32]

Fourthly, participation in the Red culture campaign was a matter of political security for many employees. Some of the activities were organized for Party members, in which case they provided an occasion to express agreement with the Party ideology. It was common practice for employees, who had jobs at stake, to conform to the tasks allotted to them by their superiors as well as activities organized by the Party committee of their enterprise. 'I didn't have a choice', said the young employee who was picked by her supervisor at work to join the chorus. '[I]t was a political task. Your superior asked you to go, and you went'. Another participant, who was an amateur singer herself, offered a similar reason for her participation in the Red culture programme. 'My boss gave me the task'.[33] It was as simple as that. For Party cadres in state-owned enterprises (SOEs), it was an 'executive order', coming from the higher hierarchy of the 'system' (*xitong*).[34] The activities organized within a particular company acted as a selection process, whereby the best of the programmes were later recommended to be performed at district- or municipal-level Red-themed shows. The 'executive order', of course, was also a political obligation. One low-level civil servant, who worked in the Propaganda Department of a district government, explained the political wisdom of her departmental director – when it came to reporting the number of Red-themed activities, it was better to be 'in the middle; no more than the others and no less than the others'.[35] 'No one was really serious about it. But you had to fill in a form every month about the numbers, which was included as part of the annual work assessment. That was the difficult part'.[36]

The participants' practices as tactics

No matter how powerful it was, the government's programme had to rely on the 'petty' existence of the dispersed practices of ordinary people. On the other hand, the practices of the participants were capable of making use of the official programme's larger pool of resources to serve their own interests. During the process of exchange and mutual appropriation, the practices of the retirees had a tactical effect on the official programme. As introduced in Chapter 2, *tactics* are practices that are dispersed, opaque, and quiet yet capable of deflecting imposing systems and dominating institutions. According to de Certeau, a tactic does not seek to escape the space in which its practitioner is constrained by the existing order and institution but poaches, and diverts, in an artful way. The success of a tactic depends on its users' creativity and, above all, their ability to catch fleeting opportunities.[37] In the case of the retirees, the tactical effect of their practices was not that it openly challenged the official programme but that they ran a course of their own that met the needs of the practitioners and served their own interests. The retirees knew well the benefits of identifying their activities with the official Red culture programme and knew exactly when to utilise this affiliation to defend their interests and leisure activities. They also excelled at picking the 'right' songs for different performances and understood how to exploit the freedom to sing songs that were their personal favourites but not typically Red. The practices of the retirees constituted 'a hidden production' of meaningful and valuable actions for themselves at the locale of everyday life. In the case of the university students, some of them knew how to catch the eye of their school officials and solicit their support for the student societies. Others excelled at making use of the opportunities to reap practical benefits, such as the development of personal skills and improving their chances of obtaining a scholarship. For the employees, participating in the Red culture campaign could mean earning extra income or opportunities for career advancement. If not, at least it was a chance to socialise with colleagues and gain political protection for one's career.

Summary

In this chapter, I have shown how the official programme and the participants interacted through the social form of exchange. The official programme provided political security, performance opportunity, and material incentives among other benefits to the participants in exchange of the participants' commitment, time, and energy devoted to the campaign. Different generations of the participants expected and received different returns from the official programme. In de Certeau's term, the official Red culture programme resembled a *strategy*, using the executive power of the government to mobilise a large amount of monetary, political, and media resources. The practices of the participants, on the other hand, show characteristics of *tactics*. They did not openly challenge the official programme while running a course of their own in service of the participants' personal interests. Despite the hugely unequal power relations between the forceful political programme and its participants, there were extensive elements of interaction and association between the two. Based on the form of interaction observed in the implementation of the campaign, there neither was forceful domination by the official programme nor outright resistance practiced by the participants.

94   *Official programme: exchange*

Notes

1 Parts of this chapter were first published in *China Perspective* 2013/4.
2 Max Weber, *Max Weber: On Charisma and Institution Building*, ed. by S. N. Eisenstadt (London: The University of Chicago Press, 1968).
3 Qianchuan Xu, 'The Red Tide' (*hong chao*), *Caijing Blog*, November 2013 http://blog. caijing.com.cn/expert_article-151567-61481.shtml[accessed 18 November 2013]
4 Interview with A04.
5 Prior to the 1990s, SOEs (*dan wei*) provided an all-around 'cradle-to-grave' social service to the employees, including medical care, child care, housing, and so on. As a result, '*dan wei*' was a significant part of the social identity of its employees. The employees often felt emotional attached to their '*dan wei*'. Since the reforms, the state has offloaded most of its social responsibilities from *dan wei* to other social organizations, such as the *she qu* (local communities). See Chapter 4 for a more detailed discussion on 'community-building' as a governance technique.
6 Interview with A07.
7 Interview with A04.
8 Interview with A05.
9 Interview with A20, female, age 55.
10 Bryant Lei Ouyang, '"New Songs of the Battlefield": Songs and Memories of the Chinese Cultural Revolution' (doctoral dissertation, University of Pittsburgh, 2004).
11 Guobin Yang, 'China's Zhiqing Generation: Nostalgia, Identity, and Cultural Resistance in the 1990s', *Modern China*, 29 (2003), 267–96.
12 Interview with A03.
13 Interview with A10.
14 Interview with A09.
15 Yang, 'China's Zhiqing Generation'.
16 Interview with A09.
17 Interview with A18.
18 Andrew G. Walder, 'Communist Social Structure and Worker's Politics in China', in *Citizens and Groups in Contemporary China*, ed. by Victor C. Falkenheim (Ann Arbor: University of Michigan, 1987).
19 '*Hongsheng guangchang kala OK tan, hou de jumin nan rumian*' (Karaoke Booth at *Hongsheng* Square Disturbed the Residents Nearby), *Chongqing Evening*, 17 August 2011.
20 Interview with B03.
21 Interview with B03.
22 Interview with a college tutor.
23 Interview with B25.
24 Interview with B25.
25 For CCP membership applicants, they must seek nomination from existing members, go through examinations by a Party branch, and get approval from the higher level of the organization to become probationary members. It takes at least another year to become an official member, during which the candidates are regularly assessed.
26 Interview with C04.
27 Interview with C17.
28 Interview with C17.
29 Interview with C17.
30 Interview with C20.
31 Interview with C20.
32 Interview with C22.
33 Interview with C06.
34 *Xitong* refers to the units within the jurisdiction of particular ministries or a group of related bureaucracies across industry lines. See Saich, p. 144.

35 Interview with C07.
36 Interview with C07.
37 Michel de Certeau, *The Practice of Everyday Life* (Berkeley and Los Angeles, CA: University of California Press, 1984), p. xix.

Bibliography

Certeau, Michel de, *The Practice of Everyday Life* (Berkeley and Los Angeles, CA: University of California Press, 1984)

'*Hongsheng guangchang kala OK tan, hou de jumin nan rumian*' (Karaoke Booth at *Hongsheng* Square Disturbed Residents Nearby), *Chongqing Evening*, 17 August 2011

Ouyang, Bryant Lei, ' "New Songs of the Battlefield": Songs and Memories of the Chinese Cultural Revolution' (doctoral dissertation, University of Pittsburgh, 2004)

Walder, Andrew G., 'Communist Social Structure and Worker's Politics in China', in Victor C. Falkenheim, ed., *Citizens and Groups in Contemporary China* (Ann Arbor: University of Michigan, 1987), pp. 45–89

Weber, Max, *Max Weber: On Charisma and Institution Building*, S. N. Eisenstadt, ed. (London: The University of Chicago Press, 1968)

Xu, Qianchuan, 'The Red Tide' (*hong chao*), *Caijing Blog*, <http://blog.caijing.com.cn/expert_article-151567-61481.shtml> [accessed 18 November 2013]

Yang, Guobin, 'China's Zhiqing Generation: Nostalgia, Identity, and Cultural Resistance in the 1990s', *Modern China*, 29 (2003), 267–96

7 How the official programme interacted with the practices of the local participants

Framing

In the previous chapter, I demonstrated how the political programme of Chongqing's Red culture campaign interacted with its participants in the form of exchange. The interactive relationship between these two critical parties concerned not only practices and resources but also how both the official programme and the participants articulated meanings of the campaign and how they appropriated and judged each other's understandings and actions. Frames are symbolic representations of events on the basis of which judgment can be made and changes can be imagined. The specific meanings that constitute judgments are often not fixed. They are rooted in multiple sources of interpretation and open to unpredictable interaction and changes. Therefore, judgment is considered capable of deflecting absolute control. Judgments contain power because they allow those who operate in highly-structured spaces to reject the meaning imposed upon them, reconfigure order, and reorganize relations.[1] In this chapter, I analyse how the government and the participants framed narratives of the Red culture campaign and how these frames were mutually appropriated and contested during the process of executing the political programme.

Framing processes by the official programme

In addition to mobilising a large number of resources, Chongqing's Red culture campaign evoked a number of principles and dichotomised value judgments in narrating the meaning of its existence. As a *strategy*, it constructed narratives of history, which were used to justify the significance of the campaign. Firstly, the Red culture campaign praised the CCP's glorious revolutionary past and criticised the spiritual emptiness and vulgar culture of the present. During the enemy evasion, it was 'March the Army' (*yiyongjun jinxingqu* 《义勇军进行曲》), 'Big Knife Marching Song' (*dadao jinxingqu* 《大刀进行曲》), and 'Defend the Yellow River' (*baowei huanghe* 《保卫黄河》) that mobilised tens of thousands of people to defend the nation. However, a crisis of the soul has emerged during the startling economic development of the past three decades. In the era of information explosion, multiple value systems existed and competed with one another. It was believed that spiritual emptiness haunted people who were now enjoying a much higher living standard than in the past. People believe in utilitarian values

Official programme: framing 97

and are influenced by Western individualism and liberalism. Many have forgotten the merits of making sacrifices for the collective. The vulgar culture of the fast-food era is eroding the soul of the general public, especially the youth. During the Red culture campaign, the young people, therefore, were encouraged to sing not only love songs but also songs that would inspire them. Moreover, they should benefit from reading classic works that will serve as a spiritual and cultural foundation upon which they can build a meaningful career. University students are advised to learn better to differentiate the 'good' and 'useful' ones from the vast amount of information in which they are now immersed on a daily basis. They are asked to preserve the glorious traditions of the revolution and wave the banner of 'serving the people'.

Secondly, the Red culture campaign criticised the swelling social inequality that has resulted from the market economy and advocated a fairer socialist approach to the distribution of wealth in society. Two points were repeatedly emphasised in the narrative of the Red culture campaign: – 'serve the people' (*wei renmin fuwu* 为人民服务) and 'common prosperity' (*gongtong fuyu* 共同富裕). Mao's renowned dictum – 'serve the people' – was argued to constitute the fundamental difference between capitalism and socialism. Chongqing's leadership argued that serving the people entailed pursuing a common prosperity. Western technology, corporate management, and the market economy were only legitimate when they served the people and brought prosperity to all. Singing Red songs was important in that it not only promoted revolutionary traditions but also helped to build an advanced socialist culture, which would boost Chongqing's economic development and benefit every citizen.[2]

Thus, the idea of 'from the masses, to the masses' (*cong qunzhong zhong lai, dao qunzhong zhong qu* 从群众中来，到群众中去) was consistently used to rationalise the Red culture campaign. The campaign was first of all considered beneficial to the people. It claimed to meet the need for both high and low culture among all strata of society. It aimed to raise the Chinese people's spirits (*jingqishen* 精气神), engender their emotional satisfaction, and provide meaning to their lives, baffled as they were by the dramatic social changes of recent decades. It opposed the influence of the decadent, vulgar culture of the fast-food era. Singing Red could evoke a spirit of unity, when large crowds gathered to sing together. With this spirit, the Chinese people would benefit from their prosperous, strong nation. In this respect, the campaign was 'for the people'. On the other hand, its success depended on the people. Bo's reinterpretation of the 'mass-line' approach started with a grand historical narration of how the masses, united under the Red spirit, had been the fundamental force underlying the founding and success of the CCP. The narrative recounted stories of how Red songs were sung in *Anyuan* (安源), *Yan'an* (延安), and at the frontlines of the anti-Japanese war by the masses, who were the true heroes of the revolutions.[3] The masses were portrayed as not only the critical force behind the CCP's revolutionary success but also the backbone of the great reform that promoted China to become the second-largest economy in the world. The success of the Red culture campaign, similarly, had to rely on the participation of the masses. The 'mass-line' approach served not

98　*Official programme: framing*

only as the theoretical justification for initiating a Red culture campaign but was also rigorously pursued in the implementation of the campaign. The participants were not professional actors and artists but 'your neighbours, your children, and your colleagues'. The performers were reported to come from a wide variety of age groups, occupations, and social backgrounds, ranging from primary school students, university students, teachers, retirees, bureaucrats, Party cadres, farmers, and workers to employees of the SOEs and private companies. The goal was for the programme eventually to become naturalised, internalised, and routinised as part of people's everyday life.

Framing processes by the participants – primary frameworks

I have mapped out how the official programme framed the meaning and importance of the Red culture campaign. Now, I will discuss how the participants framed their personal experiences and the political programme. The different generations of participants framed their experience of the Red culture campaign rather differently in accordance with the following four factors: whether participation in the Red culture campaign helped to strengthen social relationships, whether it was beneficial for self-development, whether it helped to construct an appealing identity, and whether it was capable of eliciting pleasant memories (see Appendix 3, Table 3 for a summary of the analysis). Moreover, the value that the participants attached to Red-themed activities also depended on how easily these could be replaced by other activities that could fulfill the four functions described here in the participants' social lives. On the other hand, when the participants were asked to think beyond their immediate experiences, and frame the political programme of the Red culture campaign, whether the programme was considered successful or not depended highly on their perceptions on how far the programme's effect matched its intent. These factors, which affected the participants' framing of both their own experiences and the political programme in general, were closely linked with generational differences in terms of both the participants' past life experiences and the social positions they occupy today.

The Cultural Revolution (CR) generation – retirees and older employees

Despite the sporadic complaints about being physically drained by some of the high-level performance assignments, the retirees generally had very positive framing of their experience of participating in the Red culture campaign. As detailed in the previous chapter, they experienced it as an opportunity to fulfil their interest in singing and dancing, a path taking them back to their youth, and a chance to reclaim an honourable identity for the 'lost generation'. They believed that singing was hugely beneficial to their health, and that the Red culture campaign had helped them to change their outlook on life. 'People's mental outlook was transformed vastly, and another thing was that we used to play mah-jongg a lot, you know, "building the Great Wall".[4] Now people are united, to sing Red songs'.[5] Another commented: 'It is particularly appealing to people like us, retired people who love singing. It helps to make us feel fulfilled. I almost forget my age'.[6]

Similarly, the employees in their 50s believed the campaign to be beneficial to their health, helping purify their spirits, and also valuable in teaching younger people about the past. The most enjoyable aspect was that the songs were capable of arousing genuine, deep emotions, such as patriotism and nostalgia. For example, one interviewee explained why he liked the Red songs: 'My generation still feels for these songs; for example, *"chuan hua jiang shang"* (On Chunhua River 《春花江上》) or *"wo de zuguo"* (My Motherland 《我的祖国》). My blood still rises and I feel excited. It reminds me of my childhood'.[7] Likewise, a participant who had served in the army loved the familiarity of singing Red – the unity, the momentum, and the pride, all of which he missed greatly from military life. Another participant said that the songs reminded her of when family used to watch revolution films together when she was a child. She recalled fondly her parents singing the themes of the films. 'I thought the songs were very pleasant to listen to, and really those were the only songs we grew up with'.[8] On the other hand, however, the CR generation admitted that the Red culture programme was unlikely to have much real influence on the younger generation. 'Young people are interested in different things. They like pop music'.[9] 'The effect on young people, I think, is almost zero'.[10] Despite their belief in the necessity and good intentions of such a campaign in educating younger people about the history of the revolution, the retirees were also aware of its limited influence on this younger generation.

In general, singing was an activity that was of unique benefit to the retirees. It was healthier, cheaper, and more uplifting than other popular hobbies, such as playing mah-jongg; it was more communal and had a much lower entry level than other hobbies that they might engage in, such as sports. The employees approaching retirement age were in a similar position to the retirees in terms of how they appropriated the Red culture programme in their daily practices of participating in the campaign. It is therefore unsurprising that both the retirees and older employees shared a positive evaluation of their experiences of the campaign.

The generation of youth – university students and young employees

In contrast to the retirees' overwhelmingly positive framing of their experiences of the Red culture campaign, the students' framing of their experience was mainly negative. Those students who were obliged to participate regularly in the campaign resented the fact that this was very time-consuming. For students selected to perform at the municipal-level galas in particular, their normal school hours had to be compromised from time to time. Because many of the performances clustered around the examination period, many students, busy rotating around Red-themed shows, did not have time to prepare for their exams. In some cases, they had to defer or even miss their exams. In addition, the rehearsals could be frequent and demanding. At the height of the campaign, rehearsals were often held daily, during which tasks were assigned on short notice. The students blamed the Youth League Committee of their university, who was responsible for the thought work and the organization of extracurricular activities at the university, for accepting too many assignments from the municipal government for them. 'That was their political obligation, but they had no idea what we needed to do for our studies'.[11]

100   *Official programme: framing*

The students who participated in Red-themed activities at a faculty or school level rehearsed only in their free time. Although this meant that their involvement in the campaign had far less of a negative impact on their studies, they nevertheless resented it: 'They (the government) always defend the programme, citing that the rehearsals take place in people's free time, but that is *our* free time and we have other things to do. They never realize that'.[12] One student argued pointedly: 'After all, my main task is to study, not be an actor for his (Bo's) Red programme'.[13] Other students who took part in the faculty-level activities, on the other hand, appeared quite blasé about the campaign. They treated the Red-themed activities as 'just normal school activities'.[14] These students usually had fairly vague recollections of the events. One student could not tell how long the show, in which she performed, lasted, or how many programs were staged because 'I left immediately after I'd finished'.[15] She even had difficulty remembering the number of students in her team or if her team won a prize. Moreover, singing Red was simply not cool enough. One student, who was humming the tune of a Red song that she had been practicing, was laughed at by her roommates in her dormitory: 'My roommates all wondered what was wrong with me. They thought I'd gone mad to be singing Red songs outside rehearsals'.[16] It was almost considered scandalous for young people to *love* singing Red songs.

Not all of the comments were negative, however. Positive framing of the experience of participating in the Red culture campaign included that it helped strengthen the friendships among the members of the teams, elicited pride when standing on the stage of prestigious halls, and occasionally provided pecuniary rewards. However, the positive framing was not based on any substantial element of the Red-themed activities per se. Rather the few students who claimed to have enjoyed the experience ignored the content of the Red songs as well as the political implications of the campaign in general.

> I do not understand the content of the songs. . . . I don't really care . . . but some of the melodies are quite pleasant. That is music, art. Art will never be old-fashioned. I just enjoy dancing to the music.[17]

> In terms of the songs, I do not have much appreciation for them. We simply love singing together. If these tasks weren't assigned to us, we'd still sing. . . . We treat it as art, the practice of singing. Not much else . . . Sometimes we get an assignment at such short notice that we do not have time to try to understand the background or significance of the songs. We focus on *singing* them well.[18]

The younger employees also cited aspects that they liked about their experiences, including the opportunities to learn new songs, strengthen their friendships with their colleagues, and cultivate their musical talent. Some of those who participated in the higher-level performances believed that participating in the campaign would create a special memory for them in the years to come. 'It is not like anyone can go, you know'.[19] One employee of a state-owned enterprise (SOE), an amateur singer herself, was assigned by her superior to take charge of a team composed of

Official programme: framing 101

colleagues from her department. Although it was 'an assignment from your boss', she treated it as a chance to test her capability to adapt the selected song tracks, organize the rehearsals, and direct the department's new 'chorus'. When comparing her previous role as a solo singer with taking charge of the chorus team, she commented: 'The latter was more difficult, but I'd like to try that role because I want to know if I can do it well'.[20]

For the young people, there were countless options for entertainment in which they were genuinely interested. These other activities could easily replace the Red-themed programmes, such as their Youth League Day outing. In companies, activities such as hiking and travel could easily replace singing Red as part of the effort to develop a corporate culture. Unsurprisingly, the young people liked pop music, blockbuster films, and spending time with their friends in karaoke lounges. Their framing of the Red culture campaign was therefore far more negative than that of the older generations.

When asked to provide an overall assessment on the effectiveness of the programme, the students tackled the question from a number of different perspectives. From an instrumental standpoint, the Red culture campaign helped promote the city and was valuable to the cultural industry in Chongqing, which many interviewees believed lagged far behind that of other Chinese metropolises, such as Beijing, Shanghai, and Guangzhou. When Chongqing garnered enough fame, they predicted, it would be able to attract other high-standard performances from all over the world. The Red culture campaign could be something unique for Chongqing to sell as the cultural centre of China's rising West.

Nevertheless, the students did not judge the campaign to be successful in effectively promoting mainstream values or morality. 'Who would change their personality through watching a performance'?[21] Even from the perspective of those students who admired Bo, singing Red could only marginally contribute towards improving social morality. 'It was unrealistic for it to change one's beliefs and value systems; but it would be good for the cultural atmosphere of the city'.[22] The main problem, however, was that the programme was too formalistic. Generally, the students were reluctant to criticise its content beyond pointing out that most of the programme's materials were from the distant past, and they did not have an upbringing under the Red culture that would make them feel emotionally attached to the programme. Yet, they complained about the 'form' of the programme, which was deemed to be rigid, preposterous, and hypercritical. The experience was simply boring. Because the programmes tended to be highly repetitive, many students, especially those who were involved in high-level performances, found them tedious. 'At first it was fine because we were curious. Then we were asked to do it again and again because the officials loved our programme. I got so bored in the end'.[23] 'When it (the rehearsal) lasts for more than ten days, I start to feel really irritated', confessed another student.[24] Moreover, the activities were too frequent, too extravagant, and too costly.

> The most ridiculous thing was the Chongqing satellite channel. It has been turned into a Red channel. They've replaced all the entertainment with Red

102 *Official programme: framing*

classics. No one around me wants to watch it, because it is so dated. If you ask people to sing Red songs, or participate in Red-themed activities once in a while, there may be people actually interested or willing to take part, but not in this overwhelming way.[25]

The young employees, like the university students, did not wish to sing Red songs partly because they found it difficult to build an emotional attachment to the programme. The campaign failed to interest them:

You have to tell the stories in an interesting way. What does 'mass communication' mean, if nobody wants to watch it? . . . They'd rather play Mah-jong. Indeed, the retirees, who don't have much to do, love it. You want to keep them occupied, but do you want the generation born in the 1990s to sing Red songs, seriously? How is it ever possible?[26]

Secondly, the young people claimed that they had already had their own view of the world; the effect of the campaign was therefore very limited:

People could read the classic works themselves, but it was questionable how many of them would take the texts to their hearts. They might just be faking it.[27]

You have to make it desirable to the students first if you want to influence them in any way.[28]

What I want to say is that if they want to restrict our thoughts using this method, then it is often counterproductive. On the surface, everything is fine, but off stage, people have another face.[29]

Other students, who were more politically sensitive, pointed out that they believed that Bo's intention in initiating the programme was essentially political. For Bo to attain the top position, he needed to do something spectacular to draw attention to his achievements, and he needed the support of the people:

Bo Xilai came to Chongqing and he needs to make changes, and publicize these changes. In China, people say 'good publicity is more important than actually doing things well' . . . from the perspective of the government, it must consider the whole picture. . . . [I]t has done all the work and it must show its work to the public. . . . In the 'Smashing Black' campaign, they dig up some dirty things and show them to the people. At the same time, they need to dig up some positive things, as in the Red culture campaign. The campaign is a tool, I think.[30]

Unlike the retirees, who tended to intertwine their framing of the Red culture campaign with their personal memories of the past, the generation of young people generally lacked previous experience of significant political events. Their framing processes were likely to be based on the information and ideas they were exposed to through the political analysis in the media, their teachers, or peers.

The middle-age employees

In general, the middle-age employees believed that the Red culture campaign had a very limited impact on their daily lives:

> When it [the Red culture campaign] trickles down and reaches the ordinary people, it becomes a very small wave. When it reaches to the bottom, for us, it is just something that breaks the routine, something that temporarily gets us away from the busy jobs. What the government wants to achieve has not been realized. . . . Yes, I sang the songs, but it did not make me love the country more, or love the government more, or love the Party more.[31]

For many of these employees, participating in the Red culture campaign was neither desirable nor contemptible. A sense of indifference seemed to prevail among the participants who had full-time jobs and many other 'more important things' to worry about. Their comments were conspicuously careful, mild, and balanced. For example, they would say things like:

> It is a political assignment. My supervisor asks me to go and I go; but it is not like I hate singing Red songs.[32]

> If I no longer had to sing Red songs, I wouldn't miss it; but if I am singing Red, there is nothing bad about it.[33]

> It is an executive order, yes, and we are doing whatever possible within our capacity, but it isn't like people will lose their job if they do not do very well.[34]

One participant, whose team was regularly chosen to perform on important occasions at the municipality level or above, had to attend a rehearsal the day after his daughter was born:

> Of course, I didn't want to go and felt very frustrated. But when I think back now, it was just a couple of hours. And you know what, my daughter's first song was Azalea (*yingshanhong* 《映山红》),[35] and I don't mind her learning or singing Red songs as she grows up. They are not bad songs, you know.[36]

Understandably, some employees could not care less:

> [W]hat the government wants to achieve, or how effective it has been, I don't know and I don't discuss it. At my age, I'm done with discussing the meaning of life. I just want to spend time with friends and play Mah-jongg.[37]

Similar to their younger counterparts, the benefits of participating in the Red culture campaign for middle-age employees, such as the extracurricular activities, career advancement, professional skills, and extra income, could be relatively easily replaced by other options. Sports and outdoor trips could provide a good way for a company to boost the team morale and give its employees a chance to

104 *Official programme: framing*

relax after work. Professional skills and career advancement opportunities were not, and had never been, restricted to one political programme. Young employees who needed extra cash could be assigned to other work as long as they had the right skills.

As already mentioned, the middle-age employees displayed a high degree of reservation and self-reflection when judging the Red culture campaign. Given the tradition of the CCP's enigmatic political maneuvers and covert arrangements, the employees assumed that it would be difficult to know exactly what happened behind closed doors in terms of the political struggles. 'Ordinary folk are too far from the political centre. It is hard for them to judge . . . people just follow the herd. They can't really tell'.[38]

Some admitted that the campaign was too political for them to comment on, and they had not developed the luxurious habit of 'discussing politics' because nothing 'had any real impact on our daily life'.[39] 'After the Wang Lijun incident, followed by Bo ['s prosecution] . . . the local people fear to talk about it. . . . [A]fter all, we have a job and our organization (*zuzhi* 组织), not to mention those working in the government bureaucracy'.[40] Despite their caution and reservation, people did nonetheless usually have an opinion of their own:

> At my age, I understand these things. It (the campaign) is excessive. The TV channel has become a Red channel; the radio has become Red waves. We can't just have Red culture. The economy has developed, and cultural life should reflect the economic development. . . . There is only one voice in the newspaper, (the media are) afraid of Wang's 'double indictment' pledge.[41] This is no good, and we're doing pretty poorly regarding freedom of speech. Freedom of speech is written into the constitution, so how can you go against the constitution?[42]

This was probably the most serious accusation that the employees were willing to offer as their own opinion. Some would, on the other hand, cite 'other people's views' as evidence that the campaign might have a darker side:

> Some of the teachers at my school, who teach politics, were furious. After so many years, the Party is still trying to hammer ideas into us? They created this situation on purpose, to unify people's thought, and teach people to make sacrifices, as before. It is a way of diverting attention away from our domestic social problems.[43]

Unlike the retirees, who used their memories of their past experiences as a frame of reference for judging the Red culture campaign, or the students who lacked real-life experience of political campaigns, the employees tended to make more sophisticated judgments of the Red culture campaign. Their jobs were likely to bring them into closer contact with politics and enable them to conduct a more complex political analysis. Nevertheless, this was also the generation that was far less likely to comment openly on the political significance and implications of

Official programme: framing   105

the Red culture campaign. There was simply too much at stake when it came to meddling with politics.

How frames are appropriated and contested – the keying processes

Interpreting Red

In the official narrative, the notion of Red was given a new interpretation in the Red culture campaign. 'Red' songs typically referred to propaganda songs that praised the socialist revolutions in China. Since the 1990s, the CCP has repackaged the revolutionary propaganda songs into Red songs as part of the mainstream culture. Chongqing's Red culture campaign followed the CCP's general strategy of incorporating Red songs as part of the mainstream culture. Yet there has been an increasing emphasis on the inclusiveness of the concept of Red since the end of 2010 in Chongqing, probably due to the criticism that linked the campaign to the CR. The official definition of Red songs included those from all historical periods of the CCP's development. The type of songs that were defined as Red extended far beyond the 'old songs' of the revolutionary year. They were officially designated as songs about 'saving the nation, building the nation, and strengthening the nation' (*jiuguo de ge, jianguo de ge, qiangguo de ge* 救国的歌，建国的歌，强国的歌). Chongqing's minister of the Propaganda Department argued that the decision to use the word 'Red' was because this Chinese character has very positive connotations. It implies vitality, liveliness, youth, passion, brightness, colourfulness, strength, and boldness. Red refers not only to yesterday's revolutionary martyrs but also celebrates today's good life and denotes a positive outlook about the future. During the formative years of the People's Republic, artists wrote influential pieces, such as 'Ode to the Motherland' (*gechang zuguo* 《歌唱祖国》), 'We March on the Road' (*wo men zouzai dalu shang* 《我们走在大路上》), and 'Song of Lei Feng' (*Lei Feng zhi ge* 《雷锋之歌》), which inspired people to make great efforts to rebuild their war-torn nation. In the reform era, songs such as 'The Story of the Spring' (*chuntian de gushi* 《春天的故事》), 'Marching to the New Era' (*zoujin xinshidai* 《走进新时代》), and 'National Renewal' (*zouxiang fuxing* 《走向复兴》) were testimonies to the Chinese people's hard work that made possible the spectacular economic development and ascendance of China into a major global power.[44] Moreover, every era and country had its own Red songs. Even 'La Marseillaise' (*ma sai qu* 《马赛曲》) and 'Edelweiss' (*xue rong hua* 《雪绒花》) were Red songs, according to Chongqing's minster of the Propaganda Department.

It was repeatedly emphasised that singing Red did not exclude people from singing other songs. It was argued that it was unconnected with the political struggle between the Right and Left and had nothing to do with the 'return to the Cultural Revolution'. The most popular songs during the CR, such as 'Sailing the Sea Depends on the Helmsman' (*dahai hangxing kao duoshou* 《大海航行靠舵手》) and 'It Is Right to Rebel' (*zaofan you li* 《造反有理》), were not on the list of Red songs. On the

106 *Official programme: framing*

contrary, some of songs that had been banned during the CR were now considered Red, such as 'Somewhere Far Away' (*zai na yaoyuan de defang* 《在那遥远的地方》), 'Lift Your Veil' (*xianqi ni de gaitou lai* 《掀起你的盖头来》), 'Lapping Waves of Honghu Lake' (*honghushui langdalang* 《洪湖水，浪打浪》), 'Praise to the Red Plum Blossom' (*hongmei zan* 《红梅赞》), and so on. The accusation of its affiliation with the CR was therefore considered unfounded and unjust by the leadership in Chongqing.[45]

While framing the Red culture campaign, the interviewees also offered their interpretation of the meaning of 'Red'. The interpretation of this concept by the three generations was multifaceted and relational. Firstly, Red was interpreted as referring to a specific category of cultural materials, based on their content and style. Red songs, for example, were predominantly, yet not exclusively, old songs. A small proportion that had been written during the reform era counted as well, as long as they had something to do with praising the Party, the country, and the people. Interestingly, the Red songs were often conceptualised as opposed to 'artistic songs' across the board by all three generations, especially the participants who were receiving formal singing training. Red songs were understood to be concerned with 'serious issues', such as the revolutionary wars, the nation, the Party, and the people; thus, they were political in nature and normally 'did not concern love or friendship'.[46] The artistic songs, on the other hand, were primarily about expressing private feelings. They were considered apolitical and embraced anything that was beautiful.[47] The Red songs were believed to be less sophisticated than the artistic songs. One's voice needed to be loud, strong, and sturdy when singing Red songs. To sing artistic songs, on the other hand, a higher level of singing technique was required. One needed to be able to adjust one's voice, forceful or restrained, according to the content of the song. 'There are many layers. An artistic song is rich, and it is totally different from singing Red songs. It is such a great pleasure', explained one retiree who belonged to a community chorus.[48] Students who had been professionally coached in singing echoed this appreciation for artistic songs: 'I definitely prefer artistic songs. . . . [T]hey require more techniques and musical literacy. Revolutionary songs are too simple. It is like chanting slogans. You just need to open your mouth. There are so few techniques demanded'.[49]

Secondly, Red was a symbolic reference to a positive, progressive spirit and an upbeat social morale. 'It is about faith, justice, and spiritual happiness'.[50] Borrowing a popular phrase of the day, Red songs were the embodiment of 'positive energy' (*zheng neng liang* 正能量).[51] They brought people together and made society more cohesive. In the context of today's Chongqing, Red songs were believed to be able to raise the spirits of the city. 'Red songs are about building momentum, and crafting a positive mental outlook for society'.[52] Red songs were meant to foster an appreciation of the revolutionary traditions as well as a sense of social responsibility among younger people. Even the young people acknowledged that the qualities of a revolutionary – courageous, resilient, and willing to sacrifice – were admirable. They tended to agree that society needed a dominant,

Official programme: framing   107

positive culture to battle the moral ills, the materialistic culture, and the rampant spread of rumours, especially on the Internet:

> Society does need a collective ethos. There is too much stuff on the Internet. It is sometimes difficult to judge which is good and which bad. I think there should be clear general guidelines. Society is now so materialistic, and people are no longer willing to help others. If we can dig up some good things from our past culture and promote them as the mainstream values for today's society, I suppose it is a positive thing to do.[53]

Moreover, having a dominant culture helped to ensure social coherence and solidarity. Although different beliefs and perspectives should be tolerated, nonetheless, a society needed 'a backbone', and most agreed that the government should take the initiative in this. Society would be chaotic if everyone insisted on their own beliefs. There should be consensus among people in terms of moral judgments.

On the other hand, all three generations of participants could decipher the *political* allegiance of the Red culture, seeing that it was the CCP's strategy to strengthen its political legitimacy. Most of the retirees understood that the Red songs were essentially political. 'We are led by the Communist Party, and these activities are imperative'.[54] Nevertheless, as the generation that grew up under the Red flag of the Communist Party, they seemed to accept the fact that Red was intrinsically associated with the ruling party. Despite the political connotation, Red songs above all symbolised patriotism. They were the embodiment of patriotism, the Party, the people, and one's hometown. In particular, they represented the extremely difficult but glorious history of the revolutionary past, for example, the war against the Japanese and the civil war that preceded the founding of the Republic of China.

Thirdly, the concept of Red was often framed by the participants as being in opposition to the social ills of the present, such as the materialistic culture, the worship of money, and spiritual hollowness. Dissatisfaction with the current social condition contributed to the romanticisation of the revolutionary era, when fairness was considered imperative and people had a firm faith. It was believed that the people enjoyed spiritual fulfillment despite their material want at the time. They had purer, more sympathetic hearts and were more willing to lend a helping hand. In addition to referring to the past in the context of the present social conditions, the participants relied heavily on references to 'the other' generation. To the older generation, the Red songs stood for the great effort and sacrifice made in pursuit of a good life, which they believed were significantly undervalued by the younger generation. They therefore attached a pedagogical value to the Red culture with specific reference to 'spoilt, selfish, and unappreciative young people'.[55] On the other hand, the younger generation distanced themselves from the revolutionary era represented by Red, deeming Red to be more closely associated with the morality and lifestyle of the older generation. Although they could appreciate

108 *Official programme: framing*

the values embedded in Red culture, they tended not to identify themselves as the bearers of the Red cultural tradition, nor did they aspire to a lifestyle that was associated with the past, which championed sacrifice and collectivism. From their standpoint, having a dominant Red culture should not be at the expense of the personal freedom of individuals to decide their specific life course. History lessons were valuable, yet the young people certainly did not expect to adopt the lifestyle of the past themselves; positive characters were worthy of praise, yet they should not be distorted or deified. The government had the capacity to guide, but it should not attempt to be omnipotent. The students did not buy into the almighty Red:

> Some of the reports were crazy. They said that singing Red could cure cancer, and praised people who insisted on singing Red even a family member was dying, etc. This kind of promotion was so unnecessary and fake. It's crazy.[56]

In comparison with the official narrative

The participants' framing of the value of the Red culture campaign was generally contained within the official narrative about how the campaign helped recall the glory of the revolutionary past, promoting the value of the mainstream culture which enhances social cohesion and combatting the decline of morality and domination of materialism in current society. Nevertheless, their framing also bifurcated at several critical points. Firstly, whereas the official narrative defined Red culture as 'positive' and 'healthy', as opposed to vulgar and decadent, the participants would rather evoke the contrast between Red songs and artistic songs. In comparison, Red songs lacked both sophistication and a personal touch. Secondly, whereas the official narrative devoted great efforts to justifying the benefits of the Red culture to young people, it was obvious to most of the participants that the campaign was ineffective in educating young people with the mainstream culture. The younger generation did not feel emotionally attached to the Red culture and felt entitled to pursue values as well as lifestyles that they deemed worthy. Thirdly, whereas the official narrative emphasised that the campaign would bring benefits to the people, it was clear to most of the participants that there was an instrumental, political, and possibly personal motivation behind the campaign. There were many complaints that the style of the campaign was hackneyed, formalistic, and preposterous.

Summary

In this chapter, I have shown how the official programme and the participants framed Chongqing's Red culture campaign differently. The official programme evoked a number of principles and dichotomised value judgments, such as the contrast between the glorious revolutionary past and the vulgar culture of the present, to frame the meaning of its existence in today's China. The participants, on the other hand, also constructed different narratives of the meanings of the Red culture campaign in accordance with the specific generations they belong to, that is, the CR generation, the generation of youth, and the middle-age employees. In the process of framing, the different generations of participants drew on different sources to help constructing their narratives of the campaign. For example, the CR generation was much more likely to incorporate their experiences of the CR in framing the Red culture campaign than the younger generations. Moreover, the participants were capable of judging the effectiveness of the programme from different perspectives. Whereas the Red culture campaign might help promote the cultural image of the city, it was widely considered as ineffective in influencing the youth culture. Thirdly, the participants constructed both primary frameworks and 'keyings', to borrow Goffman's terms, in interpreting the meanings of the programme. They were capable of not only knowing 'what it was that is going on' but also articulating what they thought 'was really going on'. They might not be fully aware of the political games that fundamentally motivated the initiation of the campaign, but most of the participants understood the campaign was more than what it appeared to be and was probably the result of covert political maneuvers. They had heard the ambitions of their leader, and they very much understood that their participation was part of the game that was closely linked to the political future of Bo. Lastly, as shown in the case of interpreting the concept of Red, the frames of the Red culture campaign contained both similarities and contending elements.

Notes

1 Kennan Ferguson, *The Politics of Judgment: Aesthetics, Identity, and Political Theory* (Lanham: Lexington Books, 2007), p. 142–7.
2 For example, '*Bo Xilai: chang xiang zhuxuanlu, ningju jingqishen*' (Bo Xilai: Sing Aloud and Spirit Up), *Chongqing Daily*, 23 June 2009; '*Bo Xilai: hongge changchule zanzhongguoren de zihaogan he ningjuli*' (Bo Xilai: Singing Red Enhance Pride and Solidarity of the Chinese People), *Chongqing Daily*, 8 July 2011; '*He Shizhong: 'Chang hong' shi jiankang youyi de qunzhongxing wenhua huodong*' (He Shizhong: Singing Red Is a Beneficial Cultural Activity for the Masses), *Chongqing Daily*, 11 July 2011.
3 Peng Li and Fang He. '*Hongse de liliang*' (The Power of Red), *Chongqing Daily*, 29 June 2011.
4 'Building the Great Wall' is a vernacular way of referring to play Mah-jongg.
5 Interview with A19.
6 Interview with A21.
7 Interview with C24.
8 Interview with C06.
9 Interview with A21.
10 Interview with A20.
11 Interview with B01.
12 Interview with B04.
13 Interview with B04.
14 Interview with B10.
15 Interview with B08.
16 Interview with B13.
17 Interview with B13.
18 Interview with B18.
19 Interview with C16.
20 Interview with C06.
21 Interview with B02.

110 *Official programme: framing*

22 Interview with B03.
23 Interview with B02.
24 Interview with B17.
25 Interview with B08.
26 Interview with C15.
27 Interview with B04.
28 Interview with B08.
29 Interview with B18.
30 Interview with B14.
31 Interview with C04.
32 Interview with C19.
33 Interview with C21.
34 Interview with C09.
35 'Azalea' is a folk song that celebrates the relationship between the Red Army and the local people. It was a popular choice by people during the Red culture campaign.
36 Interview with C21.
37 Interview with C11.
38 Interview with C04.
39 Interview with C21.
40 Interview with C09.
41 Wang's 'double indictment' pledge was originated from his claim in 2010 that the police should have the right to sue both the newspaper and the journalists if they produced distorted and unfair reportage on the police force. It was a response to criticisms on Chongqing's 'Smashing Black' campaign.
42 Interview with C09.
43 Interview with C26.
44 Li and He.
45 '*He Shizhong*', *Chongqing Daily*.
46 Interview with C19.
47 Interview with C22.
48 Interview with A22.
49 Interview with C13.
50 Interview with C26.
51 Interview with C21.
52 Interview with A22.
53 Interview with B23.
54 Interview with A23.
55 Interview with A21.
56 Interview with B18.

Bibliography

'*Bo Xilai: chang xiang zhuxuanlu, ningju jingqishen*' (Bo Xilai: Sing Aloud and Spirit Up), *Chongqing Daily*, 23 June 2009

'*Bo Xilai: hongge changchule zanzhongguoren de zihaogan he ningjuli*' (Bo Xilai: Singing Red Enhance Pride and Solidarity of the Chinese People), *Chongqing Daily*, 8 July 2011

Ferguson, Kennan, *The Politics of Judgment: Aesthetics, Identity, and Political Theory* (Lanham: Lexington Books, 2007)

'*He Shizhong: 'chang hong' shi jiankang youyi de qunzhongxing wenhua huodong*' (He Shizhong: Singing Red Is a Beneficial Cultural Activity for the Masses), *Chongqing Daily*, 11 July 2011

Li, Peng and Fang He. '*Hongse de liliang*' (The Power of Red), *Chongqing Daily*, 29 June 2011

8　Conclusion

This book examines the nature of Chongqing's Red culture campaign as well as the ordinary people's experiences during the execution of the campaign. It examines whether Chongqing's Red culture campaign was a genuine Maoist mass campaign and the interactive relationship between the Chinese Communist Party's (CCP's) political power and the everyday life of the ordinary people. It is an original and timely contribution to the understanding of a recent event of political significance in China. Whilst most existing studies focused on the elite politics that underpinned the fate of Bo Xilai's 'Chongqing Model', this research demonstrates that the social implications of the case went beyond the power struggles and were rooted within a more obscure and ordinary layer of social life. In contrast to the often dramatic presentation of political campaigns, this often neglected facet of the ordinariness of a campaign that was home to a wide variety of seemingly trivial acts and judgments carried out by its participants. Although the participants had extremely limited power either to initiate or terminate the political programme, their practices made up the real foundation for the social existence of the Red culture campaign during its implementation, which deflected the common assumption that the campaign was merely a tool for ideological indoctrination. Therefore, the significance of this campaign cannot be fully appreciated without an understanding of the actual experiences of the millions of participants.

Chongqing's Red culture campaign as simulation

I draw on Baudrillard's concept of simulation and argue that Chongqing's Red culture campaign was not a *real* Maoist mass campaign but demonstrated critical features of simulation. On the surface, Chongqing's Red culture campaign followed the model of a typical Chinese mass campaign. The campaign contained a series of regular and frequent operations that built up the momentum of a campaign that was grand in scale and influential in effect. Music was used as one of the most critical tools in mobilising the participation of the local people in the campaign. The 'mass-line' approach was strenuously pursued so that the dictum of 'coming from the masses, going to the masses' could be *performed*. Yet despite appearing like a classic mass campaign, Chongqing's Red culture campaign nevertheless displayed the critical features of simulation. The campaign contained a

112   Conclusion

process during which representations of reality were liquidated by the power of the political. The concept of Red, which traditionally connotes the revolutionary spirits of the Communist Party, was stretched to such an extent that it stopped making references to specific values. Moreover, Chongqing's Red culture programme demonstrated features of being a self-induced, inwardly-enfolded, and non-dialectical power circuit. The Red culture campaign relied not on a mutual understanding of the significance of the programme between the performers and the audience but on an exchange of the signs and meanings within the structures of the political power itself. Chongqing's Red culture campaign did not mobilise the masses to accomplish action that would help substantiate the concrete ideas promoted in propaganda. It did not aim to generate certain actions that would facilitate the implementation of specific policies or help achieve political goals. This is the most critical point where Chongqing's Red culture campaign differed from a genuine political or ideological campaign.

The existence of disassociative aspects within the relationship between the official political programme as simulation and its participants further raised the question of whether legitimacy is relevant in comprehending the case of Chongqing's Red culture campaign. Mass campaigns are generally considered as an important method to legitimise authority and are typically used to acquire political power. On the surface, Chongqing's Red culture campaign looked exactly like such a mass campaign. Only, as demonstrated in this book, it was in fact much more interested in *demonstrating* the existence of power by *performing* it than actually pursuing real power or using it to acquire legitimacy.

There are both positive and negative implications regarding the fact that the Red culture campaign was simulation. On the one hand, the process of liquidating the substantial representation for the notion of Red allowed some degree of freedom for the participants to sing songs of their own choice in many occasions during the campaign. In the case of the second- and third-level performances, this degree of freedom to choose songs that the performers liked was considerable. Some of the retirees chose songs that expressed strong personal emotions, such as 'Meeting at Aobao' (*aobao xianghui* 《敖包相会》) and 'Wasted Years' (*cuotuo suiyue* 《蹉跎岁月》).[1] Some of the younger people took the liberty of choosing a popularised version of an old song, such as 'Play the Drum and Sing the Song' (*da qi shougu chang qi ge* 《打起手鼓唱起歌》). This degree of liberty could alleviate some of the more normative and repressive pressure that came from a strongly enforced, top-down political programme. Similarly, because the political power that initiated the Red culture campaign was preoccupied with having a conversation within the singular circuit of political power, there was significantly less pressure on the participants actually to practice or buy into the specific ideas sold by the campaign. All they were required to do was to *perform* a superficial conformity, and they were largely left to pursue whichever ideas and values they deemed truly important in their personal lives. They were not forced to engage in practices that would significantly alter the existing social and political structures of their lives. This limited scope of social impact as a result of the nature of the programme being an inwardly enfolded and non-dialectical simulation allowed

Conclusion 113

space for creativity on the part of the participants. Because of the official programme's disinterest in the *real* mental and practical lives of the participants, they found it convenient to comply with the political performance instead of trying to fight the political pressure. At the same time, in tandem with the previous characteristics of 'liquidating the referentials', this self-induced political power of simulation allowed space for spiritual freedom, enabling the participants to make subjective judgments as well as space for the production of multiple systems of meanings for their own experiences and practices.

On the other hand, however, the process of liquidating the referentials is also associated with the danger of the 'murderous capacity' of simulation. The liquidation of the references to the real threatened the distinction between right and wrong, true and false. The real danger of such campaigns lies in the fact that people were well aware that the political campaign had stopped concerning what it appeared to be dealing with – the good and evil, right and wrong, true and false. The population is becoming increasingly disillusioned and cynical with politics.

Patterns of the participants' practice and how it interacted with the official programme

The Red culture campaign, however, was not simply a simulation. The practices of the participants, by enabling resource exchanges and the framing of meaning, broke the circuit of the singular power of simulation and provided a layer of everyday life to the political programme. With regard to the patterns of practice by the participants of the campaign, all three social groups, the retirees, the university students, and the employees, participated in the first level of participation, which required strenuous rehearsals and good connections with the organizing bodies. All three social groups participated in the second level of participation. The organization of second-level participation was highly dependent on the initiative and commitment of the organizations to which the participants belonged. Because the effect of such activities was mainly restricted within the organizing communities, there tended to be more freedom when choosing songs for such performances in comparison with the activities at a higher level. On the other hand, only retirees participated in self-organized practices in public parks and squares at the third level of participation. There was no restriction about which songs could be sung at these occasions. Voluntary participation in the campaign meant that a high level of genuine interest was taken in the activities. Yet, the investment in terms of time and energy varied significantly among the participants at this level. In general, higher levels of participation entailed higher levels of organization and higher levels of quality of the performance.

The two forms of the interactive relationships examined in this book are exchange and framing. In the case of exchange, resources flowed both ways between the political programme and the local resident's Red-themed activities. Resources here consisted of not only pecuniary investment in the staging of Red-themed shows but also media support, political endorsement, as well as the time, energy, and emotional commitment of the participants. The political programme

114   *Conclusion*

of Chongqing's Red culture campaign utilised a large amount of resources. Government directives were issued to urge the local governments as well as various social organizations to contribute to the campaign. The 'political pressure' felt by social groups and individuals to cater to the endeavours of the municipality's leadership was a critical force used to mobilise resources as well. At the same time, the practices of the three social groups investigated in this project – the retirees, university students, and employees – employed their own sets of resources. A certain amount of pecuniary resources was essential for carrying out activities. Moreover, cultural competence, performing opportunities, and the professional competence and connections of the teachers and conductors were all important resources that made the activities of the participants possible and sustainable. One of the major differences was that the retirees invested much more emotional resources, such as the sentiment of nostalgia, into their practices than the other two groups of participants.

At the same time, both the official programme and the participants also actively framed the meaning of the campaign and judged their experiences and the effectiveness of the programme. The frames evoked by the official programme consisted of a number of dichotomised value judgments, such as the progressive revolutionary spirit versus the vulgar, materialistic culture and inequality versus 'common prosperity' and corruption among the cadres versus the commitment to serve the people. In the meantime, the participants were capable of using their own criteria in their framing processes, which were intimately linked to their personal experiences, memories of the past, and hopes for the future. To the retirees, health benefits, artistic appreciation, a sense of belonging and self-worth, and the pursuit of happiness were what attracted them to the programme. To the students, the benefits in the form of self-development and friendship were what they valued. To the employees, job security, political correctness, and corporate culture were the advantages worth pursuing. The participants were also capable of distinguishing the 'keyings' from the primary frameworks. That is, they read between the lines of the official narrative and were able to identify motivations and goals of the campaign that were not explicitly articulated in public. At certain points, the local people gave interpretations of both the meaning and significance of the campaign that contended the official narrative. Judgments made in the processes of framing constitute the first step towards rejecting symbolic domination, imagining the alternative, and reorganizing social relations.

Reciprocity was thus observed between the forceful political campaign and its practitioners. This meant that the Party politics needed the people as much as the people needed the Party and the government. Yet reciprocity does not presume relations of equality. As shown in the case of Chongqing's Red culture campaign, the relationship between the political power of the initiator and implementer of campaign and the millions of participants was certainly unequal. The practices of the participants demonstrated a high level of conformity to the requirements of the official programme. No active resistance was observed. There was evidently normative pressure when people were asked to participate by their superiors at work or school. For the first- and second-level participation, the participants followed

Conclusion 115

the guidelines laid down by the performance organizers and chose the content of the performances accordingly and carefully. There was a considerable amount of sacrifice of personal leisure by the participants. Sometimes the activities were carried out at the expense of their normal working or studying hours. Nevertheless, most of the participants chose to comply with the requirements despite their complaints and dissatisfaction. Moreover, the values of the Red culture campaign, as interpreted by the participants, generally followed the official storylines.

On the other hand, relationships of unequal power do not exclude elements of resistance and deflection on the part of the weaker. As shown in the preceding chapters, the interactive processes of exchange and framing gave birth to creativity and acts of reappropriation. It provided opportunities for ordinary people to make a *tactical* effect on the official programme. Creativity was possible when the official programme and the practices of the participants engaged in a form of exchange and actively appropriated each other into their respective courses of development. The participants were capable of garnering financial and political support from a strong government and then used this to meet their own personal and practical needs. In the case of the Red culture campaign, the practices of the participants could hardly be characterised as outright resistance. Yet they constituted tactics that served the interest of the practitioners and challenged the monolithic and authoritarian power circuit of the ruling party.

Social and political implications

The examination of the interactive space between the political power and the practices of ordinary people helps us understand the discrepancies between a designed political programme or policies and what it actually morphs into once implemented on the ground. As Midgal argues, the often mixed results of policy implementation are not simply because they are poorly-designed, carried out by incompetent cadres, or resource deficient.[2] As has been shown in the case of the Red culture campaign, the implementation of a political programme or policy is often a sophisticated story about how politics, administrative power, institutional structures, ideology, collective and individual memories of the past, as well as ordinary people's most pressing needs and grievances become entangled and manifest themselves. What has often been overshadowed by the extraordinariness of political campaigns is a layer of social life that is much more banal but equally consequential in affecting the outcomes of programmes, even when the people have no substantial power over designing or terminating it. It has been shown in the case of the Red culture campaign that the different sets of resources available in the everyday lives of the participants, and the most minute but pressing needs and grievances of their personal lives, often conditioned their levels of involvement and dictated the subjective evaluations of their experiences.

Moreover, different social groups had different needs and grievances in accordance with their age groups and social positions. 'Generation' was a critical factor that affected the participants' judgment of the political programme. Although the probably non-representative samples of this research could not speak for the

116 *Conclusion*

larger population in Chongqing, far less the whole nation, some of these needs and grievances, such as how the elderly craved a sense of community, how the students struggled for self-development and better career prospects, and how the employees valued political security more than personal artistic taste, should resonate with the general social conditions under which many ordinary Chinese people deal with the political and institutional structures of contemporary society. These findings should be able to shed light on future design and evaluation of government projects and political programmes as their implementations will inevitably be filtered by this layer of social life that is composed by the conduct and mentality of different generations of ordinary people. Although the Red culture campaign as a political programme went bankrupt, as Bo was sacked from his office, the ways in which it was organized, implemented, received, and appropriated by the public and the ordinary participants shed light on deep and long-lasting questions about the ideological control of the CCP, the prospect of building a stronger social realm, and the future of political reform in China.

Lastly, the fact that the political power underpinning Chongqing's Red culture campaign demonstrated features of being a self-induced, monolithic closed circuit sheds light on how the future relationship between the CCP and its people could possibly evolve from another perspective. In Chapter 3, I discussed a rather complex and ambiguous relationship between the different fractions of political power within the CCP's leadership. It is necessary to emphasise again that despite the contradictions between Chongqing's Red culture campaign and the general direction of the cultural and ideological reforms in China, the logic of power demonstrated in the case of the Red culture campaign was inherent to the power of the ruling party. As China deepens its reforms, whether the political programmes and government policies will evolve to contain more elements of simulation, which according to Baudrillard haunts the late modern capitalist societies, will have a profound effect on how the relationship between the CCP and the people will evolve. In the short run, as shown in the case of the Red culture campaign, the fact that the political programme shows features of a simulation in fact helps enlarge the space for creative and tactical practices. In the long run, however, if the political power starts to communicate within only a small circuit of its own, it will become further detached from the lives of the masses and gradually lose its ability to adapt to the ever-changing circumstances of society, which so far has been considered a critical asset of the CCP, helping the Party maintain its resilient authoritarianism and a relatively high level of political legitimacy. Baudrillard's warnings against the domination of signs and the dissolution of moral principles are practical issues that China is facing or will have to struggle with in the coming future.

Notes

1 'Meeting at Aobao' (*aobao xianghui* 《敖包相会》) was a love song popularised after the founding of the People's Republic of China. 'Wasted Years' (*cuotuo suiyue* 《蹉跎岁月》) was produced in 1982 as the theme for a TV serial about educated youth who were sent to the countryside during the Cultural Revolution.
2 Joel S. Migdal, *State in Society: Studying How States and Societies Transform and Constitute One Another* (Cambridge: Cambridge University Press, 2001), p. 12.

Epilogue
Understanding the case of Chongqing

The Red culture campaign was only a part of the larger political project brought to Chongqing by Bo Xilai. Thus, a brief note on Bo's fate and its implications in the context of China's reform are in order. Understandably, political analysts tend to situate Bo's case within the context of China's elite politics and perceive it as the result of the political infighting among the different factions within the Chinese Communist Party (CCP). Elite factionalism constitutes a crucial aspect of China's politics. Political factions, '*guan-xi* based, vertically organized, reciprocity-oriented', form the power basis for political elites to seek 'security, material interests, and ideological and policy commitments'.[1] In China, ambitious individuals pursuing a political career within the Party establishment require the patronage of powerful figures.[2] Zheng Yongnian points out that it is almost certain that the final name list for Politburo Standing Committee (PBSC) is beyond the personal interests or ambition of the candidates. What underlie them are the entrenched power factions within the Party enterprise.[3]

In the absence of a supreme leader, such as Mao Zedong or Deng Xiaoping, it is believed the PBSC is ruled by Party officials from two rival political coalitions – the 'Youth League group' (*tuanpai* 团派) and the 'princelings' (*taizidang* 太子党). Most of the members of the 'Youth League group' climb the ladder of leadership by working for the Chinese Communist Youth League. The former general Party secretary and president, Hu Jintao, and the current premier, Li Keqiang, are believed to belong to this political camp. They tend to show a strong willingness to address social problems and are considered sympathetic to popular grievances. The 'princelings' were born into the Red families of the revolutionary leaders and political elites and tend to have much better access to high-level political and social connections than ordinary people. They are likely to develop a sense of entitlement to running the country.[4] Solidarity among the members of a particular faction is based on two possible types of connection: the value-rational relationship and the purpose-rational relationship. In the former case, the relationship itself is valued for its intrinsic significance, whereas in the latter case, connections are built to achieve certain common goals. In the reform era, purpose-rational relationships are overtaking the value-rational ones as the major types of relationships that underpin the political factions in China.[5] Of course, the real political game is likely to be far more complicated than the simple division between the

118   *Epilogue*

tuanpai and the 'princelings', which is primarily based on value-rational connections. The different factions within the Party were based on more complicated personal relations, historical lineages, as well as the constant evolution of personal interests and career prospects.

It may also be too early to fully comprehend the political and institutional implications of Bo's case for the establishment of the CCP. What happened exactly in terms of the power struggle within the circle of the political elite remains subject to speculation. At the time of writing this book, political figures of higher status than Bo (e.g., Zhou Yongkang), among a large group of officials and bureaucrats accused of corruption, had been prosecuted. Bo's case might only be a small part of a much larger and complicated case of power struggle taking place within the strata of political elites of the CCP. Nevertheless, Bo's case can still help us understand the culture of China's politics. One thing that may have made Bo's downfall particularly scandalous for the ruling party was the fact that it challenged the implicit mutual agreement among the CCP's ruling elites on unity, consensus, and discretion in public. The subculture of civility among China's political elites decrees the avoidance of the public exhibition of ideological and policy disagreement. Although factional divisions and struggles have always existed within the Party, they had been painstakingly kept behind closed doors. Emphasising unity and discretion is a major characteristic of the CCP's public image control designed to ensure 'the appearance of increasing stability and managerial competence'.[6] Yet, the 'Chongqing incident' destroyed the carefully-crafted image of unity and consensus within China's ruling stratum, which proved to be highly divided and contentious.[7] Zheng points out that Bo's scandal revealed troubled elite politics in China that still relies deeply on political instincts rather than formal competition in power transitions. He argues that China's elite politics is a defective system that is unable to resolve the power struggles at the top.[8] Moreover, Bo's case challenged the carefully-constructed logical link between the internal Party consensus and its ruling competence. The CCP has worked hard to demonstrate that Party consensus is imperative for ruling competence. In Bo Xilai's case, however, it was evident that a Party cadre could be exceptionally competent but disrespectful of the Party consensus. Hence, Party unity might prove less valuable, as the Party would like the people to believe. Even worse, Bo's popularity among the local people, even after his prosecution, might have indicated that the masses would prefer competence over Party unity. Unity and consensus, on the other hand, could rather be interpreted as signs of mediocracy and complacency.

The analysis of Chongqing's Red culture campaign, as well as Bo Xilai's larger project, should be put into the context of China's political and social reforms. To some extent, many of Bo's policies, which emphasised the decisive role of the masses in transforming society and enforced strict discipline over the local cadres, responded to some of the existing problems that had resulted from the decades of political reform or lack of political reform. The attempt to strengthen the party institutions and curb the initiatives of the 'masses' in the aftermath of the Cultural Revolution (CR) has suppressed the political and social vibrancy in China. The masses were removed from the process of formulating Party policies.

Formally designated forms of political participation, such as petitioning, have proved ineffective, and at times extremely problematic, in alleviating tensions and resolving grievances in current Chinese society. The Party has apparently been extremely wary of mass participation that is not directly controlled or carefully monitored. On the other hand, the concentration of unchecked power continues to provide the structural foundation for the rampant corruption among party officials. Individual cadres continue to tread on party regulations and formal laws.[9] The widespread corruption among its cadres has significantly jeopardised the moral legitimacy of the CCP and become a major source of anger that has been brewing among the masses, especially the lower stratum of society. Similarly, Bo's social policies, which emphasised the notion of 'common prosperity', brought about quick, tangible changes in the outlook of the city and easily won popular sympathy and support among a population that was feeling increasingly insecure in a competitive and materialistic society. However, in the case of Bo's social policies, although many of them catered for the local people's most immediate needs, these policies nevertheless helped reinforce a paternalistic image of the Party and sent out worrying signs about the personality cult of a strong leader. Moreover, the heavy restriction and censorship imposed on the media and public dissent, as well as the willingness to tamper with the rule of law, ran counterproductive to fostering a strong, lawful, and open society, as most of the supporters of China's reform would like to see. Although the Red culture campaign hardly promoted social division or political struggles, the implications associated with the revival of Maoist campaigns was troubling and detrimental to the narrative of promoting deeper political reforms. In this respect, it is unsurprising that critics of Chongqing's Red culture campaign constantly compared it with the CR.

The eventual bankruptcy of Bo Xilai's project was unsurprising. Both he and his project were too much of a maverick in the current political discourse and culture of the ruling Party. Since the 1990s, the power transitions among the top leadership have been relatively peaceful compared to previous decades. Bo Xilai's barely concealed personal ambition, as well as his willingness to step out of line, went against the tide as the Party tried to institutionalise and stabilise the power transition at the top. Moreover, Bo Xilai's repeated references to Mao's teachings and his populist appeal that won wide support from the ultra-Leftists were alarming to the ruling Party, who has categorically rejected the CR in the 1981 'Resolution on Certain Questions in the History of Our Party' (*Guanyu jianguoyilai dang de ruogan lishi wenti de jueyi*). In the post-Mao era, the CCP continues to reorient itself as a ruling party that pursues economic modernisation and better social management instead of a revolutionary party.

Notes

1 Lowell Dittmer and Yu-Shan Wu, 'Leadership Coalitions and Economic Transformation in Reform China: Revisiting the Political Business Cycle', in *China's Deep Reform: Domestic Politics in Transition*, ed. by Lowell Dittmer and Guoli Liu (Oxford: Rowman & Littlefield Publisher, INC, 2006), p. 72.

120 *Epilogue*

2 Tony Saich, *Governance and Politics in China* (London: Palgrave Macmillan, 2011), pp. 110, 112.
3 Yongnian Zheng, 'China in 2011: Anger, Political Consciousness, Anxiety, and Uncertainty', *Asian Survey*, 52 (2012), 28–41.
4 Cheng Li and Ryan McElveen, 'Bo Xilai's Poisonous Legacy', *New York Times*, 22 August 2012; Cheng Li, 'China's Team of Rivals', *Foreign Policy*, 171 (2009), 88–93.
5 Dittmer and Wu, 'Leadership Coalitions and Economic Transformation in Reform China', p. 52.
6 Lowell Dittmer and William Hurst, 'Analysis in Limbo? Contemporary Chinese Politics Amid the Maturation of Reform', in *China's Deep Reform: Domestic Politics in Transition*, ed. by Lowell Dittmer and Guoli Liu (Oxford: Rowman & Littlefield Publisher, INC, 2006), pp. 26, 28.
7 For example, Alice Miller, 'The Meaning of Bo Xilai', *Wall Street Journal*, 9 August 2012; Li and McElveen, 'Bo Xilai's Poisonous Legacy'.
8 Yongnian Zheng, 'China in 2012: Troubled Elite, Frustrated Society', *Asian Survey*, 53 (2013), 162–75.
9 Saich, *Governance and Politics in China*, pp. 131, 141, 143, 210–1.

Bibliography

Dittmer, Lowell and William Hurst, 'Analysis in Limbo? Contemporary Chinese Politics Amid the Maturation of Reform', in Lowell Dittmer and Guoli Liu, eds, *China's Deep Reform: Domestic Politics in Transition* (Oxford: Rowman & Littlefield Publisher, INC, 2006), pp. 25–48
Dittmer, Lowell and Yu-Shan Wu, 'Leadership Coalitions and Economic Transformation in Reform China: Revisiting the Political Business Cycle', in Lowell Dittmer and Guoli Liu, eds, *China's Deep Reform: Domestic Politics in Transition* (Oxford: Rowman & Littlefield Publisher, INC, 2006), pp. 49–80Li, Cheng, 'China's Team of Rivals', *Foreign Policy*, 171 (2009), 88–93
Li, Cheng and Ryan McElveen, 'Bo Xilai's Poisonous Legacy', *New York Times*, 22 August 2012
Migdal, Joel S., *State in Society: Studying How States and Societies Transform and Constitute One Another* (Cambridge: Cambridge University Press, 2001)
Miller, Alice, 'The Meaning of Bo Xilai', *Wall Street Journal*, 9 August 2012
Saich, Tony, *Governance and Politics in China* (London: Palgrave Macmillan, 2011)
Zheng, Yongnian, 'China in 2011: Anger, Political Consciousness, Anxiety, and Uncertainty', *Asian Survey*, 52 (2012), 28–41
——— 'China in 2012: Troubled Elite, Frustrated Society', *Asian Survey*, 53 (2013), 162–75

Appendix I
Research methods

This research is a case study of Chongqing's Red culture campaign. A case study is 'an intensive study of a single unit with an aim to generalise across a larger set of units'.[1] A unit here refers to a social phenomenon that is 'spatially bounded' and observed at 'discrete points in time'.[2] A case study has a unique advantage in capturing the depth, complexity, and subtlety of social processes.[3] It is adopted here to capture the processes of interaction between the political power and the individuals' practices during the campaign, which continuously unfolds, diverts, and morphs during the course of its development. A qualitative approach is employed in this research for it has a better chance of capturing the lived experiences of social actors and the nuances of their own interpretation of their experiences. It is also the only feasible approach because it was extremely difficult to obtain official permission to execute large-scale surveys due to the sensitive nature of this topic. Because this research utilises qualitative methods, thus entailing a large quantity of relatively unstructured data, it is particularly imperative for the process of data collection and analysis to be made as explicit as possible.[4]

I. The case of the Red culture campaign

The particular case of Chongqing's Red culture campaign cannot represent all contemporary political or cultural campaigns in China. I do not attempt to generalise the findings of this case to other cultural and political campaigns in China, either past or present. However, it exhibits some shared features with other mass campaigns that have occurred during the history of the Chinese Communist Party (CCP) and at the same time demonstrates sufficient uniqueness to merit special, detailed scholarly treatment. Thus, the findings about Chongqing's Red culture campaign can be compared to those other campaigns, past or future.

There are a number of reasons for choosing this particular case for scholarly treatment. Firstly, it is a highly unusual one. As Charles Ragin argues, 'it is not simply generality . . . that makes phenomena socially significant. . . . [S]ome . . . are significant . . . because they are rare, unusual, or extreme in some way'.[5] Chongqing's Red culture campaign was remarkable and significant not only because the mobilisation was carried out on an impressive scale, or that it affected relatively deeply the work and lives of the ordinary people of Chongqing, but also

122 *Appendix I*

because it occurred at a time when mass campaigns were thought to be fading out in the history of the CCP as a major source of political legitimacy. Perceived as the 'resurrection' of an old-style mass campaign, the case of Chongqing's Red culture campaign took place at a time when decades of economic liberalisation and social reform had made the memories of the Maoist-style mass campaigns sufficiently distant for today's Chinese people, especially the younger generation. Bo Xilai's decision to resurrect this method of political mobilisation seemed to be swimming against the tide of history and was thus deemed an unusual political manoeuvre. Moreover, both the initiation and termination of the campaign were associated with a political drama that involved the spectacular downfall of Bo. The event was believed to be momentous during the recent decades of the CCP's internal power struggles. Much criticism launched against Bo focused on the implications of Chongqing's Red culture campaign. Thus the significance of this case extends beyond an ideological endeavour of a local Party leader. Secondly, the case is a very recent event. This research is a timely effort to record the experiences of the participants in the campaign, which will be very difficult to retrieve as time passes. This research project does not interpret the significance of this case through the lens of the power struggles among the different political fractions among the Party elites but rather treats it as one specific case through which a sociological investigation can be launched into the interactive processes between the political power and the power of everyday life in current Chinese society.

II. Fieldwork

The fieldwork took place during two main periods between September 2011 and June 2013. The first phase lasted for seven months, between September 2011 and March 2012. During the initial stage of the fieldwork, the main task was to establish connections with the 'gatekeepers' of the field, such as the leaders of the student groups at universities, the conductors of choruses, the managers of companies, and so on. After familiarising myself with the major players in the field, I set up a schedule for visiting the targeted parks and choruses regularly – once or twice per week, depending on the frequency of the activities. Interviews were set up with the participants in the Red-themed activities. Some interviewees were invited for interview via cold-calling; others were introduced by the 'gatekeepers'.

As the fieldwork progressed, I started to explore this field in greater depth. Variation was attempted in recruiting interviewees so that the sample of participants would cover different genders, age groups, and occupations. I also attempted to contact participants whose work was intrinsically related to the campaign to gain 'insider's information' about the running of the campaign. It was particularly important to build up rapport with the participants of the programme at this stage so that some of the interviewees could be revisited later. In light of the sensitive nature of the topic, building trust with the interviewees was critical. Once trust was built, some interviewees would offer additional information 'off the record', which was used to supplement and validate the interview data. Moreover, the use of the snowballing technique also relied on a sufficient amount of trust between the researcher and the interviewee. The interviewees were often very cautious about introducing other potential interviewees, including their own family members, friends, and colleagues.

During the last two weeks of the first fieldwork period, in March 2012, I focused on verifying the existing data by revisiting most of the major fieldwork locations. It is worth mentioning here that a dramatic political change occurred in the field during February and March 2012, when the Chongqing's Party secretary, Bo Xilai, was removed from office.[6] Against this backdrop of precarious political conditions, which was making some interviewees feel anxious and confused, it proved more difficult to identify possible interviewees during the last two weeks of the first round of the fieldwork. The first round of fieldwork was thus followed by a brief, week-long revisiting of Chongqing in June 2012. Although many questions about Bo and his family remained, the initial shock resulting from Bo's downfall was beginning to subside by then. The main goal of this revisit was to gain a sense of local public opinion a few months after the political drama began to unfold. I was curious to learn whether people's attitudes about the programme had changed due to the charges being made against the municipality's leadership and also wished to observe whether any concrete changes had taken place in the cultural lives of the local residents or in the physical environment, for example, whether people still gathered together to sing Red songs in public spaces, whether the slogans and posters were still visible on the walls, and so on.

The second round of fieldwork lasted about a month, between May 2013 and June 2013. By this stage, I had begun the data analysis and formulated the key categories and some preliminary hypotheses. The goal of this trip was to acquire supplementary data about the employees, one of the three major social groups interviewed for this project. During the first round of fieldwork, the employees were more likely to be restrained about sharing their opinions about the political campaign as it was still ongoing and Bo Xilai was still the formidable Party leader in the city. It was believed that the political environment would be more relaxed a year after Bo left his post. Chongqing had a new Party secretary and was embarking on a new journey in terms of policy formation and implementation. At the same time, Bo's case was entering the final stage of trials and sentencing. I believed it necessary to revisit the site for a substantial period of time to catch up with the latest developments in the process of Chongqing's 'de-Bo Xilaization' and how people felt and interpreted the change in the political landscape of their city. Nevertheless, the data collected during this round of fieldwork (except for the formal interviews) were mainly for supplementary use. I did not attempt to make a fully-fledged comparison of the Singing Red activities in Chongqing during the Bo era and in the post-Bo era. Data were not collected as systematically as during the first round of fieldwork. The reader will be reminded whenever the participants' interpretation of the political event was obtained during the second fieldtrip period as it is likely that the subjective judgments made about the campaign would vary between the two periods of fieldwork, given that the political contexts were significantly different. Care will therefore be taken to identify during which of the three trips the data were collected.

III. Conceptualisation

The case of the Red culture campaign is treated as two different conceptual entities. It contains firstly the 'Red culture programme', which refers to the official programme as designed, or intended, by its initiator. Secondly, the Red culture campaign contains also the practices of its participants, which also consist of two components: 1) the lived experiences of it participants during the course of its implementation, that is, the patterns and levels of involvement, and 2) their subjective judgments of the experiences and the programme in general. 'Ordinary people' in this project refers to the participants who are *not* involved in the design or initiation of the programme. They are not high-level government officials. They are not engaged in narrating the Red culture campaign to legitimise its existence.

One of the key concepts used in this book is simulation. I examine to what extent Chongqing's Red culture campaign can be characterised as simulation by looking at evidence that matches or contradicts each of the main features of simulation proposed in Baudrillard's theory. I also use de Certeau's concept of 'strategy' and 'tactics' to characterise the programme of the Red culture campaign and the practices of the participants. When examining the political programme and the practices of ordinary people, I look for official, established and rationalised rules that underpin the Red Culture campaign. I investigate the particular rules and norms followed by the participants, the habits and routines brought into the practices, as well as the metaphors and assumptions evoked in the process of participation. I pay specific attention to the amount and variety of resources utilised in the campaign, including both human and nonhuman resources, such as musical instruments, rehearsal venues, performance opportunities, and so on.

IV. Sampling

Sampling techniques

The sampling techniques used in this research project include typical case, maximum variation, and snowball sampling. The participants in the campaign who were interviewed for this project consisted of three social groups of 'ordinary people': retirees, university students, and employees. They were typical examples of the local people who participated in the Red culture campaign.[7] The university students included both undergraduate and graduate students. The term 'employee' here refers to people in the workforce. They were the employees of government bureaucracy, state-owned enterprises (SOEs), and private companies. The interviewees were recruited if they fitted into these three specific social groups under investigation. Unfortunately, no reliable statistical data were available about the Red culture campaign that could be used to guide the sampling procedures. I did not attempt to generate a representative sample for the purpose of the research is to obtain an in-depth understanding of the participants' subjective experiences as well as the process of meaning making during their participation. Nevertheless, variation was attempted. Shared and differing patterns of practices were sought within and across different groups of participants. While recruiting interviewees for these groups, the snowballing technique was used. The interviewees were encouraged to recommend other candidates with similar experiences to the researcher.

V. Data collection

Three main techniques were used during the data collection process: interviews, observation, and documentary analysis. The use of a combination of techniques made it possible to gather relevant information from channels that were as diverse as possible. Five pilot interviews were conducted before the formal process of the data collection began. During the pilot interviews, several problems emerged. For example, the retirees tended to feel uncomfortable with a formal manner of questioning, and the interviewees in general tended to hold back when asked directly about their evaluation of the programme or specific politicians. Responding to these problems, I decided to modify the structure of the interview guidelines for the retirees and rewrite the list of questions on subjective judgments.

(i) Individual interviews

Interviews were conducted to access information on the practices of the participants in the Red culture campaign. Interviewing is a social occasion where the interaction between the interviewer and interviewee has an impact on the data generated. Therefore, interviews do not necessarily capture the 'genuine voices' of the participants.[8] Nevertheless, interviewing helps the researcher penetrate the participants' perspectives, which are 'meaningful, knowable, and able to be made explicit'.[9]

The interviews conducted for this research project were semi-structured. An interview guide was used to provide a set of broad themes to pursue during the conversation. However, while discussing each topic, I tried to remain flexible about exploring and probing into specific questions. There were two major subject areas of enquiry: the experience of participating in the programme and the participants' judgment of the programme. The interviewees were allowed to elaborate on topics of particular interest and initiate new themes, provided that they were related to the general subject matter under investigation. A typical interview started with questions about the relatively noncontroversial aspects of the participants' experiences, such as the frequency and routines of their participation in the Red cultural programme. After the interviewees had described their activities, they were invited to express their feelings about and judgments of the experiences. While conducting the interviews, the guideline used with the university students was more formalised than the ones used with retirees and employees. The retirees' interviews tended to be most conversational and informal, largely due to the circumstances under which they were conducted. The university students' interviews usually took place on campus and were prearranged. The students were relatively comfortable about being interviewed in a more structured manner. The

126 *Appendix I*

retirees' interviews, however, were more opportunistic, taking place in parks, public squares, or community centres and sometimes taking the form of a casual chat. The retirees were less comfortable with formal interviews and tended to hold back when confronted with 'serious' questions, such as being asked explicitly about their opinions of the government programmes and cadres. In the case of the employees, as most of the interviews took place in their workplace, the depth and length of the interviews fluctuated in accordance with their availability at the time. Due to the sensitivity of the topic, the employees tended to say far less about their personal judgment of the programme than the other two groups, especially when they were interviewed in their workplace.

(ii) Group interviews

Two group interviews were conducted with retirees from the same dancing team at the community centre where they practiced every week. The interviews were conducted in small groups (one with four people and the other with three) at the request of the team members. The interviewees knew each other relatively well and felt more comfortable chatting in each other's company than being interviewed individually. The strengths of group interviews included broader access to a variety of data from different interviewees during a single interview and improved data quality due to the interviewees placing 'checks and balances on each other'.[10] The weaknesses, however, were obvious. In both group interviews, one of the interviewees tended to dominate the discussion. This was usually someone who held a senior position in the team or had a particularly outspoken personality. Although I tried to alleviate the problem by explicitly inviting the other interviewees to respond to the questions, it nevertheless caused an imbalance in the quantity and quality of the interviewees' responses. Moreover, despite the fact that the group members' close acquaintance with each other helped to elicit more information, as they felt free to remind each other of possible answers, it still cast doubt on whether this prior relationship might have prevented some interviewees from expressing their true thoughts aloud. Therefore, unless the interviewees strongly wished to be interviewed as a group, individual interviews were preferred. In fact, the majority of the interviews were conducted with a single interviewee.

(iii) Observation

Observation was also used as a key method for data collection in this project. It was employed to gain first-hand information about the physical environment in which the Red-themed activities took place. Moreover, on-site enquiry and observation allowed the researcher to gain information that might be neglected by interviewees who were immersed in the daily routines of the settings. Thirdly, it helped validate some of the data collected through the interviews or supplement information that may have been intentionally omitted by the interviewees. Lastly, the researcher's direct experience with the setting facilitated the subsequent data interpretation.[11]

Appendix I 127

Observation took place in two main types of settings. The first kind was formal performances organized at different institutional levels. One occasion was a dance display in a public square, organized by the local government. The other was the recording of a Red-themed show. A wide variety of performers, including retirees, students, and state-owned company employees, performed in the show, which was to be broadcast on the Chongqing TV channel. On these two occasions, I was merely an observer, with no form of participation; therefore, there was little observer effect on the activities. In the case of the second type of setting, that is, observing activities in public parks and during singing rehearsals, however, I participated in some way, either as a conspicuous audience member or by actually joining in the singing practice when circumstances allowed. Overall, the level of my direct participation was low. I also made sure that my participation was as overt as possible. That is, as long as I had the opportunity, I informed the participants being observed about my intention as a researcher.

The observational data used in this project, however, were limited. The first problem encountered was accessibility. The majority of the observational data collected were related to the retirees' activities. The imbalance in the quantity of data regarding the three social groups was a result of the following conditions. Firstly, the retirees tended to gather together in public parks and community centres, which I could access far more easily than other locations. In the case of the university students and employees, they usually practiced within their own institutions or organizations. Constant negotiation with the gatekeepers, that is, teachers and school officials or company managers, was needed to gain access. Although I succeeded in securing observation opportunities at one university and one company, it proved far more difficult to observe the activities of the students and employees than the retirees. Secondly, the retirees' activities tended to be more frequent and regular than those of the other two groups. It was almost a daily practice for many elderly people. On the other hand, the university students and employees participated in Red-themed activities mainly on special occasions, such as festivals, holidays, and the anniversary of the founding of the Chinese Communist Party (CCP). When I began my fieldwork in Chongqing in October 2011, the campaign was undergoing a quiet period in the aftermath of the busy spring and summer seasons. Therefore, the students and employees' activities were significantly less frequent than before, and hence there were few observation opportunities available.

(iv) Documentary analysis

The use of documents was another data collection method employed in this research project. A key strength of the technique of documentary analysis is that textual data is relatively 'unobtrusive and reactive'.[12] This is not to say that documentary data are neutral or asocial;[13] in fact, the opposite is often true. The creation of texts is a complex process, and once produced, they are often 'multi-functional and multi-vocal'. Analysts must therefore use their own judgment when selecting specific elements of text and using them for interpretation.[14]

128 *Appendix I*

The documents analysed in this case consisted of articles about the Red cultural programme published between May 2008 and March 2012 in *Chongqing Daily*, the Party's newspaper in the municipality. As the mouthpiece of Chongqing's municipal government and the Party Committee, *Chongqing Daily* proved to be the best source for reconstructing the official narrative of the programme that was presented to the public. One feature of the 'official' documents is that they often appear anonymous, when they obviously have to be written by *someone*. As Atkinson and Coffey point out, omitting the author's name is usually an effective way to impose an aura of factual authority.[15] Most of these newspaper articles were produced by a small team of journalists who wrote under the pseudonym '*Xiao Zhu*' (肖竹). Moreover, documents and texts constituted an extremely rich source of information about the nature, organization, and official narrative of the campaign. Therefore, these documents were subjected to both 'direct' and 'indirect' uses.[16] They were directly used when I sought factual information from the texts, for example, the date when a specific directive on the campaign was issued or the number of participants and their affiliated organization for a specific performance. The data were indirectly used when I sought latent information embedded in how the information was imparted, particularly when the speeches of high-level officials were quoted in the texts. The texts were used to construct an official narrative of the Red culture campaign and provided valuable information on how the Chongqing government and its leader wished to present the campaign both to the local residents of Chongqing and the outside world. This information provided critical insights into how Chongqing wished to position the Red culture campaign in the larger context of China's political landscape and how it dealt with some of the criticisms directed at the campaign and therefore implicitly at the leadership of Chongqing.

(iv) Fieldwork notes

A diary was kept to record the tasks and events related to the fieldwork, including details about the interviews, observations, and the researcher's personal reflections and feelings. Of all the interviews conducted, 31 were tape-recorded. The interviews were later transcribed. Some of the non-verbal information, such as the interviewees' facial expressions and general emotional state, were also added to the interview transcription. The rest of the interviews were recorded by making written notes, when the interviewees declined to be recorded. I attempted to record direct quotations as far as possible. However, when verbatim note-taking was impossible, I tried to supplement the original notes with details immediately after the interviews so that as much information could be retained as possible. The researcher's personal feelings or insights were also noted when necessary.

VI. Data analysis and interpretation

Data analysis involves data organization, category generation, data coding, and assortment in accordance with categories, and proposition generation.[17] Data analysis starts with data reduction during the coding and recoding processes. Once data are properly displayed according to their categories, properties, and dimensions, a discussion and some preliminary conclusions can be produced. Data interpretation is a process that occurs throughout the research. It starts when the data collection starts. An interpretive approach helps to yield an in-depth understanding of the nature and significance of people's experiences.

Data organization and category generation

The data were firstly grouped under a few key concepts. They were subjected to a line-by-line 'microscopic examination' during the initial stage of the analysis to generate the initial categories. Categories are concepts under which 'events, happenings, objects, and actions/interactions that are found to be conceptually similar in nature or related in meaning' are grouped. It is worth mentioning that the processes of categorising and conceptualising are reciprocal. Constant adjustment and negotiation are required during the research process. The rudimentary categories that emerged from the first reading of the data collected for this project included 'levels of performance', 'cultural competences', 'resources', 'judgment', and 'memories', 'generation', and so on. A category reaches saturation when no further fresh information emerges during the coding.[18]

Data coding and assortment in accordance with the categories

The data coding involved a combination of theoretical, open, and axial coding. The data were coded theoretically in accordance with the theoretical concepts used.[19] In Chapter 7, for example, the three main social groups under investigation were regrouped into the Cultural Revolution (CR) generation, the generation of youth, and middle-age employees. This regrouping was carried out in accordance with the sociological concept of 'generation' so that the relationship between generation and judgment could be properly analysed.

The open coding, on the other hand, involved identifying concepts through data that have been broken down, examined, and compared. During this process, subcategories, as well as the properties and dimensions of the categories, were further identified and furnished. The properties of a category refer to the 'characteristics of a category', whereas the dimensions refer to 'the range along which general properties of a category vary'.[20] Comparison is a key technique for determining the properties and dimensions of specific concepts. The comparison undertaken in this research was mainly of the three social groups – retirees, university students, and employees – who participated in the Red culture campaign.

The properties of the category of 'level of performance', for example, included: the level of organizational sophistication, the quality of the performances, and the level of publicity. The dimensions of these properties of the experiences included 'high', 'medium', and 'low'. The property of the category of 'cultural competence', for instance, in this case referred to whether an individual's involvement in the programmes had any entry requirement with regard to his/her artistic

130　*Appendix I*

competency. If one had to audition to join a chorus team, the dimension of this property would be 'yes' for the category of 'cultural competence'. If not, then it was 'no' for this category.

Axial coding was also employed in the process of 'relating categories to their subcategories . . .]linking categories at the level of properties and dimensions'.[21] During the process of axial coding, data were reassembled according to the variation in the conditions and consequences of the phenomena under investigation in an attempt to grant greater explanatory power to the concepts. For example, the category of 'generation' was found to be closely associated with the framing processes of one's experience of participating in the Red culture campaign.

VII.　Ethics

Given the sensitivity of this research topic, one of the most important tasks for the researcher was to ensure the safety of the interviewees. Anonymity was strictly enforced throughout the fieldwork and data analysis processes. The researcher also respected the concerns of the interviewees and tried to ensure that they felt as comfortable as possible during the interviews. The interviews were conducted in locations chosen by the interviewees, who were aware of the purpose of the research, the identity of the researcher, and the procedures of the interviews. They were informed that their names and affiliated institutions would not be exposed to the public or appear in research publications produced by the researcher. The interviewees were asked explicitly whether they agreed to be recorded. If they declined, the researcher made handwritten notes as an alternative. The interviewees were notified that they could refuse to answer any question that they did not wish to answer or choose to terminate the interview at any point.

VIII.　Potential problems and limitations

There were a number of problems and limitations that might have affected the results of this research. The biggest threat, still, came from the sensitive nature of the topic. It would be problematic if I simply accepted the face value of the words and explanations of the interviewees. It was possible that some interviewees had chosen to hold back their opinions and genuine feelings about the Red culture campaign because they believed the issue was too political for them to comment on and they did not feel secure enough to voice any doubts or criticism. During the previous decades, the Chinese people had witnessed many political campaigns and struggles. Based on their own experience, or wisdom passed down from their parents, they had learnt about the danger of politics and the importance of self-protection. Although the political culture has become far more relaxed in recent decades compared to the period from the 1950s to the 1970s, a high-level of self-censorship remained. In other cases, a small number of elderly interviewees expressed a reluctance to speak negatively about China due to a sense of patriotism, whereas others were concerned about the fact that I was based at a foreign institution.

Appendix I   131

In general, the university students were the most open about their personal opinions. Unlike the retirees, the university students had never experienced the cruelty of political struggles. Unlike the employees, they had less normative pressure concerning job security. Still, some university students, especially those who were Party members and student cadres, had been instructed by their teachers from the Youth League Committees of their universities to be careful with what they said. A small incident that occurred during the fieldwork illustrates well the extent to which political pressure may have affected the data collection process. An interview with a group of university students who had participated in Red-themed activities was going well until one of the students went out to ring a teacher at the Youth League Committee to check whether what they were saying to me was appropriate. The student returned, saying that the teacher had instructed her to terminate the interview and request that all interview notes should be destroyed. The reason she offered for the sudden change of attitude was that she believed that the students were under constant surveillance by the national security forces, and she was worried that the comments they had made about the government and the Red culture campaign might get them into trouble. I had to terminate the interview and destroy the interview notes, as requested. Whether the incident was an accurate reflection of the potential danger associated with discussing the Red culture campaign was unclear. I had not encountered any government opposition to me interviewing participants in the campaign, so most of the difficulties, as illustrated by this incident, might have been due to the self-censorship of the interviewees.

To alleviate the problem that some of the interviewees might offer skewed answers to the questions, I employed a combination of techniques during the data collection process. For example, during the interviews, in addition to ensuring that the interviewees felt comfortable about the setting, I usually asked the more sensitive questions more than once, at different points during the interview. These questions were worded differently when I asked them more than once. If the interviewees gave different answers to the same questions at different stages of the interview, I had to pay extra attention to the context within which the answers were given and decide which answer was likely to have the higher validity. For example, some interviewees might say that they believed that the Red culture campaign was a success when asked what they thought about it for the first time during the interview. However, as the interview went on, when asked specifically about the intentions of the campaign and whether they thought the initial goals of the campaign had been fully realised, many of them changed their minds and argued that the campaign was not very successful after all. In these cases, the researcher had to make a judgment about the validity of the answers based on the context within which each was given.

During the pilot interviews, it was found out that the interviewees tended to hold back when asked directly about their opinions of the campaign. I therefore reformatted the questions. I presented a number of evaluations of the campaign as popular opinions and invited the interviewees to comment on the opinions of 'other people'. For example, I asked questions like: '**someone** says: these activities are suitable for the elderly because they feel nostalgic about the past. They

132 *Appendix I*

are detached from the life of young people. Do you agree?' Or '**someone** says: Chongqing's Red culture campaign is like another Cultural Revolution and is ultra-Leftist. Do you agree?' This technique had a very positive impact on soliciting information from the interviewees. They were very willing to comment on 'other people's opinions' and felt more comfortable about revealing their own inclinations with regard to judging the political programme. At the same time, using this technique ran the risk of 'leading' the responses of the interviewees. I therefore attempted to create a balance regarding the positive and negative evaluations of the programme. Among the six proposed evaluations of the programme, half were positive and half negative. Therefore, the interviewees were provided with both sides of the viewpoints and were far less likely to avoid making their own choice by simply agreeing with whatever was presented to them.

The second problem was connected to the method of observation. In addition to the imbalance in the observational data collected from the three social groups, which has already been discussed, it was also possible that the researcher's participant observation might have generated some level of self-consciousness and anxiety among those under observation, that is, the problem of reactivity. This problem poses a potential threat to the validity of the data.[22] Whereas reactivity on the part of the participants was almost unavoidable, observational data would be compared with the interview data, whenever possible, to cross-check their validity.

Thirdly, the case would have been more complete had I been able to conduct interviews with government officials and bureaucrats who were responsible for implementing the Red culture campaign. Although the research mainly focused on the experiences of the ordinary people who participated in the activities, more insiders' information about how the campaign was run from the perspective of the implementers would have been helpful, specifically for the section on the nature of the campaign as simulation. Unfortunately, the efforts made to secure such interviews failed, again due to the sensitivity of the topic. Moreover, most of the data were collected during the later stage of the campaign. Strictly speaking, these cannot account for the whole process of the Red culture campaign, especially the initial stage of the mobilisation. Although direct observational data are lacking, I nevertheless consulted a wide range of newspaper articles and reportage on the campaign to paint as complete a picture of it as possible.

Notes

1 John Gerring, 'What Is a Case Study and What Is It Good For?' *American Political Science Review*, 98 (2004), 341.
2 Gerring, 'What Is a Case Study and What Is It Good For?', 342.
3 David E. McNabb, *Research Methods for Political Science: Quantitative and Qualitative Methods* (London: M.E. Sharpe, 2004).
4 David Boulton and Martyn Hammersley, 'Analysis of Unstructured Data', in *Data Collection and Analysis*, ed. by Roger Sapsford and Victor Jupp (London: Sage, 2006), p. 256.
5 Charles C. Ragin, *Constructing Social Research* (London: Pine Forge Press, 1994).

Appendix I 133

6 See Chapter 1 for details of this incident.
7 Primary and secondary school students were also frequent participants in the campaign, but this research recruited only adult interviewees as it was deemed inappropriate to put children under pressure by questioning them about a politically sensitive topic.
8 Martyn Hammersley and Roger Gomm, 'Assessing the Radical Critique of Interviews', in *Questioning Qualitative Inquiry: Critical Essays*, ed. by Martyn Hammersley (London: Sage, 2008), p. 89.
9 Michael Patton, *Qualitative Research and Evaluation Methods*, 3rd edition (London: Sage, 2002), p. 341.
10 Richard Krueger and Mary Casey, *Focus Groups: A Practical Guide for Applied Research* (London: Sage, 2000).
11 Peter Foster, 'Observational Research', in *Data Collection and Analysis*, ed. by Roger Sapsford and Victor Jupp (London: Sage, 2006), p. 59.
12 McNabb, *Research Methods for Political Science*, p. 366.
13 Ruth Finnegan, 'Using Document', in *Data Collection and Analysis*, ed. by Roger Sapsford and Victor Jupp (London: Sage, 2006), p. 139.
14 Finnegan, 'Using Document', p. 145.
15 Paul Atkinson and Amanda Coffey, 'Analysing Document Realities', in *Qualitative Research: Theory, Method and Practice*, 3rd edition, ed. by David Silverman (London: Sage, 2004), pp. 77–92.
16 Finnegan, 'Using Document', p. 142.
17 Adapted from McNabb, *Research Methods*.
18 Anselm Strauss and Juliet Corbin, *Basics of Qualitative Research: Techniques and Procedures for Developing Grounded Theory* (London: Sage, 1998), p. 57.
19 Strauss and Corbin, *Basics of Qualitative Research*, p. 88.
20 Strauss and Corbin, *Basics of Qualitative Research*, p. 101.
21 Strauss and Corbin, *Basics of Qualitative Research*, p. 123.
22 Foster, 'Observational Research', p. 87.

Appendix II

Interviewee biography

Interviewees	Gender	Age at interview	Native Residence	Channel of Participation	Position	Activity
A01	F	61	Chongqing	Community Team (Spring Breeze)	Retiree	Municipality-level performance
A02	F	63	Chongqing	Community Team (Spring Breeze)	Retiree	Municipality-level performance
A03	F	59	Chongqing	Community Team (Spring Breeze)	Retiree	Municipality-level performance
A04	F	60	Chongqing	Community Team (Spring Breeze)	Retiree	Municipality-level performance
A05	F	61	Chongqing	Community Team (Spring Breeze)	Retiree	Municipality-level performance
A06	F	51	Chongqing	Community Team (Spring Breeze)	Retiree	Municipality-level performance
A07	F	63	Chongqing	Community Team (Spring Breeze)	Retiree	Municipality-level performance
A08	M	70	Sichuan	Shaping Park	Retiree	Self-entertainment
A09	F	64	Chongqing	Bijin Park	Retiree	Self-entertainment
A10	F	58	Chongqing	Bijin Park	Retiree	Self-entertainment
A11	M	68	Chongqing	Bijin Park	Retiree	Self-entertainment
A12	F	missing	Chongqing	Community Team (Autumn Moon)	Retiree	Municipality-level performance
A13	F	missing	Chongqing	Community Team (Autumn Moon)	Retiree	Municipality-level performance

ID	Gender	Age	Province	Group	Status	Activity
A14	M	70	Chongqing	Community Team (Autumn Moon)	Retiree	Municipality-level performance
A15	M	missing	Chongqing	Community Team (Autumn Moon)	Retiree	Municipality-level performance
A16	F	missing	Chongqing	Community Team (Autumn Moon)	Retiree	Municipality-level performance
A17	F	missing	Chongqing	Community Team (Blue Heaven)	Retiree	Municipality-level performance
A18	F	missing	Chongqing	Community Team (Blue Heaven)	Retiree	Municipality-level performance
A19	F	61	Chongqing	Community Team (White Cloud)	Retiree	Performance within community
A20	F	55	Chongqing	Community Team (White Cloud)	Retiree	Performance within community
A21	F	56	Chongqing	Community Team (White Cloud)	Retiree	Performance within community
A22	F	53	Chongqing	Community Team(Blue Heaven)	Retiree	Municipality-level performance
A23	F	52	Chongqing	Community Team(Blue Heaven)	Retiree	Municipality-level performance
B01	F	20	Guangdong	University A	Student	Municipality-level performance
B02	M	21	Liaoning	University A	Student	Municipality-level performance
B03	M	23	Hebei	University B	Graduated	Municipality-level performance
B04	F	19	Jiangsu	University A	Student	Municipality-level performance
B05	M	20	Shandong	University B	Student	College-level activities
B06	M	19	Shandong	University B	Student	Party work
B07	M	19	Shanxi	University B	Student	College-level activities
B08	F	19	Sichuan	University B	Student	University-level performance
B09	F	19	Zhejiang	University B	Student	College-level activities
B10	F	19	Zhejiang	University B	Student	College-level activities
B11	F	19	Zhejiang	University B	Student	Party work
B12	M	19	Sichuan	University B	Student	College-level activities
B13	F	19	Shanxi	University B	Student	University-level performance
B14	F	21	Chongqing	University B	Student	University-level performance
B15	M	21	Hubei	University B	Student	Party work

(*Continued*)

Interviewees	Gender	Age at interview	Native Residence	Channel of Participation	Position	Activity
B16	M	19	Henan	University B	Student	University-level performance
B17	F	20	Jiangsu	University A	Student	Municipality-level performance
B18	F	22	Chongqing	University A	Student	Municipality-level performance
B19	M	22	Henan	University B	Student	College-level activities
B20	F	22	Chongqing	University B	Student	College-level activities
B21	M	22	Shanxi	University B	Student	College-level activities
B22	M	20	Xinjiang	University B	Student	College-level activities
B23	F	19	Sichuan	University B	Student	College-level activities
B24	M	21	Shandong	University B	Student	Municipality-level performance
B25	F	21	Ningxia	University B	Student	College-level activities
C01	F	missing	Chongqing	University	Tutor	College-level activities
C02	F	missing	Chongqing	University	Tutor	College-level activities
C03	F	25	Chongqing	Company/Government bureaucracy	Salesman	Company training
C04	F	41	Chongqing	Company/Government bureaucracy	Department manager	Competition within company/ bureaucracy
C05	F	30	Chongqing	Company/Government bureaucracy	Department supervisor	Competition within company/bureaucracy
C06	F	35	Chongqing	Company/Government bureaucracy	Department supervisor	Competition within company/ bureaucracy
C07	F	28	Chongqing	Company/Government bureaucracy	Bureaucrat	Competition within company/ bureaucracy
C08	M	28	Jiangsu	Company/Government bureaucracy	Bureaucrat	Writer for Red-themed TV program
C09	M	50	Chongqing	Company/Government bureaucracy	Vice-secretary of the Party Committee	Competition within company/ bureaucracy

C10	M	40	Chongqing	Company/Government bureaucracy	Chief of staff	Competition within company/bureaucracy
C11	M	45	Chongqing	Company/Government bureaucracy	Department manager	Competition within company/bureaucracy
C12	M	50	Chongqing	Company/Government bureaucracy	Chief of Staff	Competition within company/bureaucracy
C13	M	50	Chongqing	TV station	Staff	Municipality-level TV program
C14	F	35	Chongqing	Company/Government bureaucracy	Teacher	Municipality-level TV program
C15	F	28	Chongqing	TV station	Editor	Municipality-level TV program
C16	F	25	Chongqing	Company/Government bureaucracy	Staff	Municipality-level performance
C17	M	45	Shandong	Company/Government bureaucracy	Staff	Department of Propaganda, Chongqing
C18	F	32	Chongqing	Company/Government bureaucracy	Department supervisor	Department of Propaganda, Chongqing
C19	F	26	Chongqing	Company/Government Bureaucracy	Staff	Competition within company/bureaucracy
C20	F	27	Chongqing	Company/Government bureaucracy	Staff	Programme production
C21	M	35	Chongqing	Company/Government bureaucracy	Staff	Municipality-level performance
C22	F	55	Chongqing	Art organization	Teacher	Municipality-level performance
C23	F	25	Chongqing	Middle School	Teacher	School-level performance
C24	M	52	Chongqing	Company/Government bureaucracy	Department manager	Competition within company
C25	F	53	Chongqing	Company/Government bureaucracy	Staff	Competition within company
C26	F	27	Chongqing	Middle School	Teacher	District Level performance

Appendix III

Data analysis: categories and dimensions

Table 1 Level of Performance

Category / Participants		Level of Performance		
		Dimensions		
		*Organization**	*Quality of Performance***	*Publicity****
Retirees	L1	H	H	H
	L2	M	M	L
	L3	L	–	–
University Students	L1	H	H	H
	L2	M	M	L
Employees	L1	H	H	H
	L2	M	M	M

*Organization:

High (H) – Involving bureaucratic efforts at both municipality and local levels of governments, residents' committees, universities, or companies

Medium (M) – Involving organizational efforts only within residents committees, universities, or companies

Low (L) – Involving individual efforts; no institutional support

** Quality of performance:

High (H) – requirements on cultural competence of the performers; high-level venues; sophisticated performance outfits and props; professional producer and director

Medium (M) – fluctuated cultural competence of the performers; venues at community centres, on campus, or within companies; special outfits and props but not necessarily for formal performances; non-professional organizer

Low (L) – no cultural competence required of the performers

*** Publicity

High (H) – coverage by local media; exposure to the wider public

Low (L) – no coverage by local media or exposure to the wider public

Table 2 Judgment

Category / Generation	Factors that affected judgment			
	Strengthen social relationships	Beneficial for self-development	Help construct appealing identities	Enticing favourable memories
Retirees	Y	Y	Y	Y
University students	Y	Y	N	N
Employees	Y	Y	N	N

Y = Yes

N = No

Appendix IV

Forty-five classic songs for schools in Chongqing[1]

重庆校园传唱经典歌曲 45 首

歌名	年代
Name	Year
1. 中华人民共和国国歌	1935
National Anthem of the People's Republic of China	
2. 中国人民解放军军歌	1939
Anthem of Chinese People's Liberation Army	
3. 中国少年先锋队队歌	1950
Anthem of Chinese Young Pioneers	
4. 没有共产党就没有新中国	1943
There'll be No New China without the Communist Party	
5. 东方红	20 世纪 40 年代初
The East Is Red	
6. 工农兵联合起来	20 世纪 20 年代
Works, Farmers, and Soldiers United	
7. 红星歌	1973
Song of the Red Star	
8. 共产儿童团歌	1957
Anthem of the Communist Children League	
9. 洪湖水，浪打浪	1961
The Waves of Honghu Lake	
10. 毕业歌	1934
Song of Graduation	
11. 五月的鲜花	1935
Flowers in May	
12. 延安颂	1938
Ode to Yan'an	
13. 游击队歌	1937
Ballad of the Green Berets	
14. 保卫黄河	1939
Defend the Yellow River	
15. 在太行山上	1938
On Top of Taihang Mountain	

16. 抗日军政大学校歌   1937
Song of the Anti-Japanese Military and
Political University
17. 团结就是力量   1943
Unity Is Power
18. 红梅赞   1962
Praise to the Red Plum Blossom
19. 英雄赞歌   1964
Ode to the Heroes
20. 咱们工人有力量   1948
Workers Have Power
21. 我们走在大路上   1963
We March on the Road
22. 革命人永远是年轻   1950
The Revolutionaries Are Forever Young
23. 学习雷锋好榜样   1963
To Learn from Lei Feng
24. 我是一个兵   1950
I Am a Soldier
25. 让我们荡起双桨   1955
Let's Paddle the Boat
26. 听妈妈讲那过去的事情   1957
Listen to Mother Telling the Stories of the Past
27. 歌唱祖国   1950
Ode to the Motherland
28. 党啊，亲爱的妈妈   1984
Party, Dear Mother
29. 我爱你，中国   1979
I Love You, China
30. 我和我的祖国   1985–6
Me and My Country
31. 妈妈教我一支歌   1981
Mother Teaches Me a Song
32. 生死相依我苦恋着你   1988
I Love You till Death
33. 春天的故事   1994
The Story of Spring
34. 在希望的田野上   1981
On the Hopeful Land
35. 年轻的朋友来相会   1980
Young Friends, Let's Get Together
36. 光荣啊，中国共青团   1987
The Honourable Chinese Youth League
37. 当兵的人   1994
We Soldiers

142 *Appendix IV*

38. 说句心里话   1989
To Tell the Truth
39. 为了谁   1998
For Whom
40. 小白杨   1983
Little Alamo
41. 十五的月亮   1986
The Full Moon
42. 大海啊，故乡   1983
The Ocean, My Hometown
43. 长江之歌   1984
Song of the Yangtze River
44. 难忘今宵   1985
Tonight Is an Unforgettable Night
45. 同一首歌   1990
One Same Song

Note

1 Chongqing Education Committee (ed.). *Homeland in My Heart: 45 Classic Songs for Schools in Chongqing* (*Zuguo zai wo xinzhong: Chongqing xiaoyuan chuanchang jingdian gequ 45 shou* 《祖国在我心中 – 重庆校园传唱经典歌曲45首》) (Chongqing: xinan shifan daxue chubbanshe, 2009).

Appendix V

One hundred patriotic songs recommended by 10 central departments, including the Department of Propaganda

2009 年中宣部、中央文明办等 10 部委推荐 100 首爱国歌曲

歌名	年代
Name	Year
1. 十送红军	1960
Seeing the Red Army Off	—
2. 红军战士想念毛泽东	—
Red Army Soldier Misses Mao Zedong	—
3. 红星歌	1973
Song of the Red Star	
4. 映山红	1974
Azalea	
5. 情深谊长	2003
Eternal Friendship	
6. 过雪山草地	1965
Crossed the Snowy Mountains and Marshy Grasslands	
7. 五月的鲜花	1935
Flowers in May	
8. 保卫黄河	1939
Defend the Yellow River	
9. 在太行山上	1938
On Top of Taihang Mountain	
10.二月里来	1939
In February	
11. 游击队歌	1937
Ballad of the Green Berets	
12. 延安颂	1938
Ode to Yan'an	
13. 南泥湾	1943
Nanni Wan	
14. 东方红	20 世纪 40 年代
The East is Red	
15. 歌唱二小放牛郎	20 世纪 40 年代
Song of Herdboy Er'Xiao	

144 *Appendix V*

16. 团结就是力量   1943
Unity Is Power
17. 谁不说俺家乡好   1961
No Place Like Home
18. 红梅赞   1962
Praise to the Red Plum Blossom
19. 没有共产党就没有新中国   1943
There'll Be No New China without the Communist Party
20. 咱们工人有力量   1948
Workers Have Power
21. 革命人永远是年轻   1950
The Revolutionaries Are Forever Young
22. 歌唱祖国   1950
Ode to the Motherland
23. 草原上升起不落的太阳   1953
The Unsetting Sun Rises on the Grassland
24. 我的祖国   1956
My Country
25. 英雄赞歌   1964
Ode to the Heroes
26. 毛主席的话儿记心上   1965
Memorising Words of Chairman Mao
27. 远方的客人请你留下来   1953
Please Stay, Guests from Afar
28. 快乐的节日   20 世纪 60 年代
Happy Festival
29. 我们的田野   1953
Our Field
30. 让我们荡起双桨   1955
Let's Paddle the Boat
31. 人民军队忠于党   1960
The People's Army Is Loyal to the Party
32. 我爱祖国的蓝天   1961
I Love the Blue Sky of My Motherland
33. 我们走在大路上   1963
We Walk on the Broad Road
34. 唱支山歌给党听   1963
Singing a Folk Song for the Party
35. 翻身农奴把歌唱   1961
Song of the Emancipated Slaves
36. 我为祖国献石油   1964
I Dedicate the Oil to My Country
37. 边疆处处赛江南   20 世纪 60 年代
The Frontier Is as Good as Jiangnan
38. 工人阶级硬骨头   1965
The Working Class Is Tough

Appendix V   145

39. 我爱北京天安门 I Love Beijing Tian'anmen	1970
40. 北京颂歌 Ode to Beijing	1971
41. 祖国颂 Ode to the Motherland	1957
42. 我爱这蓝色的海洋 I Love the Blue Ocean	1972
43. 太阳最红，毛主席最亲 The Sun Is the Reddest, Chairman Mao Is the Dearest	1976
44. 我为伟大祖国站岗 I Stand Guard for Our Great Motherland	20 世纪 70 年代
45. 我爱五指山，我爱万泉河 I Love Wuzhi Mountain, I Love Wanquan River	1970
46. 中国，中国，鲜红的太阳永不落 China, China, the Red Sun Never Sets	1977
47. 边疆泉水清又纯 Water at the Frontier Is Clear and Pure	1978
48. 我爱你，中国 I Love You, China	1979
49. 我们的生活充满阳光 Our Life Is Full of Sunshine	1979
50. 美丽的草原我的家 Beautiful Grassland Is My Home	1979
51. 我们美丽的祖国 Our Beautiful Motherland	1980–1
52. 党啊，亲爱的妈妈 Party，the Dear Mother	20 世纪 80 年代
53. 在希望的田野上 On the Hopeful Land	1982
54. 长江之歌 Song of the Yangtze River	20 世纪 80 年代
55. 我爱你，塞北的雪 I Love You, Snow at Saibei	1980
56. 鼓浪屿之波 The Waves of Gulang Island	1981
57. 嘀哩嘀哩 Di Li Di Li	20 世纪 80 年代
58. 少年，少年，祖国的春天 Youth Is the Spring of the Motherland	1981
59. 歌声与微笑 Song and Smile	1986
60. 东方之珠 The Pearl of the East	1986
61. 我的中国心 My Chinese Heart	1984

146 *Appendix V*

62. 龙的传人　　　　　　　　　　　　　　　1978
The Descendants of the Dragon
63. 大海啊，故乡　　　　　　　　　　　　　1983
The Ocean, My Hometown
64. 祖国，慈祥的母亲　　　　　　　　　　　1981
Motherland, My Dear Mother
65. 难忘今宵　　　　　　　　　　　　　　　1985
Tonight Is an Unforgettable Night
66. 小白杨　　　　　　　　　　　　　　　　1983
Little Alamo
67. 说句心里话　　　　　　　　　　　　　　1989
To Tell the Truth
68. 万里长城永不倒　　　　　　　　　　　　1982
The Great Wall Will Not Fall
69. 少年壮志不言愁　　　　　　　　　　　　1987
Young People with Aspirations Do Not Speak about Worries
70. 共和国之恋　　　　　　　　　　　　　　1988
Love for the Republic
71. 亚洲雄风　　　　　　　　　　　　　　　1990
The Revival of Asia
72. 超越梦想　　　　　　　　　　　　　　　2008
Beyond the Dream
73. 今天是你的生日　　　　　　　　　　　　1989
Today Is Your Birthday
74. 大中国　　　　　　　　　　　　　　　　1995
Great China
75. 当兵的人　　　　　　　　　　　　　　　1994
We Soldiers
76. 中国人　　　　　　　　　　　　　　　　1997
Chinese
77. 五星红旗　　　　　　　　　　　　　　　1999
The Five-Starred Red Flag
77. 红旗飘飘　　　　　　　　　　　　　　　1996
Fluttering Red Flag
79. 青藏高原　　　　　　　　　　　　　　　1994
Tibetan Plateau
80. 在中国大地上　　　　　　　　　　　　　1996
On the Land of China
81. 我和我的祖国　　　　　　　　　　　　1985–6
Me and My Country
82. 春天的故事　　　　　　　　　　　　　　1994
The Story of Spring
83. 走进新时代　　　　　　　　　　　　　　1997
Marching towards the New Era
84. 祝福祖国　　　　　　　　　　　　　　　1999
Bless the Motherland

85. 同一首歌 1990
One Same Song
86. 爱我中华 1991
Love China
87. 为了谁 1998
For Whom
88. 好日子 1997
The Good Days
89. 最美还是我们新疆 1995
The Most Beautiful Xinjing
90. 七子之歌·澳门 1999
Macau
91. 天路 2001
The Road to Heaven
92. 祖国不会忘记 1992
The Motherland Will Not Forget
93. 说中国 2007
On China
94. 红船向未来 2006
Red Boat Sailing to the Future
95. 光明行 1931
The Light
96. 共和国选择了你 2009
You Are Chosen by the Republic
97. 江山 2002
The Country
98. 旗帜颂 2002
Praise the Flag
99. 和谐家园 2009
Harmonious Home
100. 国家 2009
The Nation

Index

Note: Page numbers in italic indicate a figure or table on the corresponding page. Page numbers followed by *n* refer to notes.

activities, frames of *see* framing
Alexander, Jeffrey 44
analysis, documentary 128–9
anti-Confucian campaign 39
'armed struggle' 1–2
art, as political and symbolic tool 41–2
axial coding 131

Baudrillard's theory of simulation 25; *see also* simulation, Red culture campaign as
benefits of campaign: for employees 90–2; for retirees 84–8; for university students 88–90
bibliography, interviewee *135–8*
Bo Xilai 8; decision to use mass campaign 123; denial of existence of 'Chongqing Model' 10n1; early career of 2–3; encouragement of classic Red songs 39–40; Party factionalism and 119–21; popularity of 120; power of 116; preface to 'Reading Classics' TV series 77; as 'princeling' 118; 'Quotations for Clean Governance' 68; removal from office 10n13, 49, 124; social policies of 120; students' views of 102; *see also* 'Chongqing Model'

'Campaign to Suppress Counter-revolutionaries and Regime Consolidation' 45
capitalism: introduction of 60; politicized capitalism 22
case studies, definition of 122
categories: dimensions and *139–40*; generation of 130
CBG (Chongqing Broadcasting Group) 77

CCP *see* Chinese Communist Party
Certeau, Michel de 25
chang du jiang chuan 4
chang hong da hei 3–4
charismatic legitimacy 21
'China Red Song Concert' 48–9
Chinese Communist Party: 18th National Congress 2; control over universities 58–60; factionalism in 118–21; ideological campaigns 7–8; influence over private enterprises 60–2; legitimation of 21–2; patriotic songs recommended by 144–8; People's Liberation Army 1; Politburo Standing Committee 2, 118; relationship with people 116; Residents' Committee 57–8; 'Resolution on Certain Questions in the History of Our Party' 120; state-owned enterprises 5, 60–2, 70–2; state-society framework 18–20; structure of 10n9; as target audience of Red culture campaign 44–6; Youth League Committee 58–60, 67, 70, 118–19; *see also* Party-state; Propaganda Department
'Chinese Dream' campaign 7
Chinese People's Congress (CPC) 58
Chongqing: GDP (gross domestic product) 3; political importance of 1–2; population of 1; *see also* 'Chongqing Model'
Chongqing Broadcasting Group (CBG) 77
Chongqing Daily 129
'Chongqing Model' 1–4; controversies over 4–6; division of top leadership regarding 49; nature of 7–8; *see also* Red culture campaign activities

Index 149

circuit, self-induced 44–6
classic songs for schools: encouragement
  of 39–40; interpretations of 'Red' in
  105–8; list of 141–3
collective action, resistance and 22–4
'common prosperity' narrative 97, 120
Communist Youth League 67
community art groups, participation in Red
  culture campaign 54, 66–7
conceptualisation 125
conductors, impact on quality of
  performances 67–8, 71, 76–7
*cong qunzhong zhong lai, dao qunzhong
  zhong qu* 38, 97
contentious politics 23
'continuous revolution' 7, 21
'contract responsibility system' 60
CPC (Chinese People's Congress) 58
CR *see* Cultural Revolution
crime, 'Smashing Black' campaign
  against 3–4
Cultural Revolution: anti-Confucian
  campaign 39; Chongqing's 'armed
  struggled' during 1–2; 'eight model
  dramas' in 41; generation of 56; music
  in 41; romanticisation of 107–8
culture system 78

'Daily Red Song' programme 42–3, 67;
  see also 'Singing Red' campaign
data analysis 129–30; categories and
  dimensions *139–40*; data coding 130–1;
  data organization and category generation
  130
data coding 130–1
data collection 9; documentary analysis
  128–9; fieldwork notes 129; group
  interviews 127; individual interviews
  126–7; observation 127–8; pilot
  interviews 126
data organization 130
da xia fang 3
'Decision on Promoting Vigorous
  Development and Prosperity of
  Culture' 40
Department of Propaganda *see* Propaganda
  Department
'Directive on the Launching of Singing
  Red Classic Songs Activities' 40
disassociation 49
documentary analysis 128–9
domination: definition of 20–1; legitimation
  21; *see also* resistance

'educated youths' 54, 56
'eight model dramas' 41
Eling Park 74
elite factionalism 118–21
employees: first level of participation
  68–9; framing processes by 99–105;
  interview participants 54–5; offerings
  to and benefits received from campaign
  90–2; second level of participation 70–2;
  working as participating 77–80
ethics, research and 131
everyday practice, theory of 25
exchange: concept of 27; conclusions
  113–15; by employees 90–2; official
  programme as strategy 82–4;
  participants' practices as tactics 92–3;
  by retirees 84–8; by university students
  88–90
executive order 71
export models: 'one end outside, one end
  inside' 3, 11n14; 'two ends out' 11n14

factionalism 118–21
fieldwork: fieldwork notes 129; methods
  123–4
first level of participation: by employees
  68–9; by retirees 66–7; by university
  students 67–8
'Five Chongqings' slogan 3
'The Fragrance of Hundred Flowers –
  Holding High the Banner of the Party'
  programme 40
framing: comparison with official narrative
  108; concept of 27–9; conclusions 113–15;
  keying process 105–8; by official
  programme 96–8; by participants
  98–105; primary frameworks 98–105
'from the masses, to the masses' narrative
  38, 97–8
funding for participants 76

GDP (gross domestic product) 3
generations: framing processes by 98–105;
  middle-age employees 103–5; participation
  in Red culture campaign 55–7; retirees and
  older employees 98–9; university students
  and young employees 99–102
Goffman, Erving 27–8
'Great Leap Forward' 56
group interviews 127
*Guanyu jianguoyilai dang de ruogan lishi
  wenti de jueyi* 120
Guo, Yuhua 24

150   Index

hegemonic authority of Chinese Communist Party 22
historical context 15–16; Chinese social movement studies 16–17; collective action and 'weapons of the weak' 22–4; domination and legitimacy 20–2; state-society framework 18–20; Western social movement studies 16–17
hongjun changzheng ji 41
Horsley, Jamie 22

ideological campaigns *see* mass campaigns
implications of Red culture campaign 47–9
individual interviews 126–7
individualism 20
individual participants *see* participants
inequality, criticism of 97
institutional conditions: private enterprises 60–2; Residents' Committee 57–8; state-owned enterprises 60–2; universities 58–9; Youth League Committee 58–60
interaction with participants: conclusions 113–15; exchange 27; framing processes by official programme 96–8; framing processes by participants 98–105; keying process 105–8; offerings to and benefits received from campaign 84–92; official programme as strategy 82–4; participants' practices as tactics 92–3; *see also* participants
interpretations of 'Red' 105–8
interviews: group interviews 127; individual interviews 126–7; interviewee bibliography *135–8*; pilot interviews 126

jie qiong qin 3
jingqishen 97

keying process 27–9; comparison with official narrative 108; interpretations of 'Red' 105–8
kong su hui 38
Kuomingtang 1

labour unrest 22–4
'land financing' 3
laosanjie 56
Leftists, political ideology of 4–5
legitimation: of Chinese Communist Party 21–2; definition of 21
levels of participation *see* participation levels
limitations, research 131–3

liquidation of referential 43–4
lost generation 56
'Love the Party, Love the Nation, Love the Hometown' theme 40

'mainstream melody' 48
'managed' campaigns 31n35
Mannheim, Karl 55
'Mao fever' 48
Maoist mass campaigns *see* mass campaigns
Mao Zedong: adoption of mass campaigns 39; and concept of 'continuous revolution' 7, 21; 'Mao fever' 48; 'mass-line' doctrine of 38–9; as quoted by Bo Xilai 4; 'Some Questions Concerning Methods of Leadership' directive 38; as target audience of mass campaigns 38
mass accusation meetings 38
mass activities 15–16; *see also* Red culture campaign activities
mass campaigns: adoption by Mao Zedong 39; components of 37–9; history of 7; ideological doctrines underpinning 38–9; 'managed' campaigns 31n35; mass accusation meetings 38; music as tool in 41–2; Red culture campaign compared to 24; Red Guard movement 39; role in political culture 7–8
'mass-line' doctrine: in 'Daily Red Song' programme 42–3; Mao Zedong and 38–9; in Red culture campaign 111; reinterpretation of 97–8; social and political implications of 115–16; songs reinforcing 67; *see also* Red culture campaign activities
'The Memories of the Red Army Long March' 41
middle-age employees, framing processes by 103–5
Ministry of Education 59
model, procession of 42–3
'murderous capacity' of simulation 47
music: classic songs for schools 39–40, 141–3; 'Daily Red Song' programme 67; interpretations of 'Red' in 105–8; patriotic songs recommended by Propaganda Department 144–8; as political and symbolic tool 41–2

Nationalist Party 1
National Party Congress 2
Nee, Vector 22

new-Left 4
'New Songs of the Battlefield' 41
nongovernmental organizations (NGOs) 19

observation 127–8
offerings to campaign: by employees 90–2;
  participants' practices as tactics 92–3;
  by retirees 84–8; by university students
  88–90
Oi, Jean 22
older employees, framing processes by
  98–9
'one end outside, one end inside' export
  model 3, 11n14
open coding 130
'Open up to the West' movement, role of
  Chongqing in 2
organizational effort: mass activism and
  17; participation levels and 75–7
organization of data 130
organized crime, 'Smashing Black'
  campaign against 3–4
organized performances 42–3, 69–70; *see
  also* 'Singing Red' campaign

parks, activities in: Bijin Park 73; Eling
  Park 74; public square 73–4; Shaping
  Park 72–3
participants 42–3, 53–4; as actors of tactics
  25; categories and dimensions *139–40*;
  employees 54–5; framing processes
  by 98–105; funding of 76; generations
  of 55–7; importance to campaign 84;
  individualistic nature of practices 20;
  institutional conditions for 57–62;
  interaction with 8; interview participants
  53–5, *135–8*; keying process 105–8;
  offerings to and benefits received from
  campaign 84–92; over-reported numbers
  of 62n1; participants' practices as tactics
  92–3; primary frameworks 98–105;
  retirees 54; university students 54; *see
  also* participation levels; practices
participation levels: first level of participation
  66–9; organization and 75–7; publicity
  and 76; quality of performance and 75–7;
  second level of participation 69–72; third
  level of participation 72–5; working as
  participating 77–80
Party-state: control over universities 58–60;
  domination 20–2; influence over
  private enterprises 60–2; legitimation
  20–2; resistance to 22–4; state-owned

enterprises and 60–2; state-society
  framework 18–20; *see also* Chinese
  Communist Party
patriotic songs: classic songs for schools
  39–40, 105–8, 141–3; interpretations of
  'Red' in 105–8; songs recommended by
  Propaganda Department 144–8
patterns of participation *see* participation
  levels
PBSC *see* Politburo Standing Committee
Pei, Xinmin 22
People's Liberation Army, 'liberation' of
  Chongqing 1
performance legitimacy 21–2
performance quality, participation levels
  and 75–7
pilot interviews 126
PLA *see* People's Liberation Army
Politburo Standing Committee 2, 118
political implications 115–16
politicized capitalism 22
population of Chongqing 1
positive energy, Red songs as embodiment
  of 106–7
practices 66; conclusions 113–15; first
  level of participation 66–9; offerings to
  and benefits received from campaign
  84–92; organization and 75–7; publicity
  and 76; quality of performance and
  75–7; second level of participation
  69–72; as tactics 92–3; third level
  of participation 72–5; working as
  participating 77–80
primary frameworks 27–9; of middle-age
  employees 103–5; of retirees and older
  employees 98–9; of university students
  and young employees 99–102
princelings 118–19
private enterprises: organization of Red-
  themed activities 70–2; participation in
  Red culture campaign 60–2; relationship
  with government 60–2
problematics of repression 25
procession of model 42–3
Propaganda Department: *changdujiangchuan*
  offices 78; nomination of Red culture
  bases 40; patriotic songs recommended by
  105, 144–8; publicity efforts 83; 'Reading
  Classics' TV programme 77; reporting of
  Red-themed activities 92
protestors 22–4
publicity, levels of participation and 76
public square 73–4

152   Index

quality of performance, participation levels and 75–7

'Quotations for Clean Governance,' recitation of 68

Ragin, Charles 122

'Reading Classics' campaign 4; activities of 40; recitation of 'Quotations for Clean Governance' 68; TV series 77–8

reciprocity 27; conclusions 113–15; employees 90–2; official programme as strategy 82–4; participants' practices as tactics 92–3; retirees 84–8; university students 88–90

'Red,' interpretations of 44, 105–8

Red culture campaign activities 39–40; association/disassociation in 49; compared to mass campaigns of reform era 24, 48–9; controversies over 4–6; framing processes by 96–8; interpretations of 'Red' in 44, 105–8; lack of research on 5; as mass activity 15–16; needs from participants 84; political power supporting 19–20; 'Reading Classics' 4, 40, 77–8; significance of 122–3; 'Singing Red' 4, 39–43, 48–9, 141–3; 'Smashing Black' 3–4; social and political implications of 115–16; 'Spreading Mottos' 4, 40; strategies and tactics in 25; as strategy 82–4, 96–7; 'Telling Stories' 4, 40; see also participants; simulation, Red culture campaign as

Red culture campaign participants see participants

Red Guard movement 17, 39, 56

'Red Motto' messages 40

Red Song Gala 40–1

referential, liquidation of 43–4

repression, problematics of 25

research methods 122; case of Chongqing's Red culture campaign 122–3; conceptualisation 125; data analysis 129–31, *139–40*; data collection 126–9; ethics 131; fieldwork 123–4; interviewee bibliography *135–8*; potential problems and limitations 131–3; sampling techniques 125–6

Residents' Committee, participation in Red culture campaign 57–8

resistance 22–4

'Resolution on Certain Questions in the History of Our Party' 120

retirees: first level of participation 66–9; framing processes by 98–9; interview participants 54; offerings to and benefits

received from campaign 84–8; second level of participation 69; third level of participation 72–5

revolutionary songs see songs

Rightists, political ideology of 4–5

romanticisation of revolutionary era 107–8

sampling techniques 125–6

san jin san tong 3

sanxian 1

schools, classic songs for: encouragement of 39–40; interpretations of 'Red' in 105–8; list of 141–3

Scott, James 24

second level of participation: by employees 70–2; by retirees 69; by university students 69–70

self-induced circuit 44–6

'serve the people' narrative 97

Shaping Park 72–3

Shue, Vivienne 17–18

significance of Red culture campaign 122–3

silent majority 24

Simmel, Georg 27

simulation, Red culture campaign as 8, 37; conclusions 111–13; implications of 47–9; liquidation of referential 43–4; problematic characterisation in 49–50; procession of model 42–3; production of true symptoms 37–42; self-induced circuit 44–6; theory of simulation 25

'Singing Red' campaign 4; classic songs for schools 39–40, 141–3; compared to mass campaigns of reform era 48–9; compared to patriotic songs recommended by central departments 144–8; 'Daily Red Song' programme 42–3; first level of participation 66–9; framing processes by official programme 96–8; framing processes by participants 98–105; interpretations of 'Red' in 105–8; keying process 105–8; organization and levels of participation 75–7; performances and attendance 40; quality of performance 75–7; Red Song Gala 40–1; second level of participation 69–72; third level of participation 72–5; working as participating 77–80; see also participants

'Smashing Black' campaign 3–4

Snow, David 28–9

social exchange 27

social grievances, as motivation behind social movements 16

social implications of campaign 115–16
social inequality, criticism of 97
social movements: Chinese social movement studies 16–17; definition of 15; Western social movement studies 16–17
social unrest 22–4
'societal transition' generation 56–7
society *see* state-society framework
SOEs *see* state-owned enterprises
'Some Questions Concerning Methods of Leadership' directive 38
songs: classic songs for schools 39–40, 141–3; 'Daily Red Song' programme 67; interpretations of 'Red' in 105–8; patriotic songs recommended by Propaganda Department 144–8; as political and symbolic tool 41–2
speech contests 70
'Spreading Mottos' campaign 4, 40
state-owned enterprises 5; organization of Red-themed activities 70–2; participation in Red culture campaign 60–2
state-society framework 18–20
strategy: concept of 25–6; Red culture campaign as 82–4, 96–7
subversive behaviours 24
Sun, Wanning 24
Sun Liping 5
symptoms of mass campaigns 37–42

tactical resistance 23–4
tactics: concept of 25–6; participants' practices as 92–3; tactical resistance 23–4
teachers, impact on quality of performances 67, 69–72, 76–7
'Telling Stories' campaign 4, 40
theoretical concepts: exchange 27; framing process 27–9; reciprocity 27; simulation 25; strategy 25–6; tactics 25–6
'Third Front' development project 1, 10n4

third level of participation 72–5; Bijin Park 73; Eling Park 74; public square 73–4; Shaping Park 72–3
'Three Represents' campaign 7, 37n12
totalitarian model of social movements 17
tudi caizheng 3
'two ends out' export model 11n14

universities: participation in Red culture campaign 58–60; Party control over 58–60
university students: first level of participation 67–8; framing processes by 99–102; generation of 56–7; interview participants 54; offerings to and benefits received from campaign 88–90; second level of participation 69–70

Walder, Andrew 15
'weapons of the weak' 22–4
wenhua xitong 78
White, Gordon 22
White, Lynn 16
working as participating 77–80
'worthy' literary works 78

xibu da kaifa 2

yangge performances 38
youth, framing processes by 99–102
Youth League Committee 58–60, 67, 70, 118–19
Youth League Day 70, 101
yundong 15

zhan di xin ge 41
zheng neng liang 106–7
Zheng Yongnian 118
zhiqing 54, 56
zhongguo hongge hui 48–9
zhonghua honggehui 40–1
zhuxuanlü 48